D1189789

The Fall of the Farm Credit Empire

The Fall of the Farm Credit Empire

BEN SUNBURY

Iowa State University Press / Ames

Ben Sunbury was executive assistant to three Farm Credit Administration governors, until his retirement in 1988.

© 1990 Iowa State University Press, Ames, Iowa 50010
All rights reserved

Manufactured in the United States of America
This book is printed on acid-free paper

First edition, 1990

Library of Congress Cataloging-in-Publication Data

Sunbury, Ben.
    The fall of the farm credit empire / Ben Sunbury. — 1st ed.
        p.   cm.
    Includes bibliographical references.
    ISBN 0–8138–0046–3
    1. United States. Farm Credit Administration. 2. Agricultural credit — United States. 3.Agricul-
ture — Economic aspects — United States. 4. Agriculture and state — United States. I. Title.
HD1440.U6S86   1990
332.7′1′0973 — dc20

89–15594

Contents

Preface		vii
Abbreviations and Acronyms		ix
Introduction		xi
1	THE FARM CREDIT SYSTEM . . . A CAST OF THOUSANDS	3
2	THE BEGINNING OF THE FALL	17
3	SAY IT ISN'T SO	29
4	TWISTING THE LION'S TAIL	45
5	THE ART OF SELF-DESTRUCTION	67
6	FIGHTING BACK	85
7	LOOKING FOR HELP	99
8	GOING FOR LEGISLATION	117
9	THE FEDERAL FARM CREDIT BOARD . . . A NOBLE CONSTITUTIONAL EXPERIMENT	133
10	COOPERATIVES . . . OPPORTUNITIES LOST?	145
11	POLITICS, AS USUAL	167
12	BACK TO THE FUTURE	189
13	ONE MORE TIME	207
	EPILOGUE	233
	References	251
	Index	259

Preface

 When I left the Ohio Farm Bureau Federation in Columbus, Ohio, in 1957 to go to Washington, D.C., to join the Farm Credit Administration (FCA), I did not plan to stay long. Like most people who come to the nation's capital to work, I felt that a few years' experience with the federal government would be good for my career. I did not foresee that I would fall in love with Virginia, which is now my home, or with the Farm Credit Administration, where I worked. Not only did I stay for dinner, but for several breakfasts, lunches, and dinners (or, if you prefer, breakfasts, dinners, and suppers).

Except for my final two years at FCA, the experience was a happy one. The job was not what I expected it to be. The FCA was not a sprawling federal bureaucracy that swallowed a person up. Instead it provided pleasant, meaningful employment—something one could become a part of and identify with, namely agriculture and farmers. As a matter of fact, except for the daily commute (something that would have been intolerable had I not been a member of a commodious car pool), I really did not notice much difference from working for the Ohio Farm Bureau. Although I was perhaps a bit naive, I had the feeling that I worked first for farmers (at least for those who borrowed from the Farm Credit System), second for the Farm Credit Administration, and lastly, for the United States government. At the end, the order seemed reversed.

Many say that is as it should be, that I should not have been working primarily for farmers. You will be in a better position to judge after you read this book. For myself, all I can say is had that been the case upon my arrival in 1957, I would have stuck to my original plan and left the FCA after a few years.

Another thing that encouraged me to stay with the FCA was the fact that I was not stuck in any one job for an excessive length of time, another possible hazard with government employment. Although I was hired as and remained an information specialist for some time, the position covered a wide range of activities, including press relations, speech writing, radio and TV activity, the making of exhibits, and even motion picture work. For five years I was the foreign training officer for the FCA. I was later summoned to the head office to serve as executive assistant to three successive governors (administrators) of the FCA. Then, there was a stint as legislative officer (lobbyist). All together, I have few complaints. In any case, the variety of experience has provided a valuable background for writing this book.

Anyone who has ever produced a work of nonfiction will concur that there are a great number of people who deserve acknowledgment. Such is the case here. However, in this situation I am faced with the dilemma of not being able to acknowledge all who contributed. Many who are quoted are credited, of course, but there are others who, for obvious reasons, prefer to remain anonymous.

I would, however, like to offer special thanks to W. G. (Giff) Hoag, my friend and former mentor. Giff is a Farm Credit historian and the author of *The Farm Credit System . . . A History of Financial Self-Help,* in which he handles the monumental job of documenting "the rise of the Farm Credit empire." Special mention is also due Roger Stromberg, another former FCA colleague, whose patient counsel helped see me through the technical trauma of producing the text on a word processor. In this connection, I feel I must mention the skill of the Polaroid Corporation for rescuing my copy from a computer disk that was badly chewed up by Sissy, our resident Labrador/German shepherd. (Yes, Sissy still lives!)

Last but not least, I would like to thank my wife, Susan, who managed to persevere upstairs, despite the daily disasters that were unfolding in the basement below. All considered, the book has not been entirely a labor of love. I believe that, nonetheless, it will be well worth your time—that it will enhance and enrich your understanding of "the fall of the Farm Credit empire."

Abbreviations and Acronyms

Advertising Council of Cooperatives International	**ACCI**
Agency for International Development	**U.S. AID**
Agricultural Conservation Corporation	**ACC**
American Bankers Association	**ABA**
Archer Daniels Midland	**ADM**
Banks for Cooperatives	**BCs**
Central Bank for Cooperatives	**CBC**
chief executive officer	**CEO**
Congressional and Public Affairs division	**C&PA**
Cooperative League of the USA	**CLUSA**
Family Farm Movement	**FFM**
Farm Credit Administration	**FCA**
Farm Credit Corporation of America	**FCC/A**
Farm Credit System Capital Corporation	**FCSCC or Cap Corp**
Farm Credit System Financial Assistance Corporation	**FAC**
Farmers Home Administration	**FmHA**
Federal Agricultural Mortgage Corporation	**Farmer Mac**
Federal Deposit Insurance Corporation	**FDIC**
Federal Farm Mortgage Corporation	**FFMC**
Federal Home Loan Mortgage Corporation	**Freddie Mac**
Federal Intermediate Credit Banks	**FICBs**
Federal Land Bank Associations	**FLBAs**
Federal Land Banks	**FLBs**
Federal National Mortgage Corporation	**Fannie Mae**
Federal Reserve Board	**Fed, the**
Federal Savings and Loan Insurance Corporation	**FSLIC**
FmHA Debt Adjustment Program	**DAP**

General Accounting Office	**GAO**
Generally Accepted Accounting Practices	**GAAP**
Government National Mortgage Corporation	**Ginnie Mae**
Independent Bankers Association of America	**IBAA**
National Cooperative Business Association	**NCBA**
National Rural Electric Cooperative Association	**NRECA**
National Tax Equity Association	**NTEA**
Office of Management and Budget	**OMB**
Ohio Agricultural Financing Corporation	**AFC**
Ohio Agricultural Revenue Bond Program	**Aggie Bond**
other financial institutions	**OFIs**
Policy Coordination Committee	**PCC**
Production Credit Associations	**PCAs**
reductions in force	**RIF**
Regulatory Accounting Procedures	**RAP**
Security and Exchange Commission	**SEC**
United States Department of Agriculture	**USDA**
USDA Conservation Reserve Program	**CRP**

Introduction

"The bitter memory of what . . . was,
what is, and what must be."

John Milton, *Paradise Lost*

 Despite repeated denials throughout the summer of 1985 that the nearly seventy-year-old cooperative Farm Credit System, the nation's largest source of credit to agriculture, was in financial trouble, the rumors and newstories persisted. Congressmen in some rural areas were becoming nervous and restless, leading several (Rep. Cooper Evans of Iowa being the most vociferous) to raise the specter of the need for financial assistance from the federal government. The farmer-owned credit system (which had spent nearly half a century getting out of debt to the government in the first place) would have none of it: "Thanks, but no thanks." When it turned out later that substantial government assistance appeared to be necessary, the prospect appeared as painful to old-timers as General Lee's having to go to General Grant at Appomattox to discuss terms of surrender!

In response to the criticism, the Federal Farm Credit Board, the top policymaking body for the credit system at the time, did adopt a "Statement of Concern" on the farm crisis at its June 1985 meeting but went on to add these words of reassurance: "Based on (available) information, the Board believes—although the financial problems facing the System are severe—they continue to be manageable within System resources." This marked the first public admission by any Farm Credit official that all was not well.

Just three months later, on September 4, 1985, the *Wall Street Journal* captured the situation at the time:

Out of Options
Farm Credit System, Buried in Bad Loans, Seeks Big U.S. Bailout

Aid Could Add to the Deficit, Hurt Free-Market Goals; But Some Help Is Likely

Worry for System's Investors

Prominent in the story was this admission by Donald E. Wilkinson, governor of the Farm Credit Administration: "We've come to realize that the deterioration in agriculture has grown beyond the ability of [the Farm Credit System] to handle it. We cannot absorb the losses we face." Charles F. McCoy, the article's author, described the situation: "Whipsawed by the faltering farm economy, the System has been racing for weeks to rein in its mounting credit problems. Now, that race appears to be lost."

The breaking of this story was a shot heard around the world. The proud Farm Credit System had been held up as a role model for other (particularly developing) nations to emulate, and it was truly the envy of the entire world. Cooperative and credit specialists by the hundreds flocked to the United States to see first hand a most successful demonstration of how a government, in partnership with a segment of its people (in this case, farmers) had built such a magnificent credit facility. The System was a demonstration of the principle of self-help at its finest, and it had become the very hallmark of the U.S. AID (Agency for International Development) programs.

Further, the Farm Credit System demonstrated how a government, after assisting at the outset by providing the necessary seed capital and other encouragement, was willing not only to provide a means for these farmers to buy out the government's interest through stock investment, but, after which, to withdraw from the partnership and permit the farmers to run their own show and not be forever beholden to that government. The System also pays for the costs of its government regulation by funding the Farm Credit Administration. As Farm Credit people were fond of putting it, "the System operates at no cost to the U.S. taxpayers."

Moreover, during the period of this partnership these farmers and their cooperatives had developed a funding mechanism that served as a vehicle for moving capital (most of which is generated in the cities) into rural America. It did so by pooling the assets of farmers, used as collateral to back Farm Credit securities. These securities were sold, without benefit of a government guarantee, to investors. This enabled farmers to borrow money at the cost of money, plus the cost of carrying on the lending business. This also meant farmers could borrow at rates comparable to (or lower than) those charged other businessmen. It is said that the System had made first-class credit citizens of farmers who, historically, had to take what they could get in the way of credit. One had to admit that the whole experience was unique, refreshing.

Following September 4, 1985, or "Black Wednesday" as it is now known in Farm Credit circles, there was no consensus on what to do; only a babel of voices. Not many farmers, even though they stood to lose the most—their stock investment and a dependable source of credit—raised their voices in protest. A return to government control did not seem to concern them, perhaps because most were not around to know what conditions were like before there was a Farm Credit System. Also, they felt they had too many other things to worry about. In their Farm Credit System, farmers had the best of both worlds—government and nongovernment—and did not fully appreciate it.

The cooperative Farm Credit System was established to perform a business service. It did not, as some borrowers felt, have the divine right to lower interest rates. There was a period of time in the late 1970s when the prime interest rate was at 19 percent. The Farm Credit System at the time was lending money at around 14 percent, basing its charges, as it had traditionally done, on the average cost of money. This situation made a hero of the System at the time, but it created immense problems when interest rates did not return to a "normal" level as they had in the past.

When bad times hit, farmers tended to turn on their credit system and were inclined to vent their spleen publicly, sometimes cursing the System for what some considered to be "treasonous behavior." Moreover, it has become obvious that there had been over expectations of the System on the part of farmers as to what ownership of a banking institution meant. At the very least, there had been faulty communication.

How well the FCA has done its job has also become a subject of great debate, particularly since "Black Wednesday." There are those who charge that the regulator/supervisor was too close to the supervised. Critics from the competing agricultural division of the American Bankers Association (and even some of the System's friends) used to characterize it as being "an incestuous relationship." There was little consensus within the System on what ought or ought not be done about the FCA. There are those who contend that the changes in the structure and role of the regulator were too severe—that Congress, in its zeal to assist failing farmers, has "thrown out the baby with the bathwater." They say that, certainly, something that has served the nation so well for so many years could not so suddenly have gone sour.

In any case, enough dissatisfaction was voiced (coupled with other unsettling events) to bring drastic changes in the relationship between the FCA and the Farm Credit banks and to add to the trauma Farm Credit has experienced. Whereas the old supervisory relationship was best described as one of advocacy, FCA spokesmen all of a sudden spoke of the relationship as being at "arm's length" from the System. These changes are contained in "The Farm Credit Amendments Act of 1985," passed in a rush by Congress in December of that year as a response to growing problems, and incorporated as amendments to the Farm Credit Act of 1971, the charter act under which the System operates. As the amendments were implemented by the FCA, Farm Credit System officials, accustomed to the more friendly environs of the past, were more inclined to term the new relationship "adversarial," a description that appears to be borne out by the facts, particularly when the full implications of the credit crunch became obvious. The FCA tended to fire broadsides at the System, rather than being merely critical, as is the case with other financial regulators. In any event, the transition has proved to be exceedingly difficult.

It is obvious, too, that much has been lost in the transition—the

Federal Farm Credit Board, for instance. This thirteen-member, part-time board, oversaw the Farm Credit Administration and was responsible for appointing the agency's chief executive officer—the governor (who did the hiring and firing of the rest of the FCA staff). Such an arrangement helped minimize partisan politics within the agency. The Federal Board was the inspiration of a bi-partisan Congress—a noble constitutional experiment. Its demise, although partially self-inflicted, was also a product of the times, and was not due to its bipartisan makeup.

The Federal Farm Credit Board was replaced by a three-member FCA board, appointed by the president of the United States. As a result, the Farm Credit Administration changed drastically in a few months after the new board was installed from one of the least political agencies in government to one of the most political. A case will be presented here that this change in the long pull is detrimental to the best interests of agriculture. Such politicization, however, is not the reason for "the fall of the Farm Credit empire." Rather, it will stand as one of the stumbling blocks preventing the System from ever regaining its former independent position.

The System's fall can be attributed to one main factor—lack of farm income. The prolonged agricultural recession of the 1980s heaped so much stress on the System that it triggered a series of events and circumstances that brought the System to its knees. An accompanying decline in agricultural land prices resulted in a dramatic increase in the use of the System's loan loss reserves, leading to an equally dramatic fall in the System's income. The number of nonaccrual (uncollectible) loans skyrocketed.

Flaws in System management—and bad management in many instances—constituted the second most important factor in the System's downfall. The unfortunate timing of System bond sales and the pricing of loans in the late 1970s and early 1980s left the System with a high cost of funds. There also was a rapid expansion of loan volume, caused by liberal lending policies that were fanned by passage of the Farm Credit Act of 1971. In short, the impact of general economic factors and internal mistakes were the main causes for the System's downfall.

Lack of farm income also called attention to one of the Farm Credit System's other glaring weaknesses—an inefficient, cumbersome structure. The System had obviously "growed like Topsy" and done little or nothing to correct it own disorganized expansion. Over the years, new units were added to the System, not integrated into it. This became the root for considerable internal strife caused by internal competition. Although the need to be competitive with the commercial banking industry may have ultimately forced merger and consolidation, "Black Wednesday" dictated that such reorganization happen sooner. The System, up to its neck in lending problems, was ill-prepared to handle the trauma of merger.

This book will indicate where mistakes were made and that there is plenty of blame to go around. It should be noted, too, that the world is full of second-guessers, and events of the past many months indicate that Farm Credit has contributed more than its fair share of them. This book was not written in an effort to be added to this list. Instead, the book attempts to shed more light on the situation in an effort to learn from past mistakes; so the errors need not be repeated. As for the future, if any, of the Farm Credit System, the jury, at this writing, is still out. This account is written in the fervent hope that it will contribute to the Farm Credit System's effort to rise, like the phoenix, from its ashes.

The Fall of the Farm Credit Empire

1

The Farm Credit System . . . A Cast of Thousands

"All the world's a stage,
And all the men and women merely players"

William Shakespeare, *As You Like It*

For an institution that supplies one-third of the financing for a nation's agriculture—at its high watermark in June of 1983, well over $80 billion a year and serving well over a million farmers—it seems inconceivable that the cooperative Farm Credit System could have been so little known. It is even more surprising when you consider the part the System has played in helping the United States become the unsurpassed producer of food and fiber that it is today, an achievement that in the past has been considered a miracle. In any case, the growing problems of agriculture had enveloped the Farm Credit System and played a major role in its downfall.

The Farm Credit System did not become anything near a household phrase until it got into financial trouble in the mid-1980s. Sadly, its fame came then in the form of notoriety. Stories of United States agriculture's economic problems made headlines for some time and were the subject of many radio and TV documentaries. The topic even provided highly emotional plots for a number of movies. As a lender, the Farm Credit System bore much of the brunt of this negative publicity. Becoming aware of the cooperative Farm Credit System in such a haphazard fashion tends to confuse as much as to enlighten and would appear to be grossly unfair to an institution that has accomplished so much.

One reason for the System's past anonymity is that unfortunately it is complicated—needlessly so. To fully understand and appreciate this vast credit resource, it is essential to become more familiar with its nomenclature, operating principles, and structure even though it is destined to change. Perhaps the place to start is at the beginning, which is with the Federal Land Banks (FLBs). Congress established the twelve Federal Land Banks in twelve districts across the country, along with literally hundreds of local affiliated associations that serve as local agents for the land banks (called Federal Land Bank Associations—FLBAs). This was accomplished under terms of the Federal Farm Loan Act, enacted by Congress in 1916 to answer the crying need for long-term mortgage credit, an area that was not being serviced by the existing banking community. The success of the Farm Loan Act is indicated by the fact that it became known as the "Magna Charta of American farm finance."

The act made it possible for United States farmers to obtain a dependable source of credit for the first time. The most immediate dividend for farmers was that the Federal Land Banks, through their long-term, amortized loans made it possible for a farmer or rancher to purchase a farm over a period of up to forty years, delivering him from the need to face his local banker or other lender every one to five years to have his loan renewed. The uncertainty of the renewal could be a harrowing experience.

The Farm Loan Act was an inspired, fresh approach to lending, not only providing farmers with a source of credit, but giving them an opportunity to participate in the system of credit. Congress was committed. The act provided only the initial seed capital, but it also set forth these guiding principles, which are still enunciated in current law, the Farm Credit Act of 1971, under which the System now operates:

> It is declared to be the policy of the Congress, recognizing that a prosperous, productive agriculture is essential to a free nation and recognizing the growing need for credit in rural areas, that the farmer-owned cooperative Farm Credit System be designed to accomplish the objective of improving income and well-being of American farmers and ranchers by furnishing sound, adequate and constructive credit.
>
> It is the objective . . . to continue to encourage farm- and rancher-borrowers' participation in the management, control and

FIG. 1.1.   *The cooperative Farm Credit System got its start on July 17, 1916, when President Woodrow Wilson signed the Federal Farm Loan Act. USDA photo.*

ownership of a permanent system of credit for agriculture which will be responsive to the credit needs.

How did this ownership manifest itself? When a farmer received a loan from an association, an amount was invested in proportion to his loan (historically, five percent) in the stock of his local association. The association, then, invested an equal amount of stock in its land bank. By owning stock, a farmer became more than a borrower; he became a member and part owner at the same time. As such, farmers began managing their own credit affairs by electing directors to their local association boards. In order to be considered for a directorship, one had to be an active member-borrower. The board then was responsible for hiring its general manager, who was responsible for hiring staff and handling day-to-day operations.

For many years, some (usually three) members of the board served on the loan committee of the association along with the general manager. This presented and an interesting scenario. As a fellow farmer, a loan committee member would want to approve a loan application. Yet, as a director of the association, the same farmer was obliged to look after other borrowers' investment in the association and, therefore, would not want to make a bad loan. This put the loan committee member in the position of making loan decisions using both head and heart.

The two other units of the cooperative Farm Credit System came about later for the same reason as the Federal Land Banks — out of dire need. The Great Depression of the 1930s provided the need, and the success of the land banks provided the incentive to act. Much has been written about the catastrophic effects of the depression on American agriculture. Among the more serious of these bad effects was a lack of credit to finance planting crops. Whereas there was some of this type of credit available when the Federal Land Banks were established in 1916, in the early 1930s there was virtually no credit at all and little prospect of any in the future.

Because of the initial success of the Federal Land Banks, Congress first looked in that direction, attempting to get the land banks to add short-term credit to their line of services. But the land bank forces pleaded with the government to look elsewhere; the land banks had their hands full trying to save farmers who were losing their farms. Although the land banks' contention was an accurate assessment of the situation, in retrospect it still would have been better in the long run had these banks taken the new lending service under their wing, since cleavage and coordination problems subsequently developed (a matter that will be dealt with in detail later).

And so it was, by virtue of the Farm Credit Act of 1933, that the Production Credit Associations (PCAs) were created. The PCAs were to work much the same way in the short-term credit field (sixty to ninety days or up to a year) as the land banks worked in the long-term mortgage area. Instead of working with district land banks, however, the PCAs received their loan funds from respective district Federal Intermediate Credit Banks (FICBs).

The FICBs had been established in 1923 as a discount bank to provide funds for the making of agricultural, non–real estate loans. The FICBs were unsuccessful in fulfilling their mission at the outset, mainly because of their remoteness from rural areas. The local service concept was fulfilled through the establishment of Production Credit Associations in 1933. It not only reestablished the valid principle of bringing the loan service close to the farmer, but, as was the case with the Federal

Land Banks, provided farmers with the opportunity to participate. Oddly, the proliferation of PCAs created problems later. As communications and travel improved and the size of farms and capital needs increased, the need for so many associations diminished. Many small associations became obsolete and needed to be merged and consolidated for the sake of improved efficiency. This situation created a king-size dilemma for the System and is an integral part of the overall story. The FICBs also maintained supervisory authority over the PCAs, a responsibility that expanded greatly in the mid-1980s as the Farm Credit Administration, the government supervisory agency, assumed a more regulatory posture with respect to the Farm Credit System.

Even after the establishment of Production Credit Associations, the FICBs continued to also provide funds to other agricultural lenders, referred to in the system as "other financial institutions" (OFIs). These OFIs included agricultural credit corporations and even some commercial banks. Use of the FICBs as a source of funds for OFIs was not altogether a happy arrangement. Many PCAs resented the OFIs because they felt that farmers would be better served by their own associations. On the other hand, the OFIs often felt like outsiders—that PCAs received preferred treatment from their FICBs.

The act of 1933 also set up the thirteen Banks for Cooperatives (BCs). Twelve are district banks while the thirteenth bank, the Central Bank for Cooperatives (CBC), is owned by and provides services to the other twelve and participates mainly in financing the larger loans. Again, the BCs, like the other units of the Farm Credit System, were established out of need—to provide a dependable loan service to the nation's farmer cooperatives. The BCs have assisted in the establishment of many new co-ops over the years.

Generally, to be eligible for a BC loan, a co-op had to be engaged in (or be soon to become engaged in) one of the following functions:

1. Storing, packing, processing, or marketing farm products
2. Purchasing, testing, grading, processing, furnishing, or distributing farm supplies
3. Furnishing business services to farmers or to other eligible cooperatives, including rural electric cooperatives

Later, all such BC lending services were extended to producers of aquatic products.

In short, the Banks for Cooperatives provide a complete line of lending services to agricultural, aquatic, and rural utility cooperatives. Historically, this has amounted to over 65 percent of the financial needs of the nation's agricultural co-ops. The BCs were also affected by change — modernization, improvement in communications, shortening of distances, and the need to consolidate. There was also another reason for the BCs to consolidate. Some of their member co-ops outgrew their regional BCs. Although the BCs proved to be helpful in bringing about mergers among their constituents in some instances, they found the process difficult when they tried to apply consolidation to their own institutions.

At the time the *Wall Street Journal* exploded the "Black Wednesday" article, the lending operations of the cooperative Farm Credit System were carried on by a network of thirty-seven member-owned, regional banks — twelve Federal Land Banks, twelve Federal Intermediate Credit Banks and thirteen Banks for Cooperatives, as well as hundreds of various local lending units such as the Federal Land Bank Associations and the Production Credit Associations. Together, the banks and associations compose what is known as the cooperative Farm Credit System.

It is pertinent to point out that as of the close of 1987 the Farm Credit System was not one huge bank, but rather a loose federation of many banks. It was, in fact, a federation of separate corporations. It was a system mainly in the sense that it operated under the same charter, dedicated to the same purpose of meeting the financial needs of farmers and their cooperatives. The banks were otherwise bound together for the purpose of funding.

As the accompanying chart illustrates the cooperative Farm Credit System is organized on a regional basis (see Fig. 1.2). However, Congress has mandated severe changes in this structure, as outlined in the Agricultural Credit Act of 1987. The 1987 act prescribes a decrease (merger) in the number of districts, with the Banks for Cooperatives likely being reduced to one bank.

Perhaps the most interesting and significant facet of this story is the extent of people involvement that exists — farmers managing their own credit affairs. In addition to electing their own boards of directors at the local (association) level, borrowers also had a voice in electing their district boards. Each of the three groups (PCAs, FLBAs and co-ops) that borrowed from their regional BC participated in electing two members to the seven-member district Farm Credit Board. Until passage of

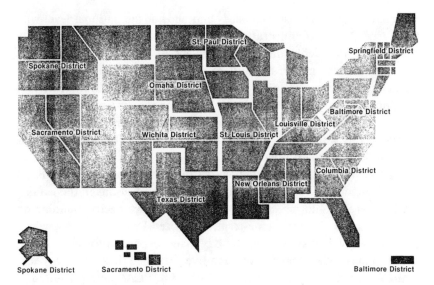

FIG. 1.2. *For many years the cooperative Farm Credit System was divided into twelve Farm Credit districts. This structure was greatly changed by the Agricultural Credit Act of 1987, which called for a number of mergers. FCA map.*

the Farm Credit Amendments Act of 1985, the seventh director was appointed by the governor of the Farm Credit Administration. Now the seventh board director is elected at large in each district.

The Farm Credit System even had input in the naming of the Federal Farm Credit Board, which was the top national policy-making body until passage of the 1985 act. Although twelve of the thirteen federal board members were appointed by the president of the United States with the advice and consent of the United States Senate, the president was required to consider the nominees advanced by the System in making such appointments. With three exceptions all selections to this board have been made from the System nominees since the Federal Board was established by the Farm Credit Act of 1953. The thirteenth member of the Federal Farm Credit Board was appointed by the secretary of agriculture and served at his pleasure.

As indicated by its charter act, there was a deliberate effort within the System to maintain a bottom-up structure. This philosophy is obvious in examining one of its organization charts (see Fig. 1.3). This chart places the farmer-borrowers at the top and flows down through the associations and the district boards and ends at the national level with the Farm Credit Administration and the Federal Farm Credit Board. Also, there was deliberate encouragement of using a "we" approach when referring to any of the System institutions. This fostered the frequent use of the word "cooperative" when referring to the System. This terminology proved to be an asset in building the System because most farmers considered themselves members, not just borrowers. Doubtless, however, this philosophy added to the System's difficulties when the structure started to crumble in 1985.

By having control over its own destiny in the credit area, the Farm Credit System was able to make a number of innovations in the lending field, generally tailoring credit to the farmers' own needs. Building on the land banks and their long-term, amortized loan, the PCAs, which started mainly with sixty-to-ninety-day loans, expanded to yearly loans, then to intermediate loans of three to five years and then to seven years. Ultimately, with the Farm Credit Act of 1980, PCAs were permitted to make loans with terms up to fifteen years, a move that further alienated the PCAs from their FLBA brethren.

If there was a perceived need, the System generally managed to expand its service to cover it, even if such enlargement required congressional action. Prior to the fall, bipartisan congressional support was usually automatic, given sufficient consensus within the System and little or no outside opposition.

Another critical element of the Farm Credit System is the manner in which it obtains its loan funds. The System, in cooperation with groups of security dealers and dealer banks, had for many years gotten its loan funds by selling securities to the investing public through a joint fiscal agent in New York City. So popular and accepted were Farm Credit securities among investors for many years that the System was able to obtain its funds at rates comparable to those charged the government without a government guarantee. The System's fiscal agent is called the Federal Farm Credit Banks Funding Corporation, with headquarters in the heart of New York City's financial district.

System securities were the joint liability of all thirty-seven Farm Credit banks, a matter that has been under heavy dispute as some of the troubled banks sought financial assistance from their healthier sister banks. This is a matter that will, if not resolved by the Agricultural Credit Act of 1987, most likely be settled in the courts. The main problem rests with the fact that although each bank is a part of a Farm Credit

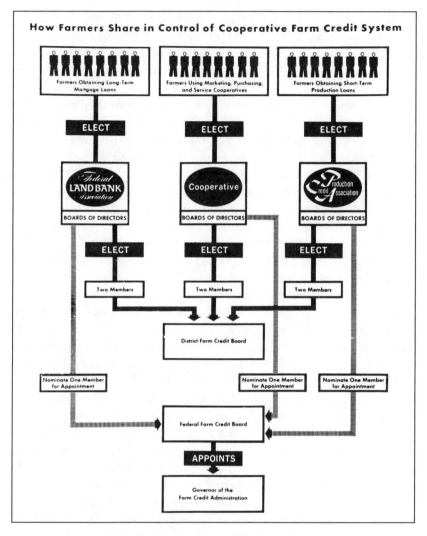

FIG. 1.3. *Farmer-members were immensely proud of their cooperative Farm Credit System. There was a feeling of ownership and control. As is illustrated in the flow chart, a bottom-up control philosophy prevailed. FCA chart.*

System for the purpose of funding, it is also a separate corporate entity with fiduciary responsibilities to its respective stockholders. Although a well Farm Credit bank might prefer to assist troubled banks as a way to maintain the System as a system, such an action could (and has in some instances) place a bank in a position to be sued by its stockholders. In other words, the Farm Credit System for many years was strong because it was perceived as a nationwide credit system. However, when trouble struck, the banks of the System were not able to hang together in many instances.

As is true for all banking institutions operating under a federal charter, there is a government agency, the Farm Credit Administration (FCA), designated to supervise and regulate the Farm Credit System. The Farm Credit Administration was established in 1933 by an executive order of President Franklin Roosevelt. At that time all Farm Credit System institutions were placed under its supervision. The FCA remained an independent agency until 1939 when, for the second time, it was made part of the United States Department of Agriculture (USDA). FCA was returned to independent status by the Farm Credit Act of 1953, which also paved the way for the System's eventual complete farmer-ownership status. This corporate independence was achieved amid great fanfare in 1968. Although the land banks had been completely farmer-owned by 1947, a few PCAs and BCs did not achieve member-ownership status until 1968. Actually, there really was no great financial incentive to gain self-ownership; it was tempting to be able to continue to make use of cheap government capital. It was more a matter of pride and the desire for independence that goes with cutting the umbilical cord.

Although the FCA is an official agency of the United States government and the funds to cover costs are appropriated by Congress, all FCA expenses are passed along and paid by the banks and associations of the System, which were then able to claim that Farm Credit was completely self-sufficient. The primary functions of the FCA are to maintain the System's integrity by assuring that its units operate according to the law and the regulations governing its activities, to examine the institutions that compose the System, and to attempt to coordinate some of the System's activities in a manner that serves the public interest and the best interests of the borrowers at the same time. The FCA carried out these duties for many years, with little hint of impropriety or scandal. FCA's performance was rarely questioned — that is, until 1985.

So, there you have it — the entity that was generally considered to be Farm Credit for many years. Although the term "Farm Credit" was often used to indicate only the Farm Credit Administration, its common use was more generic and encompassed all Farm Credit institutions, including FCA, an agency of the United States government. However flawed such a definition may have become in many respects, the latter definition for Farm Credit shall be its usage here.

Farm Credit has made very little change in its structure since 1933. However, some other organizations have been added to the Farm Credit System over the years. A few of them were established quite recently to help assist the System through its crisis. Since their names will be mentioned in the telling of the story, additional farm credit institutions are briefly described below.

The Farm Credit Corporation of America (FCC/A) was chartered in 1985 basically to fill the void left by the FCA. FCC/A provides a mechanism for formulating System policies and guidelines. It was to serve as a vehicle for System policy development and for promoting self-regulation and self-discipline within the System. At least at its outset, FCC/A was often referred to as the "central entity" within the System. Headquartered in Denver, FCC/A also served as the System's voice on issues of national importance (a particularly delicate and critical function formerly handled by the FCA) and provided System banks with a number of services in the areas of risk management, human resources management and training, communications, and research. Other responsibilities included managing the systemwide planning process and setting system standards and guidelines in the areas of credit, finance, and information and reporting.

Owned by the Farm Credit banks (with the exception of Texas banks at this writing), FCC/A is governed by a board of directors elected by and from the boards of the Farm Credit districts and the Central Bank for Cooperatives. FCC/A's continued effectiveness depends largely on the willingness of the Farm Credit districts to give up some of their individual sovereignty, a sacrifice that has not come easily. At this writing, there are many who say that the Farm Credit Corporation of America has yet to realize its potential or to achieve its expectations. If that be true, then it is largely because its members have not permitted it to do so.

The Farm Credit Council is the trade association for the Farm Credit System and other agricultural cooperative lenders, taking over another role formerly handled by the Farm Credit Administration. The council began operations in 1983 and "serves to protect and promote its members' interests in the nation's capital." Most Farm Credit districts have a council of their own, which assists the national organization and works with state legislatures in their respective districts. As a federated trade association representing an industry (cooperative agricultural lenders, not just the cooperative Farm Credit System), the Farm Credit Council technically is not an entity of the System and, therefore, is not subject to FCA regulation. The Farm Credit Council and the FCC/A have a common board of directors and at one time it was assumed that the council would become an integral part of the FCC/A and, combined, become more of a trade association.

The Farm Credit System Capital Corporation (FCSCC) gained official status under the Farm Credit Amendments Act of 1985, after it was established on an ad hoc basis months earlier by the FCA. The FCSCC was designed to deal with troubled Farm Credit institutions by providing financial and technical assistance to Farm Credit banks and associations experiencing severe financial difficulties. The FCSCC was authorized to purchase problem loans and acquire properties from troubled System institutions, using capital from assessments made to the System's stronger banks and associations. These assessments were designed to be repaid by the FCSCC in proportion to the dollar amount generated from the liquidation of the assets used for the purchases and acquisitions. In view of events surrounding the System in the 1980s, it goes without saying that the FCSCC was very busy indeed. The FCSCC was headquartered in Kansas City, Missouri, not in Denver with the FCC/A. (It was assumed by the System that the two agencies would be housed together. This provides an interesting sidelight that will be covered later.) The FCSCC was governed by a five-member board, three members are elected by the System and two were appointed by the chairman of the Farm Credit Administration Board.

The operations of the Farm Credit System Capital Corporation became academic with passage of the Agricultural Credit Act of 1987, with the FCSCC succeeded by the Farm Credit System Financial Assistance Corporation (FAC). The FAC's functions remained substantially the same, as it oversees the infusion of government capital. Initially (until January 30, 1992), the new Financial Assistance Corporation was to be operated by a three-member Assistance Board, made up of the secretary of agriculture, the secretary of treasury, and a member appointed by the president. Ultimately (when the federal assistance funds are repaid by the system), the new Financial Assistance Corporation will have the same board as the Federal Farm Credit Banks Funding Corporation.

The Farm Credit Leasing Services Corporation was established in 1983 and provides leasing services to agricultural producers and

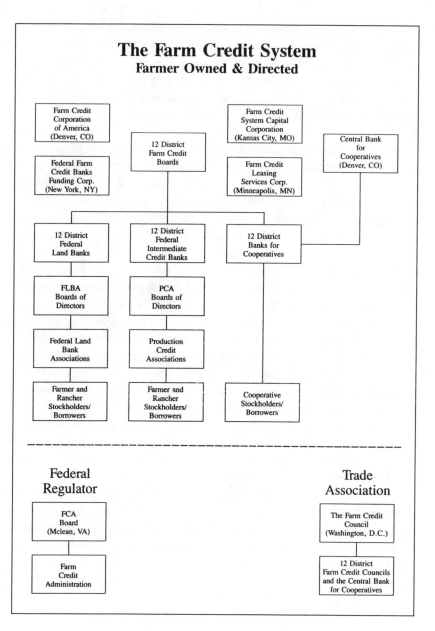

The Farm Credit System
Farmer Owned & Directed

Farm Credit
Corporation
of America
(Denver, CO)

Federal Farm
Credit Banks
Funding Corp.
(New York, NY)

12 District
Farm Credit
Boards

Farm Credit
System Capital
Corporation
(Kansas City, MO)

Farm Credit
Leasing
Services Corp.
(Minneapolis, MN)

Central Bank
for
Cooperatives
(Denver, CO)

12 District
Federal
Land Banks

12 District
Federal
Intermediate
Credit Banks

12 District
Banks for
Cooperatives

FLBA
Boards of
Directors

PCA
Boards of
Directors

Federal Land
Bank
Associations

Production
Credit
Associations

Farmer and
Rancher
Stockholders/
Borrowers

Farmer and
Rancher
Stockholders/
Borrowers

Cooperative
Stockholders/
Borrowers

Federal Regulator

FCA
Board
(Mclean, VA)

Farm
Credit
Administration

Trade Association

The Farm Credit
Council
(Washington, D.C.)

12 District
Farm Credit Councils
and the Central Bank
for Cooperatives

FIG. 1.4. *The Farm Credit System, table of organization. FCA chart.*

cooperatives, mainly to rural electric and telephone organizations and Farm Credit entities. At the close of 1988, the corporation had a portfolio of $285 million, with assets of nearly $181 million. The Corporation is owned by the Farm Credit Banks. It has a nine-member board—five members elected by and from the owner-banks and four elected by and from the customers of the corporation.

It is well to recognize that Farm Credit is more than a group of institutions; it is people. The emphasis has always been on people. The Farm Credit "empire," like motion pictures based on its Roman counterpart, can also literally boast "a cast of thousands." First and foremost were the borrowers. At its high-water mark in loan volume (1983), the PCAs and the FLBs had upwards of a million borrower-members, even taking into account any duplication of those who had both a PCA and FLB loan, as well as those who had more than one loan. In addition, the BCs had well over three thousand loans outstanding to farmer cooperatives, accounting for thousands of other farmers affected by the System. Add to this number the hundreds of employees at the association, district, and national level as well as employees of other agricultural cooperatives, and you come up with an even more impressive figure.

As W. Gifford (Giff) Hoag, longtime Farm Credit Administration employee and writer, described in his history of Farm Credit, "the Farm Credit System has been highly successful dollarwise. But even more importantly, it has been highly successful peoplewise. It has been instrumental—the catalyst supplying much of the financial power—in helping farmers increase the food and fiber supply for more consumers on this earth at a reasonable cost."

All true. Or, at least it was when Hoag's book was first published in 1976. Historically, people have provided the Farm Credit System with its greatest strength and resource. As things are turning out, however, too much people involvement may turn out to be the Farm Credit System's Achilles heel. In any event, all members are a part of the story of the Farm Credit empire.

2

The Beginning of the Fall

"Watch out w'en youer gettin' all you want.
Fattenin' hogs ain't in luck."

Joel Chandler Harris, *Uncle Remus: Plantation Proverbs*

Looking back, there were just not many issues that concerned the cooperative Farm Credit System in the early 1980s. Well, perhaps there was one—the perennial issue—a renewed threat to its continued open access to the money market. The American Bankers Association (ABA) kept grousing about the "unfair advantage" the System had because of its "agency status" and brought it up before congressional banking committees at every opportunity. At the time, it did not appear that the ABA would get very far with its complaint, probably because few people took the time to figure out what they were talking about. When things appeared to be going well, why bother? The ABA longed for the day when the banking committees would share joint jurisdiction over Farm Credit along with the agriculture committees. With the rumored agreements that went on behind the scenes in gaining passage of the Agricultural Act of 1987, joint jurisdiction was a growing probability.

Agency status is a difficult thing to define because it is not any one thing but several. Dr. George Irwin, chief economist for FCA for many years, had the question put to him regularly by the FCA staff and the Federal Farm Credit Board. This is the substance of his explanation:

> The Congress has provided a number of unique characteristics that help ensure that financial markets will remain receptive to the

amount of FC System securities that need to be sold. Taken together, this set of characteristics is commonly referred to as "agency status." These, along with the strength the System has built for itself—the sound capitalization, impeccable payment record, recognized skill in agricultural lending, and broad diversification of loan risks within agriculture—enable the System to sell large volumes of securities at favorable interest rates, even in times of adverse economic conditions.

Some of those unique characteristics are:

1. issuance of securities under authority of an act of Congress,
2. exemption from registration under federal security law (Thus, the FCA approves terms and rates, not the Security and Exchange Commission—SEC.),
3. issuance and payment of securities through facilities of the Federal Reserve,
4. legal investments of federally-supervised financial institutions,
5. eligibility of Farm Credit securities as collateral for advances and discounts from the Federal Reserve System,
6. unlimited purchase of Farm Credit securities by national banks,
7. purchase and sale of Farm Credit securities as part of the Federal Reserve's open market operations,
8. qualification of Farm Credit securities as collateral for public deposits,
9. exemption from state and local taxation on interest income, and
10. eligibility as investments by credit unions and savings and loan associations.

The Farm Credit System is not truly unique in this respect. Agency status is shared with other government-sponsored financial agencies such as the Federal National Mortgage Corporation (Fannie Mae), the Government National Mortgage Corporation (Ginnie Mae), and the Federal Home Loan Mortgage Corporation (Freddie Mac). As a matter of fact, all banks operating under a federal charter are granted some sort of special status, including the commercial banking industry. The System's agency status was granted on the basis of its public purpose, as outlined in the preamble of its charter act. At the same time the System was otherwise limited by its purpose—obliged to serve in all farming areas at all times and under all economic conditions. The System could not, as is true for commercial banks and insurance companies, jump in or jump out of agriculture as the market indicates.

Both Republican and Democratic administrations have challenged the System's agency status, particularly during times when, for various reasons, they felt it desirable to get a firmer grip on the money market. However, as soon as a crisis subsided, so did the hue and cry to strip the System of its status. It is true that the Reagan administration has been the most persistent in its efforts to gain control, but the Carter White House also expressed similar sentiments on the subject. The Reagan administration, however, came up with a new strategy intended to reduce the benefits of agency status — a user fee, a charge for the use of agency status privileges.

The Reagan administration also brought a new term into common use. As explained by the Heritage Foundation:

> A new word — privatization — has entered the lexicon of federal budget making. Put simply, privatization means the transference of federal assets and activities to the private sector. Facilities owned by the federal government can be sold to the private sector; these same facilities can be kept in federal hands but managed by private firms or groups; federal services can be provided, under contact by private firms; or low-income Americans can be given the means to obtain services in the private sector.

The administration made no secret of the fact that the Farm Credit System was one of those groups being targeted, arguing that the System should be public or private, but not both.

The Farm Credit System, therefore, had something very constructive for the newly installed Farm Credit Council to do. The council proceeded to haul out some old ammunition to counter this threat, claiming that charging a user fee would amount to running up the price of food and fiber. It would have an impact on interest rates to farmers, the cost of which would have to be passed along to the consumers. The council also argued that upping the cost of food would have an impact on the international market, making farm products from the United States even less competitive.

Agency status is a privilege bestowed by the government. However, the System felt that such status was something it had earned over the years. What's more, it had worked well for all concerned. So, the System also used another agreement that came into common use during the

1980s "If it ain't broke, don't fix it." This seemed to make a lot of sense to Congress and others. So before September 1985, the pleas of the System's critics seemed to fall on deaf ears. The push for a user fee in the Office of Management and Budget (OMB) and Treasury did not prevail either, at least not yet.

So it was that in 1985 the Farm Credit System could afford to feel a bit smug—like it could take on all comers. After all, the System was fresh from another recent victory on the legislative battlefield—the Farm Credit Act Amendments of 1980—that it had won (albeit in the eleventh hour) against rather considerable odds. The 1980 act contained a number of new lending authorities, the most widely heralded of which was permission for the banks for cooperatives to finance the foreign transactions of U.S. farmer co-ops. It was felt at the time that this authority would not only increase the amount of agricultural exports, but would enhance the farmers' share of the profits. Unfortunately, the new lending authority had not worked out that way by 1985. It was something of a disappointment even though, since that time, things are looking better. In January 1988, for example, the Central Bank for Cooperatives, which provides this lending service, showed loans outstanding of over $1 billion, and it had not shown a loss in its first five years of operation.

The early disappointment in the international lending authority was unfortunate, however. The cost to the System in getting the legislation had been quite high because the System at times had to do battle with longtime friends. Although all farm organizations were strongly in support of enhancing foreign agricultural trade, there were a few that were dead set against some other features of the 1980 legislation, particularly the proposal to permit the System to expand its credit-related business services (mainly insurance) to its member-borrowers. Most farm organizations provide their own insurance services to farmers, a practice that tends to bind a farmer to a certain farm group. To a volunteer farm organization, having a farmer holding your insurance not only makes the annual membership drive much easier, but the insurance premiums help fund the organization.

Despite the hazard of alienating some farm groups, the System proceeded with its legislative efforts in 1980 and, with an assist from the agriculturally-oriented Independent Bankers Association of America (IBAA), was able to defeat the powerful ABA in the halls of Congress. The System had to feel pretty good about that and could not be faulted for thinking that in its own bailiwick, at least, there was not much it could not do, once it put its mind to it.

Despite increasing signs of diminishing agricultural prosperity, there appeared to be little concern in the System over worsening farm prices. Apparently, there was a feeling that this recession, like the others since World War II, was only temporary. It, too, would pass. It was easy to revel in the past. After all, the cooperative Farm Credit System was among the nation's more innovative and enlightened financial achievements, and it served an industry — agriculture — whose production ability was being described as a miracle. The System was also content with the feeling that it had wisely built up sufficient surpluses and reserves over the years to protect it from any eventuality, an assessment that proved to be invalid.

The System's rise was not only unique; in some respects, it was breathtaking. In the early years, particularly during the worst years of the Great Depression when much of the System was established, there was an indomitable, pioneering, self-reliant, yet cooperative, spirit that seemed to inspire farmers to press ahead against what must have appeared to be insurmountable odds. The new banking units added to the System in the Great Depression were not given much of a chance for success at the time. After all, what did farmers and college agricultural specialists know about finance? As was pointed out by this author in *Bank for Cooperatives: A Quarter Century of Progress,*

> At best, these banks and associations were considered an adventure in courageous lending. But the time was ripe for experimentation. It was less a sin to try and fail than not to try at all. People had become disillusioned with the order of things. Fortunately, among these new people were many who, not realizing something was impossible, tried it and discovered it possible after all.

Knowing about this legacy helps one understand more readily why the System felt so confident. System borrowers of the early 1980s were proud of this heritage. They were also somewhat resentful that the commercial banking industry in the past had not come to their aid. Many farmers relished hearing stories about how the bankers had pretty much ignored farmers as a source of business. As my father, a dairy farmer, was fond of recalling, "Now, old [local banker] is a fine Christian gentleman, but he wouldn't loan me a dollar if I was starving!"

Such bitter memories tended to whip up farmers' competitive spirits and make them want to do things on their own. Through the development of the cooperative Farm Credit System, farmers were provided the opportunity to become their own bankers. Once given this chance, the upstart farmers had the bad manners to destroy the myth that had surrounded the banking industry all these many years—that finance is a very specialized business, best left to the experts. In retrospect, it can be said that in the field of agriculture there are not many experts around either. The same goes for finance, and not just agricultural finance.

Almost immediately, the farmers with their new piece of credit machinery started messing around with loan terms and other instruments of credit and, in general, tailoring loans and terms to fit their own special needs. Also, once they established a good reputation with their security sales, the System banks were able to supply credit to farmers at rates comparable to (or below) those charged their business counterparts on Main Street. The commercial banking industry, which had either ignored farmers altogether or treated them with benign neglect, began to sit up and take notice. This initial success (particularly that of the PCAs in short-term credit) began to draw attention from the bankers on Main Street, who began voicing their concerns about Farm Credit to their trade associations and who have since not been inclined to underestimate the Farm Credit System. However, until 1985 Farm Credit generally considered ABA protestations a minor annoyance.

System pioneers would admit, although sometimes grudgingly, that an understanding, benevolent United States government had extended them a helping hand in getting the System started by advancing seed capital and offering considerable encouragement, aid, and comfort along the way. But these same farmers and farm leaders would quickly remind you that not only has this debt been repaid, but that it has been repaid manyfold through services performed to American agriculture that brought badly needed capital into rural America. Despite the early government seed stock investment, these farmers felt their legacy to be one of self-help—that the government wisely "helped farmers to help themselves."

This "self-help" image played well to a budget-minded Congress. For years, the Farm Credit Administration, during its House Appropriations Committee hearings testimony to gain annual budget approval, was highly praised and told to continue its chores as the Farm Credit System supervisor and to pass along their undying gratitude and best wishes to the supervised. Ironically during this period, if the System was criticized at all, it was for not lending enough to farmers. Congress could afford to be generous. Unlike the USDA, which had the bad fortune of having to present its budget requests at about the same time, FCA costs, although appropriated by Congress, were merely passed along to the System to pay. The Farm Credit System not only funded its own supervision (the FCA), but also everything else connected with its operations.

If you think there was "Farm Credit magic" in Congress and the White House, consider the effect on the United States State Department, which after World War II became deeply involved in foreign aid programs—"Point IV" and P. L. 480 Programs, whose very essence was in "helping people help themselves." Needless to say, the cooperative Farm Credit System principles were advanced as a model to follow, with System leaders constantly called upon to spread the gospel of cooperation to the rest of the world. This was as it should be, since the United States had borrowed rather liberally from foreign countries (largely England and Germany) in developing concepts for its own, fully developed cooperative Farm Credit System. That was what was so special about it, sharing ideas—cooperation—is free! Well, almost free.

The U.S. Agency for International Development (AID) program brought literally thousands of foreign nationals to the United States to see first hand what their rugged individualist, self-reliant American counterparts had done for themselves. Many of these foreigners found their way to the Farm Credit Administration, which—after proper introductions—hied them off to the System, where they could observe this miracle for themselves. Almost without exception, the banks and associations of the System accepted the foreigners with open arms, gave unselfishly of their time, energy, and, in most cases, enthusiasm. Many even volunteered to carry their expertise overseas personally. Some may still be doing it. Now, however, in view of foreign trade deficits, some may wonder if they did their job too well.

One of the toughest obstacles in preparing such training was bridging the gap between the United States and developing nations, since United States farmers enjoy at least a two-generation head start in development over most countries. It was a Pakistani cooperative specialist who explained this communications gap to a veteran U.S. cooperator who, at the time of this visit by foreign nationals, was rounding out his career as secretary to the Wichita Bank for Cooperatives.

Although greatly enthusiastic and evangelistic in carrying out his

FIG. 2.1. *The Farm Credit System participated in a massive program of training foreign nationals on the elements of cooperative farm credit. The program was sponsored by the United States Agency for International Development (AID) and was aimed at assisting developing nations. The author, who served as the FCA foreign training officer from 1965 to 1969, is shown preparing two Philippine marketing specialists for a trip to visit a cooperative port facility in Houston. FCA Photo by Donald W. Drilling.*

assignment of informing the foreign co-op specialists on how farmers in the United States had built their own banks and how they were now benefitting from these services, he was painfully unaware of the current state of cooperation in the developing countries. For the most part, the countries represented at this training session did not yet have cooperatives in the classic sense. Their countries were desperately trying to do something to help their farmers pull themselves up by their bootstraps. Thus, they invested some money in developing cooperatives. Pouring funds into developing co-ops was considered to be a highly speculative investment. However, based on the American experience, foreign governments felt it was worth a try. These governments harbored a hope that the principles might one day take hold and that cooperative enterprises would "blossom forth." This venturesome philosophy was not unlike the hope that had existed in the United States in the 1930s.

The Pakistani student felt compelled to restrain his American teacher's expectations. Borrowing from Voltaire, Junab Kazi Maziruddin said to the teacher: "You must understand, Mr. Terpening, that cooperatives in my country at this juncture are not really cooperatives at all. You might compare them to the Holy Roman Empire, which was 'neither holy; nor Roman; nor an empire!' "

But in America, the Farm Credit System certainly one of the most successful, if not the world's largest, cooperative had truly reached empire proportions, providing more than one-third of the credit used by farmers and well over half of that used by their credit cooperatives. The System had reached its highwater mark in June of 1983, when it supplied $82.6 billion in loans to farmers and their co-ops. What's more, the thirty-seven banks of the System had $6.75 billion in reserves and surpluses, in answer to anyone who might have started worrying about losses. Yes, things were seemingly going well, with no end in sight.

After all, according to many observers, System losses were ridiculously low. Historically (and even as late as 1982) FICB/PCA losses were almost minuscule—only $160,435, or 2/10 of 1 percent. FLBs/FLBA losses were even less—2/1000 of 1 percent! This was worrying some Congressmen, all right, but not for the obvious reason. Often when a constituent was turned down for a loan (which until 1985 was not often), the System was criticized for not doing its job by not loaning (and losing) enough money! FCA officials sometimes felt this slap on the wrist when testifying before Congressional committees. Senator Mark Andrews of North Dakota, for one, claimed that the best way to tell how good a job Farm Credit was doing was to look at its loan losses. At that time (prior to 1985), Senator Andrews sometimes commented that System losses were not high enough.

It is not difficult to see why the Farm Credit System could become so smug and self-satisfied, so overconfident, and, in some instances, so arrogant. Like most other lenders, Farm Credit got caught up in the frenzy of spiraling inflation and doubtless contributed to it by providing credit. As it turned out, loans were made on the basis of unrealistically high asset values—in this case, land prices—that could not produce enough income to pay the interest.

Meanwhile, the Farm Credit System had become one of the most respected and sophisticated members of the agribusiness community. A few decades ago, a graduate from one of the nation's agricultural colleges would probably first seek employment with the Agricultural Extension Service, in the old county agent tradition. By the 1980s, this had all changed — agriculture graduates who did not plan to return to the family farm, would more likely turn to agribusiness, where the pay and prestige were much higher. They might then be surprised to find they faced the fiercest competition for such jobs from graduates in finance, particularly from those who could also boast a farm background. Before 1960, it was almost a given that a person without a farm background and a degree in agriculture need not apply.

Once launched in a Farm Credit career, the chances were good for a young credit officer to become lulled into complacency, like the farmers the System served. Being a second or third generation removed from the start-up of the System, it was understandable that a new employee would rationalize and become convinced that the success of the organization was due more to his own innate skills than to anything else. Something similar can be said of some farmers who were inclined to think that their success was entirely due to their pluck, rather than to rich natural resources and a temperate climate. Whatever the cause and effect, most Farm Credit people were inclined before September 1985 to discount and dismiss the circumstances of inflation and other storm signals that were beginning to flash around them.

By the late 1970s, the Farm Credit System had lost much of its pioneering zeal. It reminded this writer of the spread of evangelistic churches in his native northeastern Ohio from the mid-1930s through the mid-1940s. Pastors and members of these fledgling churches started out preaching on street corners. Encouraged here, it was not long before they moved inside, "graduating" to rented or donated quarters. Continued success soon had them constructing their own building and, later, expanding their facilities, until ultimately a magnificent edifice graced the community. It was at this point that the churches often changed. With something now to lose, they became conservative — or "more respectable," as it were, content to serve only the current members and others of equal standing in the community. At the same time, these churches also seemed to become less vital, less compassionate, and less their brother's keeper. And so it may have been with the Farm Credit System as the years went by. For example, the System was sometimes accused of having a snobbish attitude toward the Farmers Home Administration (FmHA). FmHA, an agency within the U.S. Department of Agriculture, served as a government-subsidized credit source of last resort for farmers. In some areas, it appeared that Farm Credit wanted to distance itself from FmHA. In any case, the two agencies appeared to be unwilling to cooperate with each other in serving farmers. Presumably, a farmer was to be nursed along by FmHA until his farm operation developed to a point where government help was no longer required. He was then to be "graduated" to the Farm Credit System or another lender. This procedure always sounded better on paper than it worked in fact. Understandably, FmHA often was not anxious to turn over a borrower that it had brought along successfully. Other lenders generally were not eager, depending upon economic circumstances of the moment, to receive them. In fairness to Farm Credit, government rigidity often caused red tape problems in dealing with FmHA that discouraged the orderly transfer of borrowers, and cooperation in general. One could often cite instances of lack of cooperation on both sides. Despite the problems, some Farm Credit people in some areas will readily admit that FmHA has been extremely helpful at times in taking bad loans off their hands.

Even so, it was not unusual for people in Farm Credit to be critical of FmHA programs. This included a former chairman of the Federal Farm Credit Board—Dwight Tripp of Auburn, Maine, who had a New Englander's contempt for anything smacking of government subsidization of credit. Tripp, a longtime Grange official in his home state, was featured on the cover of the May 1984 issue of *Farm Futures* magazine. The story was entitled "Easy Money Is No Favor," and read: "Dwight Tripp, a 500–acre Maine dairy farmer, is no fan of current FmHA loan policy. He is tired of seeing farmers bearing the costs of Farmers Home loans 'at least twice over.' In his view solvent farmers not only pay for FmHA's subsidized interest rates, but also suffer lower incomes because these loans subsidize surplus production."

There was nothing legally binding that forced cooperation between the System and FmHA. The obligation was a moral one. But it was a situation that frustrated secretaries of agriculture, both Republican and Democratic. Most would have liked to have seen the two organizations combined, with the System handling the "hard" credit, but overseeing a "soft credit window," available to farmers who could not otherwise qualify for credit. In view of the latest crisis, there are many who believe this combination and coordination should yet take place.

But during the 1970s and the early 1980s there was no way in the world this would happen. The Farm Credit System was riding the crest of its success and was being protective of what it had gained. As indicated earlier, there was some truth to the charge that the System had allowed complacency to set in. Certainly, the winds of change were lost upon it. Like the hog in the barnyard parable, the System had become fat, vulnerable to slaughter.

3

Say It Isn't So

"There are times I almost think I am not sure
of what I absolutely know."

King Mongkut in *The King and I*

 You really cannot say that Farm Credit (FCA and the Farm Credit System) did not get sufficient warning. Storm signals were everywhere. It was just that they were a long time believing what they saw, so incredulous did it all seem. Ironically, nearly the whole unfolding scenario was outlined in a paper developed three years earlier, in 1982, for the annual planning conference of the Federal Farm Credit Board.

The paper was made to look like a reprint from the October 1995 issue of *Affluence Magazine,* a fictitious publication but clearly an imitation of *Fortune Magazine.* The article was titled, "Failure: The Farm Credit System . . . A Funny Thing Happened on the Way to Dominance." It has proved to be amazingly accurate in predicting and describing the fall of the Farm Credit empire. The first reaction to the paper was a demand to know who was responsible for this tomfoolery. The author's name was a pseudonym—"Fredrick Blaine," a composite of C. T. (Terry) Fredrickson, then senior deputy governor of FCA; and Blaine B. (Ben) Sunbury, senior staff associate in the Office of the Governor, FCA.

For the most part, the Federal Farm Credit Board was not amused. Federal Board members were generally not known for their sense of humor, and they lost what little they did have as "Black Wednesday" drew nearer. Like most other leaders in Farm Credit, Federal Board members took particular umbrage to any derogatory remarks about the sacred Farm Credit System. For some reason, this board and other Farm Credit officials were a bit more indulgent toward Terry Fredrickson, perhaps because he was easily the nimblest wit in the whole of Farm Credit. As for Sunbury, he was approaching retirement and could afford to be more daring.

When it came to politics, Fredrickson was devoutly bipartisan, criticizing each party with equal candor. It was always assumed that he was a moderate Republican like his uncle, former Senator Frank Carlson, of Kansas, but one could never be certain. An accomplished devil's advocate, Fredrickson often would take the opposite view with almost anyone, if only to help crystallize his and their thinking. His keen sense of humor and sharp tongue tended to keep one on one's toes, a stance that not everyone appreciated. This, along with his youth, probably cost him the governorship of the FCA when the job came open in 1977. The Board went instead for the older, more sedate Donald E. Wilkinson, even though he was from outside Farm Credit.

FIG. 3.1. *Traditionally, Farm Credit developed its own leadership. Among the most outstanding of these was Terry Fredrickson, shown above making one of his many speaking engagements. Fredrickson was one of the few Farm Credit leaders who by the early 1980s foresaw deep troubles ahead for the Farm Credit System. Farm Credit Banks of St. Louis photo.*

In any case, after a bit of persuasion from Fredrickson, the Federal Board agreed to accept the reprint when assured that, after all, it was for purposes of stimulating discussion only. Also, in return for accepting the paper for that year's discussion, the board extracted a promise from the two authors that they write a counterpart "success" piece for the planning conference the following year. True to their word (and, perhaps, for the love of their jobs), "Fredrick Blaine" did produce the sequel. The following year the Federal Board's planning conference featured a reprint — also from the October 1995 *Affluence Magazine* — entitled, "Success: The Farm Credit System . . . Where the Best Provide Themselves the Best." It was much more in keeping with the Federal Board's sentiments on the matter, and it went over very well. The pity is that the board did not take the "Failure" article seriously, a grievous error and an early opportunity lost.

The "Failure" article featured a report of hearings being conducted by "Chairman Ted Greenback" of the "House Subcommittee on Rural Affairs," who had proposed Farm Credit legislation that among other things, called for "an infusion of government capital . . . in an apparent vain attempt to revive the nearly moribund Farm Credit System." The article made reference to passage of a Farm Credit Act of 1985 (which turned out in real life to be the Farm Credit Amendments Act of 1985). The Act was described in the *Affluence* article as "an unmixed defeat . . . of very substantial proportions." The article noted that "the independence of the FCA was essentially eliminated with the requirement that the governor of FCA be appointed by the president, with the advice and consent of the Senate."

The article also described the decline of the System empire in considerable detail: how it had lost loan business to competitors because it could no longer "measure up to the other giants of the agricultural finance industry," pointing out further that "the System's reputation in agriculture is now as a second class lender, one to whom borrowers turn when other alternatives are not available." The article noted further that "Ironically, one of the long-standing claims of the System was that it made first-class credit citizens of farmers by demonstrating, through successful operations, the credit-worthiness of farmers, as borrowers."

The prediction of borrower flight from the system also turned out to be accurate. In July 1986 the FCA reported that for the thirteenth consecutive quarter, commercial banks increased their outstanding farm real estate loans, while the Federal Land Banks continued a six-quarter

slide in their total loans outstanding. FLB loans outstanding peaked in
the summer of 1984 at $52.4 billion, but fell dramatically by $6.3 billion
to $46.1 billion by March 31, 1986, a 12 percent contraction in an
eighteen-month period. Over the same time frame, commercial bank
outstandings have risen from $10 billion to $11.8 billion, a 17 percent
increase. As it turned out, this was only the beginning of a long decline.

There had been a number of other harbingers of problems to come
that should have been taken more seriously, but these warnings were
often discounted out-of-hand. For example, over a year before the
earth-shaking *Wall Street Journal* story, there was an article in the
August 1983 *Farm Journal* on the Farm Credit Banks of Louisville,
Kentucky. The article, written more in newspaper exposé style, detailed
for Farm Credit System borrowers "Why You May Pay For Millions in
Bad Farm Loans," adding that "It May Take the Entire Farm Credit
System To Keep the Lights on in Louisville."

We cannot speak for the readers, but the article did get the attention
of the Farm Credit Banks of Louisville, whose presidents at the time
(Raymond L. Schlader, Federal Land Bank; Alton B. Cook, Federal
Intermediate Credit Bank; and Thomas N. Farr, Bank for Cooperatives)
expended most of their energies in heated denials. Under the then chairman of the Farm Credit District Board — Ray Moss Tucker — the banks
fired off a memo to their PCA and FLBA presidents and the chairmen of
the boards and managers of borrowing co-ops. The memo advised them
of "several extremely misleading implications and inaccuracies" in the
Farm Journal article, including: "It implies that the Louisville District is
close to requiring national assistance through triggering of the national
loss sharing agreements . . . [and] . . . it implies that the Louisville District is close to depleting its reserves for bad debts."

Suffice it to say that several months later, the Louisville district was
among the first of the Farm Credit banks to seek financial assistance
from the rest of the Farm Credit System! Indeed, help *was* needed "to
keep the lights on in Louisville."

Even before the September 4, 1985, press announcement, it was
beginning to appear to outside observers that the System ". . . doth protest too much." "Where there's smoke, there's fire" was an oft-repeated
cliche every time there was a story even remotely hinting of the possibility of financial troubles in any of the banks. Adding validity to such
rumors was the increasing number of "horror stories" that were drifting

into the national news from the Spokane Farm Credit District to the effect that PCAs there (along with their FICB) were in deep trouble.

FCA supervisory officers, particularly those who had served in the Spokane district in recent years, were not at all surprised. "Why shouldn't they be in trouble! First, they've got a Populist for a president, one who feels that every farmer and fisherman who wants a loan has the constitutional right to get one. When we raise hell with him, he goes to his board, which, in turn, jumps all over the governor of FCA, charging unwarranted government interference. Then, the governor, in turn, caves in and questions our actions as if we are at fault. So, what's the use?"

The reference was to the amiable William F. (Bill) Barratt, a farmer, who was also president of the Spokane FICB from March 1970 until he retired under fire in 1984 because of PCA loan losses. Barratt was thrust into the limelight by virtue of being president of the first Farm Credit bank to seek assistance. He was made even more visible because of his leadership in gaining passage of P.L. 95–443 in 1978, which permits PCAs to make loans of seven to fifteen years to fishermen.

Lending to fishermen was one of those things that seemed a great idea at the time. To be sure, a very good case was made to the System to extend loans to fishermen. They were portrayed as American "Farmers of the Sea" being out-maneuvered and sometimes harassed by Russian, Cuban, and Japanese fishermen (mostly because of their smaller and lower-powered boats). Fishermen witnesses recited the details before the House Agriculture Committee and were particularly persuasive. As a result, the legislation zipped through Congress in record time. There was virtually no opposition, and voting for the measure almost appeared to be a patriotic duty. Representative James Weaver of Oregon (one of the five states making up the Spokane Farm Credit District) was the bill's chief sponsor in Congress and proved adept at waving the flag for this bill.

As losses on loans to fishermen mounted, passage of the legislation cast further notoriety upon the Spokane district and its lending acumen. The Farm Credit System, for the most part, was inexperienced at making such loans. An extended recession hit the tidewater fishing industry. Coastal PCAs generally, and the Spokane district in particular, suffered heavy losses on loans to fishermen, adding further to the System's woes. On the other hand, loans to fishermen may have shared disproportionately in the blame because a few inland associations in the Spokane district were faring no better.

In November 1984, under considerable financial and political duress, the Spokane Farm Credit Board gave up the ghost and submitted for the FCA's approval a plan that would "restore financial viability to the FICB/PCA System in that District." The early plan contemplated handling the problem internally (within that Farm Credit district) and included a proposal for the merger of a number of PCAs. That immediately stirred up a hornet's nest within the district, but, even so, it was becoming obvious that Spokane could not handle the job alone.

After weeks of deliberations, including the holding of two special meetings of the Spokane board with the Federal Farm Credit Board, the FCA cut an interim loss-sharing agreement between the FICB of Spokane and the other thirty-six member banks of the Farm Credit System "not to exceed $25 million." Ominously for the rest of the System, the agreement also contained a proviso that five of the seven members of the Spokane district board (all those who had served while the credit deterioration was taking place) were to resign "upon the first advance of funds . . . and agree not to stand for re-election." Removal of Farm Credit directors for any cause was initially unusual and extreme, but such removals became less rare later, as the full impact of "the fall" began to be felt.

The Spokane directors who were forced to resign were all farm leaders in their respective communities and areas. The list included the FCA governor's appointee—Everitt D. Foust, Moiese, Montana; PCA-elected directors Ronald Bokma, Conrad, Montana; Eugene C. Davis, Bruneau, Idaho; FLBA Director Frank Niessner, Royal City, Washington; and BC Director Harold Behler, Lewiston, Idaho. Not affected were the newly-elected FLBA Director Clarence Hollifield of Hansen, Idaho, and BC Director Fred Shannon of Wenatchee, Washington. The Spokane board also agreed to merge the management of its three banks in early 1985. Kenneth P. Krueger, FLB president, was selected as president and CEO of all three banks.

Although being the first district to seek aid from the other Farm Credit banks was a dubious honor, there were those in the Spokane banks who will tell you in retrospect that getting the early warning was probably a blessing in disguise. It provided them a head start in managing of their problems. Early action probably held down losses in the long run. On the other hand, you probably would not hear the same thing from those who became caught up in the rash of lawsuits and other hassles resulting from restructuring. In addition, there were a number of lawsuits brought by some farmers who were unable to get their loans renewed because of a general tightening of credit policies. Association mergers were deemed necessary to make operations more efficient, the better to put the district back on its feet. However, this theory was hard to sell to a longtime borrower of one of the associations involved. Like it or not, the Spokane district situation proved to be a trailblazer, particularly since it provided a number of test cases.

Although the "Spokane problem" created quite a stir at the time, it was generally considered a special, isolated situation. It took rumors of similar financial troubles in the Omaha district to get Farm Credit's full and undivided attention. First, the Omaha banks served some of the nation's most fertile farm land — Iowa! In addition to Iowa, the Farm Credit District of Omaha also includes Nebraska, South Dakota, and Wyoming, pretty fair farm states in their own right.

Secondly, its banks — notably the land bank — were considered among the best in the country. How could they be in any kind of trouble? Still, if it were not so, many reasoned at the time, why was the Omaha district targeted, along with Spokane, for special attention by the Federal Farm Credit Board? The federal board had called a special meeting with the directors of the two districts while they were attending the annual meeting of the National Council of Farmer Cooperatives in San Antonio in January 1985. Word of this rendezvous spread throughout Farm Credit country like wildfire. And the advice at the time among FCA supervisory troops was: "If you think Spokane has problems, wait 'til Omaha blows!"

And blow it did! The scenario was not unlike what had transpired in Spokane. In mid-1985, the System approved a financial assistance package of well over $300 million to help buoy the ailing Omaha FICB. Later, the Omaha FLB was obliged to seek similar help, an event that shook Farm Credit to its very foundation. The Spokane and Omaha FICB assistance packages were proposed by the System's Finance Subcommittee, made up of a president each from the three banking groups. Whatever the subcommittee decided still required the approval of FCA and the other Farm Credit district boards, an agonizing, time-consuming process that came at a time when fast action was essential.

Members of the Finance Subcommittee were presidents of the Farm Credit banks. Service on this subcommittee, once considered an honor, suddenly became a drag, a thankless task, particularly after the need arose for the Farm Credit banks to come to the financial assistance of other banks in distress. The subcommittee was stuck with the task of proposing the terms under which such assistance would be granted. It was much like prescribing rigid therapy for a brother, even though in the final analysis, the Farm Credit districts had no choice in the matter. The System banks were committed to joint liability on their bonds.

Joint liability meant that the banks were all in this thing together and were responsible for each other's obligations up to the limit of their resources. None of the districts, of course, wanted to lend assistance — particularly the more solid banks. Their officers could easily visualize what was in store for them when other banks queued up for assistance. It was at this time that the realization dawned that the cooperative Farm Credit System was only a system insofar as dealing with Wall Street was concerned (getting the loan funds). Otherwise, the banks were separate legal entities with fiduciary responsibilities to their stockholders — stockholders who, by the way, had the right to sue (and many did) when they realized that their bank might have to help bail out other banks. So, it was not so much that the well banks did not feel obliged to come to the aid of their brethren; it was that they dared not. Joint liability was an issue that was left to Congress and the courts to decide.

Service on the subcommittee was an additional drag because its members often felt that it was becoming too big a job. They felt they ought to be home devoting full time to handling their own problems. Thus, the responsibility of reviewing requests for assistance from Farm Credit districts and coming down with recommendations was soon delegated to a newly organized group called the Farm Credit System Capital Corporation. The capital corporation concept received official status in the 1985 act.

In human terms, the toll on the Farm Credit districts in financial trouble was high, both for farmers and bank and association management. The Omaha Farm Credit Board, following the Spokane lead, elected to go to joint management. Two of the System's most highly respected presidents — Donald L. Hovendick of the Omaha FICB and Arthur C. Buffington of the Omaha FLB — were among the first of many to lose their jobs (or to take early retirement) as a result of the problems.

Both Omaha retirements were particularly shocking to Farm Credit. If one were to clone the ideal Farm Credit official, it would very likely have been in the image of Donald Hovendick, a Nebraska farm boy whose father had once served as a PCA loan officer. Hovendick was a graduate in agricultural economics from a land grant university (University of Nebraska) who had worked his way up to the presidency starting as a loan officer and rising to general managership of a PCA and then moving to the regional FICB headquarters as vice president of public relations. Handsome, articulate, aggressive, and with an innate, home-grown desire to serve farmers, Hovendick appeared to be a natural for the post, except for the fact that he was considered a "PR" person not a "credit" person. In Farm Credit, such a label usually proved to be an insurmountable stumbling block, precluding any bank employee from ever hoping to rise to the presidency. Doubtless, Hovendick's public relations background was used against him because many of the FCA supervisory officers harbored the same prejudice.

Hovendick later explained his downfall in a letter. "Farm Credit was facing two fatal flaws in 1980 — (1) a one-industry/one-purpose business; and (2) a panicky bent to turn and run, fatal not only to itself, but near fatal to agriculture." The fact that land prices in Iowa had dropped to less than half also had to contribute, Hovendick suggested.

There was perhaps some truth in another analysis made by one of Hovendick's close friends: "Don Hovendick probably was just too nice a guy to be a Farm Credit bank president. He was inclined to make other's problems his own and was let down by some members of his staff. He's probably better off in getting out." The "nice guy" image, however, has not hurt Hovendick in his work overseas. He has been in constant demand for foreign assignments, and has accepted a few for Agricultural Development International, notably in Israel.

FLB President Art Buffington presented a somewhat different image. Buffington was a credit man, with experience not only in Farm Credit but in the Farmers Home Administration as well. He was at one time sought by the FCA to serve as deputy governor, presumably as a stepping stone to the FCA governorship. Buffington was highly regarded by his fellow FLB presidents, representing them on the management group of Project 1995, an extensive study made by the System of its operations that will be discussed in more detail later. For a long time, Buffington was almost worshipped by some members of his board, a relationship that deteriorated with the stress of loan problems. Although Buffington had announced to his board his plans to retire within a certain period, the date was in effect advanced by the board when it announced its plan to go to a joint president for all three Omaha banks.

As was true in other districts, the Omaha board opted for its BC president—John Harling—to take over the helm of all three banks. Preference for the BC president was probably because during this period the BC was the only bank in the district that was solvent and the board hoped that this magic could rub off on the other two banks. The impression of BC managerial superiority often did not prove to be the case, and certainly not in the Omaha district. Harling suffered the same fate as Buffington and Hovendick by September 1986.

In the matter of management consolidations of Farm Credit banks, it was not just some of the presidents who became superfluous, but many of the lesser staff members, as well. Many hard personnel decisions needed to be made in the name of gaining greater efficiency. Just as a district needed only one president, so, too, did it need only one secretary, one treasurer, one vice president in charge of credit, and so on down the line. As a board and a new CEO agonize over painful staff-pruning decisions, things can get a bit hairy, as anyone who has ever been through the experience can attest. Certainly, it was traumatic in Omaha. Severe cutbacks created instant trauma, which not only affected the people involved, but the community as well. There was a feeling, particularly in the smaller cities that were sites for district Farm Credit headquarters, that if layoffs can happen to Farm Credit, they can happen to anyone. The well-being of the whole community was at stake.

The Omaha district was not the only one to suffer such a large number of employee casualties. There were deep employee cutbacks in nearly every Farm Credit district, a process that continued into 1988. In the neighboring Wichita district, for example, 109 jobs—or one-fourth of the district's employees—were eliminated in the three banks during the fall of 1985, following consolidation of its management. Even more cuts came later. These figures do not include the cut in the number of employees that came about as a result of mergers of associations. Also, at Wichita some of the banks' real estate was to be sold, including the sale and lease-back of the banks' new headquarters building that opened in February 1986. There were sales, too, of some PCA and FLBA property around the district.

In Omaha, the staff reduction was the subject of much publicity—as were the other indicators of an austerity movement. For example, one of the first acts of the newly named, three-bank Chief Executive Officer Harling was to announce the cancellation of the long-planned construction of a new Farm Credit building in downtown Omaha. This was an indication that perhaps the Farm Credit System was taking a cue from its member-borrowers, who by this time were beginning to show signs of becoming restless. A public announcement explained the cancellation as in keeping with its policy not to spend money for such purposes . . . during the current difficult times facing farmers and ranchers."

Word was getting out. In a Sunday edition of the *Des Moines Register,* Jerry Perkins wrote: "Time is running out for Omaha Farm Credit Banks, the number one lender to Iowa agriculture. For two years, the lender upon which thousands of Iowa farmers rely for credit has been buffeted by a persistently bad farm economy and a downward spiral in land values."

The Omaha press exposure stirred an investigative urge with the press in other parts of the country to see if what was going on in Omaha was also true locally. Thus, other district Farm Credit banks received inquiring phone calls and got knocks on their office doors. In some cases, the efforts of the press were rewarded with news stories, thereby fanning the flames even further, blowing things up into nationwide proportions.

The whole farm situation, of which the credit picture was an important part, tended to upgrade the status of farm news in the media—not only bringing it back, but, thanks to Farm Credit, sometimes getting it on page one. This was enhanced greatly by some top farm writers in Washington—Jim Webster and Ed Curran, newsletter publishers; veteran Washington farm columnist Jay Richter; Ward Sinclair, of the *Washington Post;* and ag wire reporters Don Kendall of Associated Press and Sonja Hillgren of United Press International. A number of farm-oriented dailies were also heavily involved—the *Des Moines Register,* the *Omaha World Herald,* the *Minneapolis Star and Tribune,* and the *Louisville Courier-Journal,* among several others from coast to coast. There also were the usual unsung heroes—the farm radio directors and the newspaper farm editors. In addition, there were writers for a number of farm magazines, such as Marcia Zarley Taylor of *Farm Journal,* who authored a number of in-depth stories during the months that followed.

It should be noted further that the performance of the farm press throughout this period was generally fair and a credit to the profession. In a farm crisis, the writers close to the scene tend to be sympathetic to agricultural producers, yet such a prejudice did not appear to interfere with objective reporting. They wrote the news and were also able to interpret it. For example, Jim Webster was a former staffer for Sen.

George McGovern of South Dakota and also served on the Senate Agriculture Committee staff. While serving as assistant secretary of agriculture under President Carter, Webster was able to obtain an added insight into Farm Credit, having had to handle the staff work on Federal Farm Credit Board appointments.

By 1985 interest in credit stories was heightened by the fact that the situation had become so emotion packed. As an example, there was the story about a forty-nine-year-old Nebraska farmer who opened fire on three sheriff's deputies when they tried to serve legal papers. The story was wired to all parts of the country and was even featured in the February 18, 1985, issue of *Business Week* magazine:

> The four-year farm depression has yielded many sad sagas, but the story of Arthur Kirk of Cairo, Nebraska stands out. Like many farmers, he battled huge debts and heavy losses as farm prices fell. Last fall, he finally gave up and sold off $100,000 in machinery, livestock, and grain. But the embittered Kirk refused to pay even a penny to the bank holding his $300,000 mortgage. A confrontation with a sheriff's deputy serving a foreclosure notice escalated into a gun battle. When the shooting ended, Kirk lay dead.

As a result of increased interest, a number of similar stories were developed by the TV networks and run on prime time. For example, CBS' Dan Rather was among those to go on the road, and he reported on the crisis on his weekday, prime-time evening newscast. For a while, there was also a rash of movies in which the plot usually centered around a young farm couple being foreclosed, resulting in sheriff's sales, divorces, and suicides. "Country" and "The River" are probably the best-known among these. Although these motion pictures tended to place farm lenders in a bad light, they helped put across the farmers' plight to city people, most of whom, if they thought of farmers at all, either pictured them as existing in a serene, pastoral setting or as indolent country folk feeding at the government subsidy trough.

In addition, members of Congress representing rural areas were getting considerable feedback from the folks back home. Anxious to prove to constituents they were doing something about it, they staged field hearings. Sen. John Melcher of Montana was one of the early adapters. He held a hearing in Helena in mid-January 1985 that attracted a standing-room-only crowd of four hundred people. The audience gave the speakers their rapt attention, responding emotionally to a report of two farm couples who were losing their farms. These were among the first of many harrowing stories that were publicized around the country.

One of the first representatives to visualize the extent of the Farm Credit problem and to become openly critical of the Farm Credit System was Rep. Cooper Evans of Iowa, who was making offers of government assistance to the System. When his overtures were turned down, Representative Evans snorted prophetically, "The question is not whether we [Congress] have to do something, but what and when!" The sincerity of Representative Evans' concern was further evidenced by the fact he did not plan to seek reelection. A bonafide maverick and an intellectual, Cooper Evans was an independent thinker who often contributed to the clarification and full discussion of issues.

In 1985 the Farm Credit Administration was still considered to be the official voice for the Farm Credit System and, as such, was receiving its share of attention from the press. By early 1985, Ron Erickson, the FCA's chief press officer, reported receiving upwards of fifty press queries in a matter of a few days, easily a year's quota during "normal" times. So intense was the interest in Farm Credit after the September 4, 1985, *Wall Street Journal* story, that a press conference was hastily called at the FCA's McLean, Virginia headquarters on the following day. It attracted upwards of one hundred newspersons, including eight TV cameramen from every major network. As one who had literally pleaded with the press to attend Farm Credit press conferences in the past, I felt this press conference should qualify for entry in the Agriculture Hall of Fame!

The FCA's position as the national news source for the System proved to be a sore point, as the bad news mounted. The rapidly of unfolding events, along with the FCA's bent to develop an "arm's length" relationship with the System, was a constant source of irritation and consternation between the FCA and the Farm Credit System. Traditionally, the FCA would have checked signals with, or given advance warning to, the System before releasing anything of such great significance as very negative loan statistics. Now, the FCA was not checking, partly because there simply was not enough time, but also because the agency was beginning to act like a government regulator. "Surprise" announcements from the FCA seemed inexplicable acts of sabotage to some System people. Things were beginning to get out of hand.

In any case, increased press interest proved enough to smoke out the agency's governor, who felt obliged to reassure the public. Governor Wilkinson selected the American Institute of Cooperation, the closest thing to an annual family reunion for cooperatives, including Farm Credit, as his platform. On August 1, 1985, on the campus of Kansas State University at Manhattan, Governor Wilkinson vowed that the System, although admittedly faced with some serious problems, could pull through without any government help, thank you. "From a realistic standpoint, I don't think it would be appropriate to ask the Congress or the Administration for any kind of financial assistance unless and until the System has done everything in its own power to alleviate its problems," Governor Wilkinson said.

The need to ever go again to the federal government for help was highly unlikely, Governor Wilkinson implied. To back up his claim, he cited year-end figures showing the System's thirty-seven banks had $5.1 billion in capital stock, and its PCAs had $1.9 billion of their own. Earned net worth, he added, totaled $4.1 billion for the banks and $2.5 billion for the FLBAs and PCAs. Overall reserves for possible loan losses totaled $1.3 billion. The implication was that a sufficient cushion was available to meet any eventuality. No one quarreled with him at the time.

Even so, the nation's tenth and final FCA governor seized upon the occasion to give the Farm Credit districts a bit of "in case of disaster" procedural advice. "Capital should be consolidated in those FC Districts where PCAs [the FLB problems, although equally severe, did not surface until later] are having severe financial troubles and must be consolidated in those districts that face the prospect of requiring financial assistance from other parts of the System." And, for those faced with the trauma of having to merge their PCAs, the governor encouraged them to do so, observing that such action "will permit individual Farm Credit districts to maximize earnings and capital management." For Governor Wilkinson to associate himself publicly on the side of association mergers was considered, at that time, an act of bravery.

Governor Wilkinson's pronouncements must have been well received by the Reagan administration. With farm program budget problems of its own, the administration was casting about for any help (or good news) it could get from agriculturalists who might contemplate asking for help from the U.S. Treasury. While addressing the annual convention of the National Corn Growers Association in Cedar Rapids, Iowa, on July 29, 1985, Secretary of Agriculture John R. Block, a land bank borrower himself, was asked whether the administration planned to lend the System a helping hand. His responded "The Secretary of Agriculture and the administration are prepared to do something if we are asked to. . . . Most everyone thinks the Farm Credit System is federally supported, and that the government is obliged to save the day, and certainly there is no question about it that a system with $80 billion in loans is not going to be allowed to go down the tubes."

These were welcome words for the Farm Credit System and they gave a boost to the sale of its securities. Even though it was fairly widely known in the money market that Farm Credit securities are not backed by an explicit, legally-binding, government guarantee, there was, as Secretary Block indicated, a feeling that the government would not stand idly by and let the System go bankrupt. Even so, it was comforting for the System to have this reconfirmed from time to time.

In the FCA, there was increased "burning of the midnight oil." History should record that this small band of professionals performed rather well, often above and beyond the call of duty. The word "stress" had taken on new meaning—personal as well as economic. A stress committee was named within the agency—to gauge the System's stress, not the committee members'. The committee spent a good share of its time on the road rummaging through Farm Credit banks' and associations' loan files to determine if things were really as bad as rumors claimed. The reports the committee members brought back to the agency were not at all reassuring.

Perhaps the person under the most stress at the agency was its governor, Donald E. Wilkinson, who by mid-1985 was being bombarded from all sides. Governor Wilkinson generally was liked by the rank and file of FCA employees, although he was less highly regarded by the credit and finance professionals, who regarded him as a marketing man who did not really understand credit. Most of the supervisory officers who dealt with System officials were not too certain of his backing at all times. Wilkinson was less respected at the executive staff level, particularly during the last days of his FCA tenure. At a time when support and loyalty were needed most, a couple of his top staffers were open in their criticism, even carrying some tales to Capitol Hill. Strangely, it always seemed as though Wilkinson listened more to his staff detractors than to his supporters.

In his instructions to the staffers studying economic stress, Governor Wilkinson made what may turn out to be one of the greatest understatements of the century: "The Farm Credit System faces economic strains unprecedented in recent memory." Meanwhile, at its February 1985 meeting, the Federal Farm Credit Board, following a meeting with Secretary of Agriculture Block regarding the worsening farm situation, adopted a resolution on "Dealing with Stress in Agriculture."

The resolution directed the FCA governor "to develop, in concert with industry representatives, specific proposals to deal with . . . agricultural credit problems of farmers and their institutions [and] to work with the administration leadership, appropriate committees, members of the U.S Congress and other organizations in this regard and to make available to Congress the assistance of the FCA in fashioning appropriate remedies."

Also, in the finest American tradition, the Federal Farm Credit Board resolution called for the naming of a committee to stay on top of the situation and keep the board apprised of further developments. The events that followed, however, were not in the best American tradition, since they ultimately led to passage of the Farm Credit Amendments Act of 1985, one of the provisions of which was the abolishment of the Federal Farm Credit Board and of the governor of the FCA!

In any event, the clear threat to the Farm Credit empire was, at this point, becoming a worst-kept secret.

4

Twisting the Lion's Tail

"We grow tired of ever but turning others into ridicule,
and congratulating ourselves in their defects."

Hazlett, *The Plain Speaker*

 Back during the days of a mighty, seemingly omnipotent British Empire, it was common practice and sport, particularly among oppressed nations, to attempt to embarrass the giant through a show of independence or an act of contempt or defiance. The Irish were the most adept at this, perhaps because they had so much practice. This activity was often referred to as "twisting the lion's tail." One could discern a certain parallel with the cooperative Farm Credit System in the mid-1980s, as its troubles mounted.

The System, an institution whose reputation in United States agricultural politics was almost akin to sainthood, was suddenly under fire. Politicians who had historically ridden the System's coattails were suddenly becoming estranged, trying to separate themselves from the System. Instead of "pointing with pride" to the System, they were "viewing with alarm." A similar phenomenon was developing among farmers. Historically, farmers had pointed an accusing finger at the commercial banker for their financial woes; now, they were naming their own Farm Credit System as the culprit, since it had become the dominant, most visible lender.

Word about the System's problems was getting around on Capitol Hill from back home — either through stories in the newspapers or direct from farmers who were experiencing difficulties getting their loans renewed. There was a public outcry and a demand that something be done—that agriculture simply could not survive in the United States without its greatest resource for capital and credit, the cooperative Farm Credit System! In fairness to the System, it should be noted that some of the people who were so critical of it for not loaning them enough were now claiming that they were loaned too much and that the System's generosity had gotten them into trouble.

There was a period of several weeks in 1985 during which the nation and the world were bombarded with news on Farm Credit and the American farmers' plight. Public and commercial TV and all types of magazines and newspapers, including the Paris edition of the *New York Herald-Tribune,* the Russian news agency Tass, the *National Enquirer,* *Parade* magazine, and even the *Village Voice* were reporting on the farm crisis. Most of the news, of course, was bad news; some of it could qualify as "bad mouthing."

An article entitled "Heartland Rebellion" in the *Village Voice* did not even try to distinguish the System from regular commercial banks, claiming that "the bankers [are] behind the farm crisis," pointing an accusing finger at the Farm Credit System. "Behind this populist revolt lies a real villain—the Farm Credit System—an immense hidden banking operation with roots in Wall Street that reach far beyond the farms to bondholders in commercial banks, state governments, insurance companies, pension funds, and thousands of individuals, including many foreigners, who buy the securities as nest eggs." The *Voice* even scolded the System further for its heretofore anonymity, referring to it as "an immense hidden banking institution." If nothing else, the *Voice* article offered further evidence to prove the old axiom that only bad news about an organization gets around and is worth printing.

Even the *National Enquirer,* better known for publishing matters of a more ribald and off-beat nature, took an editorial plunge into agriculture with an "expose"—"Government Fat Cats Harvest Big $$$ As Farmers Sink in Red Ink." The article, bylined by Rep. Pete Stark of California, was erroneous in a number of respects, starting with an indication that the Farm Credit System was a government institution.

As the story spread around the world, England's *Economist* felt obliged to comment and do some interpretation for its readers about "Elephant High Farm Debts" in the United States.

> America's farm debt is as big as Brazil's and Mexico's debt put together. It needs to be rescheduled, not met by higher crop prices. America's family farmers are facing their worst financial troubles

since the dust-bowl years of the Great Depression, when they burnt their maize to keep warm because they could not afford to buy wood.

As you read further, however, you got the feeling that the *Economist* was not so worried about American farmers, but what effect all this would have upon Britain.

Farm lobbyists are pretending the farms face an insolvency crisis. They are demanding higher government-backed crop prices to keep farmers out of the bankruptcy courts. If these lobbyists get their way, wave goodbye to the chances of a more rational world agricultural system.

Even so, the *Economist* appeared right on with its summary:

In any event, it is clear that the years of over-lending and over-investment are coming home to roost. Barring a miraculous turnaround in farm prices, or reckless generosity in the new farm bill, it is likely that the administration will sooner or later have to swallow its free-market principles and intervene.

Not surprisingly, the most damaging publicity during this period came from the *Wall Street Journal* on the eve of Gov. Wilkinson's memorable "cannot absorb the losses" admission. This article served as an indicator that the financial newspaper was moving ever closer to the System's jugular. Again, the *Wall Street Journal's* headlines enticed the reader:

Blighted Ledgers

Farm Credit System Relies on Accounting That Hides Bad Loans

But the Truth Might Rattle Investors Who Fund It; They Cite 'Hassle Factor'

The Cost of Credibility

For the first time, the System's bookkeeping procedures came under public scrutiny. The article spoke of the System's "home-brewed accounting standards" and how they had "masked bad lending and lax regulation." The article went on to claim that such standards had "kept alive loans that accountants and commercial bank regulators say other lenders would have been forced to give up as hopeless." Such inaction by Farm Credit, the article speculated, appeared to have "left the System with hundreds of millions of dollars of still-unrecognized losses and only a hazy notion of where its finances really stand."

The article concluded, probably rightly, that

> In calmer times, the System's tangled bookkeeping would be little more than grist for esoteric debates among accountants, and the mess could be straightened out with gradual tinkering. But the farm economy's collapse has suddenly turned subtle accounting anomalies into the difference between modest losses and catastrophic ones.

The same could be said for a lot of things Farm Credit left undone, such as consolidation.

Although exaggerated and unfair to the scores of conscientious and competent Farm Credit accountants who have labored in Farm Credit for many years, there was some truth in the article, making it difficult for Farm Credit to categorically deny it. Unfortunately, in situations such as this, the innocent get tarred with the same brush as the guilty. Some Farm Credit officials even seemed to go along with the accusations. One former Farm Credit bank president (not identified in the article) admitted, "We fiddled while loans burned." An unidentified System farmer-borrower was quoted in the same *Wall Street Journal* article as describing the System lending policy as "like a soap commercial. They were giving money to whoever passed their way, and they didn't ask many questions."

The System, although staggering, could seemingly absorb such blows; what injured the System most was the effect of such statements in the money market. Just in case investors were not drawing the proper conclusions, the *Wall Street Journal* very graciously helped them along. "The loss of credibility has already been costly [to the Farm Credit System]. It has turned what had been blue chip obligations into the 'junk bonds' of so called agency issues. That's dangerous because the traditional buyers of the System's securities have been risk-averse bank trust departments, insurers, pension funds and municipal treasurers."

If System securities were not endangered before, the article helped make them so. Invariably, it seemed that during this period whenever a "bad news" article on Farm Credit problems hit the financial press, the cost of Farm Credit bonds would edge upward. "Every time one of these stories comes out, it's like shooting yourself in the foot," Mike LaVerghetta, veteran FCA finance officer, moaned. For example, on October 30, 1985, the money market, already jittery and sensitive about the market for Farm Credit securities, received the System's third-quarter financial data. Once digested, the spread (difference between the rate of Farm Credit securities and those of the U.S. Treasury securities) on six-month bonds went to 110 points (1.1 percent), up from 84 points (.84 percent) on September 25, 1985, and up from only 15 points a month earlier. Normally the spread, if any, was more in the range of 20 basis points (where each basis point equals 1/100 of a point).

On October 30, 1985, an article appeared in the *Wall Street Journal,* stating that the secretaries of treasury and of agriculture had gotten together and recommended to the president that a U.S. Treasury line of credit be made available to the System, thus confirming long-held view that the government would not let the System topple. The article claimed that Treasury Secretary James Baker and Agriculture Secretary John Block had already agreed on a plan to aid the Farm Credit System by establishing a line of credit for the System.

The article quoted the two cabinet members as agreeing that something was needed to show that the System "had underlying support from the federal government." A compromise was that this might be accomplished by providing the System authority for a line of credit from the Treasury. All the plan needed was the endorsement of the White House, which was eventually given. Even without the president's instant approval, the market reacted quickly to this news. By 2:30 P.M., pricing time for that Farm Credit issue, the spread had narrowed to 84 basis points, thereby saving the System (and, therefore, farmers) about $1.5 million on its new $1.25 billion issue.

Then, on November 1, one of Agriculture Secretary Block's assistants—Frank W. Naylor, Under Secretary for Small Community and Rural Development—who by this time had become a self-styled USDA ambassador without portfolio to Farm Credit, testified on Capitol Hill that the president was not ready to make the line of credit available until FCA and the System "instituted some reforms." As soon as this news hit Wall Street, the spread again widened to 100 points by the end of the day.

Again, the System was being whipsawed by a mere statement—this time from a USDA spokesman.

In fairness to the press, all of its dispatches were not of a sensational nature. There were some calm, studied analyses, perhaps the most thoughtful of which at the time came from Chet Currier, AP business writer, on October 18, 1985, entitled "Tough Times for the Farm Credit System." Currier's column must have drawn some loud "amens" throughout the System and all of agriculture:

> The problems of American agriculture have turned a harsh spotlight on the large, but little known network of financial agencies that makes up the Farm Credit System. . . . The names are familiar . . . to private institutions, state and local governments, and more than a few individual investors who own bonds known as federal agency securities issued by the System to raise the money for those loans. For most of its history, however, many other denizens of the nation's cities and suburbs scarcely knew the Farm Credit System's existence, much less how it worked or the possible problems it might face. That is changing now, to many people's chagrin, as front-page headlines tell of what the System's regulatory official [Wilkinson] describes as "the most severe crisis since the Depression" facing it.
>
> To a large extent, analysts say, the FC System's problems coincide with those of many individual farmers, who are caught in a web of massive debt, declining land values and prices for farm products that have fallen far short of the expectations raised in the inflationary 1970s.
>
> When big borrowers get into trouble, so do their lenders. Donald Wilkinson, Governor of the FCA, a government agency that regulates the System, declared last week that parts of the network might have to be liquidated in 18 months to two years, if the economy's problems keep getting worse. Some other observers say the moment of truth may come even sooner.
>
> These are unsettling words to investors in securities issued by the System, which—though not guaranteed by the Government in the same way as Treasury bonds, bills and notes are—have long been considered almost as safe and solid as Treasury securities. But the situation is not just a problem for farmers and bankers . . . the fortunes of farmers penetrate deeply into the nation's economic infrastructure.

Currier also made another pertinent observation—that the Reagan administration had shown a reluctance to rush in and rescue the Farm Credit System, despite the growing clamor for it to do so. However, most observers felt that ultimately there would be no choice, that the stakes were too high for the government to let the situation get much worse. This, too, proved to be prophetic.

If, indeed, the administration was not responding appropriately, it was not for a lack of congressional proposals and suggestions. Congressmen from both parties were responding to their constituents, introducing new bills almost daily. Things were heating up. Protest groups were springing up everywhere, but particularly in the Midwest where you began hearing new names, such as the Iowa Farm Unity Coalition, Prairiefire Rural Action, Midwest Emergency Action League, League of Rural Voters, National Organization of Help the Farmers, Inc., and the Family Farm Movement.

Curiously, but perhaps not surprisingly, farmers tended to organize new protest groups, rather than turning to the old, established ones. One might assume that the protest groups were of an ad hoc nature, but that is not necessarily the case. It is possible that a few may survive for some time. For example, in an ad in the London, Ohio, *Madison Press,* the Family Farm Movement (FFM) recruited for professional organizers in the Midwest and described the kind of person they were looking for as one who is experienced in "citizen action, community outreach and fund-raising." The offer sounded as though the position might lead to future things.

The FFM at that time had received a grant from the Catholic Rural Life Conference, which was to be used to set up "a family crisis hotline for families that are facing debt problems. They can get advice based on the experiences of farmers that have successfully negotiated debts to allow continued operation." It was probably no coincidence that the London, Ohio, branch of the Columbus PCA was one of those credit associations that was stormed by a small group of irate borrowers in 1983.

So many farm protest groups sprang up, that there was some joking about it. For example, Curt Donaldson, columnist for the *Lincoln, Nebraska Star,* wrote tongue-in-cheek: "There have been a few hopeful signs. Back in 1982, I established the first chapter of Farmers Anonymous, a self-help group for chronic farmers. The way it works is, when you get the urge to plant a little, to go into town and borrow more money than the crops will ever repay, you call me or another recovered farmer, and we'll go drinking."

Another pertinent observation came from Jerry Pepper, Executive Director of the Iowa Institute of Cooperation, who said, "Farmers attitudes toward credit are greatly different today. They appear willing to utilize unsecured credit and walk away from it." Pepper hit on a key point. Perhaps the easiest way to explain it is to differentiate between those farmers who came along before and after the depression of the 1930s. Most depression types, like my father, vowed that if they somehow were ever able to climb out of debt, they would never borrow again. My father did not and neither did most dairy farmers of his vintage. They did not have to borrow. However, conditions changed with World War II and the agricultural boom that followed it. The philosophy of borrowing changed right along with the times, with the substitution of capital for labor.

In any case, actions of farmers are sometimes hard to explain to someone who has not lived among them, and even to some who have. As Drake Mabry commented in the *Des Moines Register:* "What kind of madness is this? Nobody in his right mind sells something for less than it costs to make it, except the farmer. The farmer, little understanding the strange forces arrayed against him, fights his banker, his supplier, the weather, Congress, the marketplace, the value of the dollar, the world."

Of course, it's dangerous to generalize about anyone, particularly farmers. To illustrate this point, during the period of deepest economic stress for farmers, there were a number of stories on farm foreclosures that hit the wires nationally. It was interesting, albeit sometimes tragic, to note how these farmers reacted differently at the prospect of losing their farm. Here are examples of three such stories that broke during the same week in February 1986 and were carried in the February 20 issue of *Inside FCA,* under the heading, "What Would You Have Done?":

Farmer Number 1, from Georgia, after exhausting all possibilities to save his farm, "handed his wife his insurance policies, walked into the bedroom of their mobile home and shot himself to death." Later, his wife explained philosophically to the local newspaper editor, "Farmers have a lot of hope. We lived on hope. Leonard always said 'Wait 'til next year.' It was always next year that the crops would be better—that's what kept him going." As one of his two sons sized it up, "Daddy has given his life to pay his debts."

When the Spokane PCA filed suit against Farmer Number 2, a Washington State cattle baron, to recover what it could on an $11.9 million note (other creditors, including a national bank, sought an additional $2 million), the farmer gathered up all his credit cards and what cash he could muster and headed for Caesar's Palace in Las Vegas. When questioned about what the family and she were going to do, his wife expressed hope that they could make a go of a Christian bookstore she had established. About the downturn in the family fortunes, the wife shrugged: "At least what we have lost is only what we accumulated. We started with nothing." Easy come, easy go!

Farmer Number 3 employed dual tactics. Being from Iowa, he utilized Governor Terry Branstad's newly installed loan moratorium to gain some time, while fighting the foreclosure proceedings in court. On the whole, he was not too comfortable with his course of action nor about its possible outcome. For one thing, his Farm Credit lender was a bit mystified about him going to court in the first place. "It has been our practice for a long time never to foreclose on a borrower who is keeping his interest payments current," a Farm Credit spokesman commented. Later, the Iowa farmer conceded it was pretty much a delaying action. "Eventually, you still got to pay the bill," he conceded.

It should be noted that of the examples, Farmers Number 1 and 2 were not typical, but there were many suicides. The most typical borrower was a class not listed. This group, composed of people who got out of agriculture for a variety of reasons, did not make the papers, only the statistics. One would have to conclude that what was bad for farmers has proved to be good for lawyers. A great number of farmers sought help through the courts, like Farmer Number 3. So many cases went to court that Dun and Bradstreet began a listing of farm or agricultural services (agribusiness) failures that involved court action. The list includes farmers who ceased operations following bankruptcy, farmers who ceased operations with losses to creditors after foreclosures or other actions, or farmers who withdrew, leaving unpaid debts:

	Crop farmers	Livestock farmers	Agricultural services
1985	1,655	573	430
1986	1,695	443	449

Figures for the first six months of 1987 indicated that the rate of such court actions would continue at at least a similar pace and would perhaps increase slightly.

As usually happens, there were a few writers during this period who were not very forgiving of farmers and their problems. Anytime Congress is working on farm legislation (here, it was working simultaneously on a farm bill and a credit bill), a hue and cry is raised against subsidies for agriculture. Here's one from Doug Bandow of the Cato Institute, whose article, "Way to Help Farmers Is to Cut All U.S. Aid," appeared in the August 16, 1985, issue of *USA Today:* "Agriculture has no need for subsidies. Farmers, like other businessmen, claim to be special in order to garner government support. Rural USA sups more mightily at the federal trough than other industries because of its greater political clout, not its stronger case."

Although there is perhaps some validity in Bandow's remark, comments such as this tend to raise the hackles of former farm boys, like myself. It begs the question—if farming provides such easy pickings, how come more people aren't taking advantage of it? Farmers, after all, are not the only people in our society receiving government subsidies; it's just that they get most of the publicity. Government subsidies should be judged on their own merits.

A far more caustic commentary came via an editorial cartoon printed in the September 21, 1985, issue of the *Hagerstown* (Md.) *Herald-Mail,* depicting the scarecrow of *The Wizard of Oz* as the "Farm Credit System," walking with Dorothy. The caption reads: "Brains?! Who needs brains when you can ask for a government bailout?!"

"BRAINS?! ... WHO NEEDS BRAINS WHEN YOU CAN ASK FOR A GOVERNMENT BAILOUT?! ..."

FIG. 4.1. *By the fall of 1985, the Farm Credit System had come under heavy editorial fire, even from cartoonists. Reprinted with special permission of NAS, Inc.*

However, in general, most of the publicity that spotlighted farmers during this stress period seemed to have had a positive effect on the general public. *USA Today* devoted a whole page of its September 9, 1987, issue to farm subsidies, replete with guest columns, results of a public survey, quotes from experts and an editorial cartoon. Perhaps the most commonly held view was best summed up by the newspaper's own editorial, entitled, "Phase Out Subsidies; Don't Pull the Plug."

> The government can't just walk away from our family farms. . . . But large-scale giveaways must not continue. We need farm programs that make sense, that have clear goals and firm timetables to phase out subsidies. Government can help by supporting research to develop new uses for old crops. And developing export markets.

And, then ironically, in a phrase that could have been lifted out of a Farm Credit history book, *USA Today* continued: "Above all, farmers must help themselves. They must manage their businesses better. Many may have to switch to unfamiliar new crops for which there is a demand and ready markets."

The editorial concludes:

> Most U.S. farms are operated by individuals, couples, or partnerships. They're worth saving. We need them. But it won't help anybody to make farmers more dependent upon the government. They must become more independent. And that won't happen until the government decides to give farms in trouble a hand up, and not a handout.

Again, it is hard for almost anyone to argue with this. Yet, realistically, I concur with one of those experts quoted in the same piece—Dr. Neil Harl, agricultural economist at Iowa State University: "I don't think you will see government completely out of agriculture in our lifetimes. After all, food is too important to be left entirely at the mercy of the marketplace."

Subsidies would never have been much of a public issue during the days of the old Farm Bloc. Or, at least they would not have been in jeopardy. Agriculture was particularly powerful during the Farm Bloc days, prior to and during World War II, when a larger proportion of the population was on or close to the farm. This translated into a greater proportion of rural-oriented congressmen. The Farm Bloc was a bipartisan coalition of legislators who united, despite other differences, on farm issues because they realized that their rural numbers in Congress were diminishing. Comparatively speaking, by the 1980s any semblance of the old Farm Bloc had all but eroded away. Rural congressmen now need to resort to swaps and trade-offs with their urban brethren in order to garner enough votes to support an issue. The bottom line is that farm population has shrunk to the point where farmers' influence in Congress has been greatly crippled.

Since 1985 Congress has been bombarded by antiagriculture constituents on one hand and frustrated cries for help from farmers on the other. About the only points upon which both factions seemed to agree was the need for more export and the necessity of at least maintaining the national school lunch and food stamp programs. These were issues in which some common meeting ground could be reached, and they were crucial in agriculture's garnering city support for farm legislation many times in the past. Urban representatives favored having the School Lunch Program for the children in their districts, for example, while farmers are always happy to have such a good market for their products.

Farmers were going to need all the help and understanding they could get as frustration and despair set in. One farm wife explained her plight in a letter of appeal sent to her representative on the Federal Farm Credit Board in late 1985:

> Our national anthem closes with the words, "the land of the free and the home of the brave." Who'd ever think it to look at the farmer? My husband is neither free nor brave, anymore. He's paying with his blood and is chained to a farm program that is helpless, hapless and hopeless. He's so scared he's going to lose his farm that he can't sleep nights. There's no gun at his head, but he's a hostage just as surely as those that were at the airport at Beirut! And who cares? The Government? It says — "you're too good a farmer, shame on you for begging for help." The consumer? "I want cheap food, you hear?" The loan agencies? "File for bankruptcy — there's no other choice."

During 1984–1985, the protest groups busied themselves staging marches and demonstrations — mainly at local Farm Credit Associations, FmHA offices and local banks, at the statehouses, and, funds permitting, at the nation's capitol. There were several examples of a group of farmers storming Farm Credit Association offices, but they did not confine it to this. For example, in Chicago in January 1985, in a protest of low farm prices, twelve farmers were arrested for attempting to disrupt the activities at the Board of Trade. At most such demonstrations, the farmers spared no adjectives in expressing their thoughts on the Farm Credit System and other lenders, often creating civil disorders in the process. Although such rallies did not accomplish much beyond drawing attention, they did provide a safety valve through which farmers could blow off steam. Also, they helped pinpoint for Farm Credit, Congress, and the public the issues that were uppermost on the farmers' minds — high interest rates, increased foreclosures, acquired property, and differential interest rates.

Some senators and representatives responded to such protests and pleas from farmers by calling a public hearing in concert with some of their congressional colleagues. All the aggrieved parties were invited to these hearings. The agendas were much the same. The sponsoring officials would express a few words of welcome, mostly to establish their presence and concern, introduce the representatives of the lenders present, who would do much the same, and, then, open up the meeting to questions and statements from the audience. What followed was an outpouring from individual farmers about the problems they were facing with credit, not unlike the one from the farm wife above.

Perhaps the most memorable of these public hearings was one called by Sen. Charles Grassley of Iowa in Ames, Iowa, in August 1985, at the urging of the Iowa Farm Unity Coalition and Prairiefire. The hearing was billed as an "Emergency Statewide Meeting on the Farm Credit System." As it turned out, there was no one at the hearing from the System. The Farm Credit Banks of Omaha, apparently a little gun shy by this time, declined to send anybody. This was understandable in a way because the Omaha banks were already under siege, even from their own board of directors. Under such conditions, it did not seem unusual to take the bureaucratic approach — why stick your neck out any further? Why, indeed?

Not to be denied his opportunity, Senator Grassley put the finger on FCA/Washington, which, as a government agency, was more obligated to respond to such requests from congressmen, however difficult. Whereupon FCA responded by offering up Ron Erickson, veteran communications officer, and Jeff Katz, a young credit officer from the agency's Office of Examination and Supervision. Katz was relatively new on the staff and, therefore, in no position to beg off, but he also could boast previous experience with FmHA in Arizona.

True to congressional form, Senator Grassley, who was running for a second term and was careful not to align himself too closely with the administration or Farm Credit, delivered what was described as "an inflammatory speech in which he pressed all the hot buttons," fielded a few questions, turned it over to his colleagues, and adroitly departed the scene. Even though these hearings were often heart-wrenching, they were not always without some humor. During the Ames hearing, just as one of the most aggrieved farmers was summing up his arguments and accusations in which he, like many others, blamed most of the farmers' problems on "those so and sos in Washington," Katz, with a twinkle in his eye, leaned forward to Rep. Jim Leach of Iowa (who earlier had told the audience, "I'm going to stop talking because I'm interested in hearing what the FCA people have to say") and asked, "Do you want to field this question, Mr. Congressman?" After recovering, Representative Leach smiled, as much as he dared, and declined, later observing, "You (in FCA) have an impossible job." Members of Congress, it appears, are quick to recognize a "no win" situation, having been there many times themselves.

As pure theater, the congressional "road shows" ranked high. However, they were outdone by one Capitol Hill production orchestrated by perhaps one of the most skilled tail-twisters of them all—Oklahoma Rep. Glenn English. Apparently not content with the stage time allotted him for questions as a member of the House Agriculture Committee, Rep. English, as chairman of the Government Information, Justice and Agriculture Subcommittee of the House Committee on Government Operations, called a special hearing of his own on April 26, 1986. He invited three members of the FCA staff—Governor Wilkinson, Deputy Governor Larry Edwards, and General Counsel Fred Medero—and, as one congressional staffer described it, "proceeded to grind out their valves." It was much like an inquisition.

Unfortunately, the hearing had little to do with the actual extension of credit to farmers. It concentrated on the System's organization structure. When it comes to Farm Credit, Rep. English had the advantage of growing up in a home steeped in knowledge of the subject. His father had been a director of his local FLBA in Oklahoma and was a veteran of the old battle over FLBA/PCA coordination, a subject that will be examined more fully later. This feud may still be smoldering in some parts of the Wichita district, as it has been for many years. FLBAs in some areas just did not care to be associated with those "upstart PCAs," while

PCAs deeply resented the cozy referral service that some FLBAs had going for them with commercial banks. Some FLBAs would refer their borrowers to commercial banks for their short-term credit, rather than to their sister PCAs. Representatives from some other parts of the country would also get caught up in similar disputes between the two types of System units. This was particularly true of Wichita's neighbor to the south, Texas. As an issue, it was no longer germane, rather like continuing to fight the Civil War during its centennial year.

Representative English's subcommittee report cited FCA in some seven findings, three of which had to do with the merger and consolidation process. Representative English maintained that the System had violated the stockholders' rights to local control. According to the report: "FCA supervised the merger election process in a manner which allowed district bank officials to use misstatement of facts and threats of coercion to persuade stockholders to approve districtwide mergers."

English's side comment on this at the hearing was, "We are talking here about coercion, misinformation, people being lied to." The subcommittee report further charged that FCA, by claiming mergers were necessary to consolidate capital and had the authority to move capital, was attempting to consolidate System power at the district level by approving plans to merge all local associations of a district into one. In cases where a local association decided not to join in a districtwide merged association, the report claimed, "FCA gave the districtwide association authority to compete for business in the dissenting association's chartered territory."

Despite all efforts by the System to keep the association merger and consolidation issue separate from that of federal relief, it would not be an easy matter. For one thing, Representative English was not, by any stretch, the only congressman ensnared in this issue. What was worse for the System, the issue of consolidation and merger was often advanced as one of local control, traditionally a sacred cow in most rural areas.

It was as Jim Webster reported in his October 4, 1985, issue of his *Agricultural Credit Letter:* "That simmering opposition to mergers of PCAs and FLBAs—stimulated last year by FLBA officials in Texas after management of the three Texas banks were merged, and egged on this year by proposed single-district PCAs in Wichita, Omaha and Spokane— could complicate efforts in Congress to provide financial help for farm leaders."

Another representative to jump on the local control bandwagon was

Virginia Smith of Nebraska, who in mid-July 1985 issued a colorful "Dear Colleague" letter to try to influence her fellow legislators, urging them to join her in cosponsorship of a joint resolution. In her letter, Representative Smith claimed that "this very serious situation has been exploited by those who wish to remove local control from farmers and ranchers and create a huge multi-billion dollar . . . national farm credit bank."

In her proposed resolution, Representative Smith claimed "the FC System is actively pursuing the merger of land bank and production credit associations without borrower approval or authorization . . . wide-scale consolidations and mergers of FLBAs and PCAs should not be pursued by the FC System or accomplished through coercive action such as the threat of liquidation of dissenting associations."

Even the normally cool, unflappable Rep. Cooper Evans, who had admitted earlier that "centralization may, in fact, be essential for some of the financial pressed banks and associations of the FC System," retreated to neutral ground when confronted with a memo drafted by System attorneys, raising concerns that farmer-borrower stockholders may be forced to accept consolidation of their banks and associations even if they vote against it. Representative Evans decided to go along with those who wanted to turn this hot potato over to the U.S. Department of Justice.

Congress has another method for applying pressure on such governmental subjects as the FCA. That is through the General Accounting Office (GAO), its investigative arm. Needless to say, the GAO was put to use during this period, with what seemed to be an endless number of investigations into the FCA and the System. The GAO made some twenty studies involving Farm Credit between 1970 and August, 1986. Generally, however, Farm Credit scored rather high with the GAO. As an example, a 1985 GAO study, "FCA's Liquidation of Production Credit Associations," indicated that the FCA's liquidation procedures were "consistent with those used by other financial regulators" and, otherwise, found the FCA's performance acceptable.

It was understandable why rural politicians could not escape being drawn in to the "credit crisis." However, it would appear many politicians tended to overplay it by projecting themselves into the issue. High on this list one would have to put the governor of Iowa, Terry Branstad, who made noise above all others. Governor Branstad dragged out the threat of a loan moratorium, which, as newsletter editor Jim Webster explained, was "designed more for show than substance . . . [but which] sends shivers through farm lenders worried that it could delay necessary foreclosures in Iowa and that it could be a precursor of even stronger action in other hard-hit farm belt states when their legislatures meet in January."

Loan moratoria was one issue upon which all lenders seemed to agree. For example, the Iowa Bankers Association president during 1985 — J. Bruce Meriwether, of Dubuque — was quoted by the *Northwestern Banker Newsletter* as stating flatly that "Iowa bankers are very disappointed." A loan moratorium, Meriwether claimed, "has several negative implications for farmers, bankers and the State of Iowa. Farmers are not really being helped by the action," he said, "the Governor is simply delaying the inevitable. [The moratorium] will only temporarily assist a limited number of them." What's more, Meriwether concluded, it "sends negative signals to the rest of the country and the world regarding economic growth in Iowa."

Governor Branstad did not send the message to Washington; he carried it there in person, something he did at least twice during the height of the Farm Credit crisis. Although being a Republican probably helped him gain an audience with President Reagan, party affiliation did not stop him from firing a few uncomplimentary salvos at 1600 Pennsylvania Avenue. In any case, he received an audience with the president, and with just about everyone else he asked to see. Whatever else one might say of the Iowa governor, he demanded and got attention, something that is not often easy in the nation's capitol. In any case, for a few weeks, political scientists and historians were able to witness a state governor stealing the show on what was obviously a national issue.

One of Governor Branstad's trips was made in October 1985. His main message was that "the Farm Credit System is so overloaded with debt that it will sink by the end of the year, if a Government bailout is not arranged soon." An October 17, 1985, AP dispatch carried this headline: "Branstad Urges Reagan To Endorse System Bailout and Sign Farm Bill." Before visiting the White House the governor stopped by to see officials of the Farm Credit Council. Council officers were glad to get the Iowa governor's support for their legislation, but probably differed with him on the timing as to the need for government help. The Farm Credit Council also failed to convince Governor Branstad that a loan

FIG. 4.2. *Many state governors were involved in efforts to save American farms from foreclosure in the mid-1980s, but none figured more prominently than Iowa's Gov. Terry Branstad, shown (at right) discussing the plight of Iowa farmers with President Reagan at a meeting in the White House in June of 1984. Others at the conference included (left to right) Secretary of Agriculture John R. Block, Vice President George Bush, and Sen. James Abnor of South Dakota. White House photo by Jack Kightlinger.*

moratorium would wreak havoc upon a lender like Farm Credit that relies on loan funds from investors, and that it also had the clear potential of drying up credit in a "close call" credit situation.

Commenting on Governor Branstad's visit, Farm Credit Council chairman Ray Moss Tucker noted that "we understand Gov. Branstad's concern for compassionate treatment of distressed Iowa farmers, but other farmers may have to pay the bill." Tucker claimed that there could be substantial costs associated with a moratorium on foreclosures. There could be increased losses as land values declined further while lenders were unable to proceed with foreclosures, Tucker pointed out. He noted further that the lender has to pay on money it has borrowed to make loan funds available and that there would be increased reluctance on the part of lenders to assume the risk of making farm loans. In addition, Tucker observed, there would be higher costs of Farm Credit bonds, as investors perceive additional risk.

The FCA decided not to take any chances with Governor Branstad, nor any of his fellow state governors who might follow his lead and push for a loan moratorium. The FCA decided to resort to its ultimate weapon — federal supremacy over state's rights. Although this precedent had been fairly well established by and since the Civil War, the Federal Farm Credit Board decided to take no chances. It would go on record anyway, just in case there were any out there who were not up on the Constitution. At its October 1985 meeting, the board approved a regulation that explained how federal law "preempts any state law from interfering with the terms of a Farm Credit System institution loan contract with respect to repayment of principal and interest, or remedies in collection thereof."

This approach may have brought the Federal Board instant victory, but it did not play too well around the country, particularly among farmers. The feeling at the time was that even though Farm Credit might escape the tentacles of loan moratoria on the basis of operating under a federal charter, Governor Branstad was successful in gaining one objective — getting the attention of Congress, the president and, most important to him, his constituents back home in Iowa. As Joe Terrell, vice president for public relations for the Farm Credit Council, noted on the results of one of the Iowa governor's Washington visits: "News reports carried interesting twists on what was said, but this much is clear: a message of concern got to the president." The Iowa governor did, however, receive some backlash later on because of the new image he had projected of his home state on the basis of the agricultural bad news. So poor had he painted conditions in the "tall corn state" in his effort to qualify for federal aid that many felt that people and industry would be reluctant to move to a state in such a state.

Governor Branstad's example also was the stimulus for a group of eleven state attorneys general from the Midwest and Kentucky to confront the FCA with a series of questions dealing mainly with the rights of Farm Credit System borrowers. The attorneys returned from Washington with multiple pages of answers to their questions dealing with such matters as disclosure terms, access to documents, fairness in the System, the right of review, the doctrine of forbearance, and the rights of stockholders.

The visit to the FCA by the midwest attorneys general was another indication that, although the Farm Credit System took most of the heat, the FCA was not exempt. The regulatory agency came in for its share of criticism and tail-twisting during these months of trial for Farm Credit. Among those to zap the agency was a top professional at this trade — Jack Anderson, columnist, former partner and successor to the late

Drew Pearson. Pearson, who at one time had owned and managed a dairy farm in suburban Maryland near Washington, D.C., until "giving up the ghost" during an earlier agricultural recession, was very understanding of farmers' problems and often wrote in their behalf. Not so Anderson, who devoted a whole column in July 1984 to the FCA's new office building in the Washington suburb of McLean, Virginia. He wrote in the column that the agency had gone "on a multimillion dollar spending spree for office construction at a time when thousands of farms are being foreclosed."

The column was something of a cheap shot. There were those, like myself, who thought the building was not particularly elegant, but drab—that on the outside it resembled an army pillbox, which was an image entirely appropriate at this time of siege. The column neglected to

FIG. 4.3. *Farm Credit Administration Office Bldg., McLean, Virginia. Quite a furor erupted when the Farm Credit Administration erected its own office building in McLean, Virginia, a suburb of the nation's capital. Although the timing for the new construction was bad, the building actually has proved to be a good investment. FCA employees' biggest complaint is the location—near the Capital Beltway and a huge shopping complex, one of the most congested areas in the country. FCA photo.*

point out that although, historically, the FCA was housed (by law and rent-free) in the United States Department of Agriculture, the new charter act (the Farm Credit Act of 1971) had provided considerably more freedom and independence for the System, including the "freedom" to pay for the housing of its supervisory agency—the FCA. From past experience and for the purposes of its identity, the first thing the System wanted to do was to get the agency out of the USDA's South Agriculture Building, even if it had to pay for housing. In 1972, space was leased in the L'Enfant Plaza complex near Capitol Hill. When its lease ran out and L'Enfant proposed to hike the rent considerably, the decision was to build. From a purely business standpoint, it was an excellent decision as the property has appreciated considerably. One must concede, however, as Jack Anderson brought out in his column, that the timing was bad. Other writers—some in earnest, others in jest—referred to the FCA building as either the Taj Mahal or "the McLean Hyatt." Both descriptions are gross overstatements.

In the mid-1980s Farm Credit found its formerly good public image rather tarnished. It seemed as if when the System was not being held up for ridicule, it was being made a scapegoat. Nothing seemed to be going right. Worst of all, the System, despite all its protestations and explanations, was unable to convince most of its farmer-members that it was still working in their behalf. Nor could Farm Credit convince many of its members that badmouthing the System was absolutely of no value—that by so doing, they were twisting the wrong tail!

5

The Art of Self-Destruction

"We has met the enemy and it is us."

Walt Kelly, *Pogo*

 Undoubtedly, in no area in Farm Credit has more time, energy, money, and animosity been misspent than in fighting merger or consolidation of the Farm Credit System's banks and associations (FLBAs and PCAs). Consolidation usually meant joint management of two legally distinct entities. Merger meant the ultimate step, creating a new entity of two separate corporations. There were those within the System who were dedicated to a no consolidation/no merger policy and who would apparently continue to proclaim that policy in a eulogy at the System's funeral, so strong does the feeling run in some quarters. The closest the System came to officially proclaiming any kind of consolidation policy on its own was in 1987 when the Farm Credit Council adopted a voluntary policy, which was of little value. In Farm Credit, permissiveness seldom gets the job done.

The advantages to joint management appeared obvious to most outsiders—foreign visitors, economists, commercial bankers, farm writers, agriculturally oriented politicians, and even farm organizations (groups that do not have a very good record in this regard, either). Why do you have three banks? was the question most often asked by visiting foreign nationals (most of whom had less than the equivalent of a high school education).

During a training session for a group of foreign nationals in the

Spokane Farm Credit District, the designated spokesman, Joseph Muleta of Ethiopia, was pressed by one of his Spokane host instructors to
admit that the concept of having three banks, as practiced in the United
States, was the route to take. Not wanting to appear disrespectful or
unappreciative, Joseph smiled and said, "Yes, that is, if your country can
afford it." As it turns out, Joseph's observation was quite prophetic.

For many years the official response (excuse) for the three-bank
mode was supplied by Robert B. Tootell—the man who served as FCA
governor the longest (and such diplomacy was probably one of the reasons for his longevity). His explanation went something like this: "Well,
if we had the opportunity to put the Farm Credit System together again,
we would do a number of things differently (implying that having one
bank would have been one of them). Unfortunately, the banks were
started at different times for what seemed at the time to be for different
reasons." Ironically, the System did get the chance to put itself together
again, but it was forced by circumstances of the 1980s to do so. The
System did not reorganize of its own volition.

One of the prime reasons for the separation of the banks was the
fact that when the Production Credit Associations were organized
during the Great Depression, the Federal Land Banks and FLBAs (then
called National Farm Loan Associations) felt they had their hands full
with trying to prevent farm foreclosures. Additionally, there were several
thousand NFLAs, some of which were rather weak. Thus, the FLBs did
not want to be bothered with short-term production loans and declined
the opportunity. Although there were a few cases locally where the same
secretary-treasurer headed both lending activities (notably in the St.
Louis, Berkeley, and Columbia districts, and later in the Springfield and
Baltimore districts, when most associations were fully coordinated),
these were the exception, not the rule. Thus, the System moved ahead
with separate institutions, with the thought that the two could be joined
down the road. Certainly, that was the intent of Henry Morgenthau, Jr.,
who served as the FCA's first governor and as secretary of treasury
under President Franklin D. Roosevelt. Obviously, consolidation never
happened and, later, after the PCAs were organized and entrenched, it
seemed to be too late to change.

One of the most important reasons for the System's delay in merger
and consolidation was a very common and natural one—self-interest
and survival. Put simply, jobs and prestige were at stake. Three sets of
banks and associations mean staffs and boards to match. For the most

part, farmer-directors were of little help in the drive for consolidation. Board members were quite honored to serve and developed a fierce loyalty to their respective associations. This could be detrimental to harmonious working relationships with the other association, even though in the case of the FLBAs and PCAs, the two associations presumably served the same farmers.

As a foreign training officer for five years, I made use of this situation and drove home this point to foreign nationals: "Let this be a lesson to you as you develop co-ops in your country. Use great care in putting your organizations together because, as you can see here in the Farm Credit System, it is easier to do it right in the first instance than to make changes later on." Not only did foreign nationals understand the point, but they also appeared comforted to learn that the Americans, even with their fine credit system, were capable of making mistakes—that they were not infallible.

Intramural strife within the Farm Credit System occurred largely between the Federal Land Bank and Production Credit units. At district headquarters offices, the Banks for Cooperatives often had to serve as referee between the other two units. Normally, the three banks were housed on different floors in a headquarters building. This seemed natural enough, but it was not unusual in some districts for middle and lower level staff members to never become acquainted with their counterparts on other floors. In some cases, they were discouraged from doing so.

So intense did this rivalry become in some associations that, though jointly housed, each office had its own entrance door, thus requiring a farmer to enter each association separately. Once inside, a partition usually further separated the two associations. Even so, this arrangement was better than another common situation, one which found FLBA and PCA offices on opposite sides of town, or even in different towns. Often, too, this divisiveness was encouraged from the Farm Credit district headquarters and not always discouraged firmly by the FCA.

As if the association people could not carry on separatism well enough on their own, district and national organizations were there to make sure they did. Each district usually had an association of FLBA and PCA general managers (presidents). They met periodically to discuss matters of mutual concern, including such things as credit policy and joint advertising and promotion, but there was also time for feuding. Nationally, there was the National Federation of FLBAs, which, until relatively recently, took on all issues that would in any way infringe upon the sovereignty of the Federal Land Banks. The Federation started going and growing—particularly in the midwestern Louisville, St. Paul, and Wichita districts—right after the FLBAs (National Farm Loan Associations) lost the right to elect from among their numbers to the district Farm Credit boards. Yes, that's right—at one time it was possible for a general manager of a local FLBA to be elected director of his Farm Credit district board! This practice was abolished by provisions in the Farm Credit Act of 1955, which precluded service on the district boards by salaried persons working for any Farm Credit organization.

The federation was something of a company union for FLBA managers, but it also attracted association directors, if for no other reason than to fight the PCAs and to get a free trip each year (paid for by his association) to the annual convention. This probably explains why supervisory action was taken by the FCA, albeit belatedly in the waning months of Wilkinson's FCA governorship, to preclude association personnel and directors from paying the expenses for attending, at Farm Credit expense, what the FCA considered a self-serving, nonofficial meeting. Needless to say, the FCA's action had a devastating effect on the federation's strength and stability.

The federation lost its punch in the seventies, partly because it came out on the losing side in the battle to gain passage of the Farm Credit Act of 1971. This legislation, a modernization and updating of the System's charter, enabled the Farm Credit System to considerably broaden and liberalize its scope of services. For example, it enabled the land banks to lend up to 85 percent of the appraised value of the farm property and, in general, to use more credit judgment in making farm mortgage loans. For years the FLBs were limited to loaning only 65 percent of the normal agricultural value of the farm or ranch, plus the amount needed to buy stock in the FLBA. With years of continued inflation, normal values lagged behind current market prices, making it almost impossible for a land bank to be much of a factor, particularly in assisting young farmers trying to get into agriculture.

Thus, the 1971 act was heralded widely as emancipating the land banks, permitting them to get back into the farm mortgage market in a big way. In retrospect, the 1971 act was blamed as one of the main factors that got the System in trouble. Sen. David Boren of Oklahoma, for one, in hearings for the 1987 act described how the excessive liberal lending policy of the land banks drove up the price of farm land, which eventually led to the collapse of land prices. It is a charge that the System is hard put to deny. It could be said that the 1971 act made it possible for the land banks to lose money and they took full advantage of the opportunity.

A much more controversial provision in the 1971 act was the one that permitted the FLBs and the PCAs to make loans to nonfarm rural home owners. This feature was strongly opposed by the savings and loan associations for reasons of turf. Another provision that was equally controversial was the broadening of the System's authority to provide loans to businesses providing farm-related and credit-related services to farmers. Even the farm organizations did not want this because it violated a widely held tenet of theirs—that Farm Credit is for farmers only—a view also strongly shared by the National Federation of FLBAs.

Passage of the 1971 act brought an erosion of the federation's issues that resulted in attrition of its leaders. What turned out to be an almost mortal wound was the departure of one of its most assertive generals— Sam G. Eberly, Kansas livestock farmer who also ran a farm recreation business and who served as executive secretary of the federation for a number of years. Apparently, Eberly, like a lot of other federation members, decided if you can't lick 'em, join 'em—that there's not much you can do on the outside looking in. In any case, Eberly was a successful candidate in 1983 for a director of the Wichita Farm Credit Board and since has risen to the chairmanship of that board, as well as to high national offices in the system.

Perhaps in desperation, the federation of FLBAs then ironically opened up its membership roles to the PCAs. The federation's main promotional appeal was a commonality of interest against districtwide mergers of associations. For whatever reasons—perhaps the accumulation of too much bad blood over the years—this invitation did not have much appeal and did not result in the salvation of the federation.

Do not get the impression that the Federal Land Banks and the FLBAs were the only heavies in the consolidation hassle. The PCAs were fully capable of making their own contributions. For example, when first organized, PCA loans were primarily for a seasonal term—thirty to ninety days. The progression was to an annual term that was then increased to three- and then to five-year intermediate loans, then to seven. The loan period was increased to fifteen years in its latest lunge. Needless to say, these progressions caused consternation on the part of the land banks. The FLBAs noted vociferously at times that the PCAs were often utilizing first mortgages as collateral, a clear infringement on their territory. Rather than discussing the matter with the PCAs or Federal Intermediate Credit Banks (FICBs), or even before the district boards, the land bank presidents invariably complained to their government regulator-supervisor, the FCA, thus turning attempts at supervision by the FCA into a nightmare.

Perhaps one of the author's colleagues had the most positive analysis of this situation. "Not to worry. Look at it this way. The PCA loans are getting longer, while the FLB loans are getting shorter. Pretty soon, no one will be able to tell the difference, and — presto — our consolidation problems are solved, thereby becoming another striking example of enlightened FCA supervision!"

Why didn't the Farm Credit districts do more to force the issue of consolidation sooner, rather than wait until the System was in such disarray? Well, the National Federation's views were symptomatic. True, people wanted to hold on to jobs. But, it was also true that many were fiercely proud of and loyal to their own organizations and saw no real reason to change. Why, for example, would a FLBA risk offending local commercial bankers by associating themselves with PCAs? This perhaps made good short-term business sense to the FLBAs in some areas, but in the long term it was injurious to a cooperative, family attitude within the System. To many land bank supporters, real estate lending at that time was relatively simple and clearcut. Why complicate it with PCA short-term and intermediate-term loans? The PCAs, on the other hand, were able to get around the FLBs because they were able to make the longer-term loans on their own. In short, why hassle? At least, why hassle openly?

Nobody knew better than district bank officers how the seven members of the Farm Credit board got their posts — two each were elected by the PCAs and FLBs and the stockholders of the Banks for Cooperatives (BCs). The seventh was appointed by the governor of FCA and served at large. Even though a director might well be a PCA and a FLB borrower and be a member of one or more other co-ops that borrowed from that district's BC, he was wise never to lose sight of the constituency that had put him where he was. For example, although each district director was presumably a director of all three banks, generally in a board meeting, when a subject about PCAs came up, the other directors deferred to the PCA-elected directors for any proposed action that affected the PCAs alone. Maybe this was not how things were supposed to be on paper, but this was how it worked and it contributed to board harmony.

Suffice it to say that the countryside was strewn with incumbent district Farm Credit directors who took up the banner of consolidation while in office. These people were not reelected. And, keep in mind for later reflection, that it is the membership—the farmers—who do the voting in the Farm Credit System. They, too, were not immune to such blind loyalty and devotion to their associations and were either oblivious to or ambivalent about what the cleavage between the associations might be costing them. Until the mid-1980s crisis, the matter could be avoided, and it was.

What about the supervisory agency? For many years, FCA, even though supposedly representing the public interest, did not perform much better than the Farm Credit System on the issue of reorganization. The FCA did not make any waves. It merely reflected and, in some cases, imitated the System's structure and rationale on such matters, the better for working relations and supervision. Upon occasion, someone in FCA—usually from the information office—would try to use moral and other suasion, talking up the advantages of joint housing (one-stop credit service) for the farmer-members that the System was set up to serve. Occasionally this sort of common sense would be picked up and repeated by other interested parties in agriculture, such as farm groups, but not often. Interference smacked of meddling, something that sophisticated organizations were loath to do, at least publicly.

While Charles B. Shuman was president of the American Farm Bureau Federation (AFBF), that organization adopted a policy resolution, urging greater coordination (one-stop credit service) for farmers who borrowed from the Farm Credit System. As a Sullivan, Illinois, farmer, perhaps Shuman had personal experience with having to go to separate offices for long-term and short-term credit. Doubtless, Shuman regarded this as rather foolish. After Shuman retired from the AFBF, the resolution (which was never on the front burner anyway) was finally dropped.

Too bad there was not more editorial comment like that of Lane Palmer, editor-in-chief of *Farm Journal,* who, in the August 1985 issue, thoughtfully explained "Why Mergers Are Necessary."

> The feuds between local PCAs and FLBs are petty and senseless. . . . Where once the missions of the two types of banks were clearly separate, change has forced them into each other's backyards. . . . So, we should merge PCAs and FLBs into a single bank that

can finance land, machinery, cattle, buildings — anything. . . . Private banks have adjusted to this changing market
through failures and consolidations. But Farm Credit hasn't adjusted, so its overhead is so high it is no longer competitive.

This plethora of separate entities is also why the System has
been so slow to react to the current crisis. As the ancient Greeks
learned, there is such a thing as too much democracy. That's why
our Founders chose a democratic republic with representative voting. FCS members needn't lose local control when they consolidate.
They have simply to elect to district boards directors who will truly
represent them.

On second thought, it was probably wise on Palmer's part to have
waited until 1985 to publish such an editorial. As it is, it has not projected him into knighthood within the System. Had he penned the editorial much earlier, there would have been some cancelled subscriptions,
or, worse yet, some cancelled advertising. Even in 1985, there were some
veiled threats of this. What's more, it would have stirred up the System
pot even more.

Consolidation was not really a new issue in Farm Credit. The Federal Farm Credit Board, in one of its more daring and inspired moments,
selected an outsider, E. A. (Ed) Jaenke, from USDA's Agricultural Stabilization and Conservation Service (ASCS), as its governor in March of
1969. During his stormy tenure, Governor Jaenke was called a number
of things, depending upon one's views, but all would concur that he was
most often pragmatic, and always "a stubborn Dutchman." Governor
Jaenke, like the foreign credit and cooperative specialists, could see no
merit in the three-bank setup. Unlike his predecessors, however, he was
determined to do something about it.

In an obvious show-by-doing effort, the new governor reorganized
the FCA along functional lines, eliminating the separate, but almost
equal, service divisions. (Actually, the Federal Land Banks appeared to
have an edge on the basis of seniority, tradition, and the strength of
some of its leaders.) Jaenke made other similar moves that failed to win
many advocates within the System, but he made believers of any diehard
separatists on his own staff. At least, he convinced those who either were
not eligible for immediate retirement or in a position to move through
the revolving door — back to the Farm Credit System. After gaining
success in the FCA, Jaenke decided to press matters with the System by
making a frontal assault on the well-fortified bastion of "dual directorship."

FIG. 5.1. *E.A. (Ed) Jaenke. No man made a greater impact upon Farm Credit in such a short time as did E. A. (Ed) Jaenke, FCA governor from 1969 to 1974. He made a valiant attempt to modernize and consolidate the System and succeeded in gaining the passage of the Farm Credit Act of 1971, a new charter act. Photo by William E. Carnahan.*

Dual directorship is a term given to a situation that permits a farmer-borrower of the System to serve simultaneously as a director of a local association (PCA or FLBA) and on the district board. To many, and particularly to Governor Jaenke, being a director on a district board that has direct supervisory authority over an association board, of which one is also a director and is in a position to have a voice in such things as setting salaries and other terms of employment, was intolerable and a blatant conflict of interest. To most leaders in the System, whose power base was through the local associations, the practice was considered customary and, among honorable men, they saw no reason to change. In fact, they were prepared to fight to the hilt for dual directorship. To question such a sacred philosophy was treason. Jaenke's attitude, right or wrong, proved to be his undoing as FCA governor.

Governor Jaenke used all the means at his disposal. He reasoned, lectured, pleaded, cajoled, and threatened — all in a vain attempt to convince the Farm Credit System that dual directorship was morally wrong and should be abolished forthwith. There followed many months of debate and skirmishing. At one time, dual directorship advocates threatened Jaenke that if he persisted in his campaign, they would move to have salaried co-op officers precluded from serving on the district Farm Credit boards on the same basis as salaried Farm Credit people. This had great appeal to those farmer-directors who resented co-op officials serving on the boards. The Sacramento district actually precludes a salaried officer of a co-op from serving on a district board. If applied throughout the System, this preclusion would have denied the System of badly needed management expertise. With all due respect to many excellent farmer-directors, co-op managers have made great contributions to System progress. Others, including a couple of Jaenke's staffers, sought a compromise that would have permitted dual directorship to be "grandfathered" out, that is, to permit those already serving on boards to continue to be eligible to serve, but not to extend the privilege to their ultimate successors. Jaenke steadfastly refused, insisting that "If it [dual directorship] was wrong yesterday, it's wrong today, and it's wrong tomorrow!"

There are those who argue that when Ed Jaenke resigned the FCA governorship on Halloween of 1974, his ouster was politically motivated. He was a prominent Democrat serving during a Republican administration. It was true that there were three or four partisan, Nixon-appointed directors on the Federal Farm Credit Board who openly sought Jaenke's removal on partisan political grounds. As a matter of fact, a motion was made for Jaenke's ouster at each Federal Board meeting during the months immediately prior to his departure. However, FCA staffers close to the scene maintain that partisan, external politics were not the deciding factor. Politics were involved to be sure, but mostly of the internal variety. Ed Jaenke was mainly guilty of upsetting the peace and tranquility of the cooperative Farm Credit System, an unforgivable sin! On the other hand, it was only a matter of time before Jaenke would have been booted out because a prerequisite to being considered by the Nixon administration for a Federal Board appointment was to pledge to vote for Jaenke's ouster. When it comes to politics, Ed Jaenke is a realist and he got out. He could see the inevitable—as soon as the Federal Board had sufficient votes—so he resigned and went on to establish a very effective lobbying firm on Capitol Hill.

An indication of the Farm Credit System's inborn resistance to change is that after all the debate and hassle, at this writing dual directorship was still permitted in seven of the twelve Farm Credit districts. Three districts (Springfield, Omaha, and Spokane) acceded to Governor Jaenke's wishes and to their consciences and voted to preclude dual directorship, while Wichita and Louisville have done so since that time.

On the other hand, the Farm Credit banks in all twelve districts had moved to joint management rather quickly after hard times hit in 1985.

However, since that time, the Texas district was unable to withstand pressures within the district to maintain three separate presidents and reversed itself. When the announcement of joint management in the Farm Credit Banks of Texas was made in August 1984, a group from the Lone Star State (including a former FLB president and a former state governor) carried their protest to Congress. Failing there, the group filed suit (*Holman et al v. FCA*), which was later dismissed by the courts. Even so, the board of the Texas banks relented on their own in 1986 and went back to a president for each of its three banks, so powerful and relentless was the opposition.

Again, in retrospect, it is regrettable that the merger-consolidation issue and other internal issues did not get resolved during less troubled times. Instead, the controversial matter got dropped on the System's doorstep at a time when it could least afford to take the time to deal with it—smack in the middle of the worst farm depression since the 1930s. Now consolidation could no longer be ignored or set aside because it had become an integral part of the System's survival formula. Strongly confirming this view were the undeniable results of the most intensive, thorough study ever made of the System—Project 1995, about which more will be said later.

Up until the September 4, 1985, announcement, the brouhaha over merger and consolidation had been fought largely at the management/director level. The mass of System farmer-borrowers did not really get involved until credit matters started coming unglued. Farmers watched their associations being merged at the same time that more and more members were being turned down for their loans, and those who could get loans watched their interest rates go up. Farmers did not like this and made no bones about it. Worst of all, some farmers felt they had lost their most priceless possession—control of their associations.

Things were just moving too fast. There simply was not time for the usual periods of discussion and debate. There was need to act and not time to observe all the amenities that normally go with being a democratically controlled, cooperative organization. As *Farm Journal's* Lane Palmer pointed out above, there is such a thing as "too much democracy." Another problem was the fact that local control had never seemed important until farmers felt they were losing it. By not attending meetings and keeping up with activities of the association, most members simply lost touch and were not able to know the best course to take in an emergency situation. One might attribute this lax attitude on the part of members to laziness or to a blind faith in their credit cooperatives. Likely, it was a combination of the two.

In any case, it would be fair to say that many Farm Credit System stockholders had voluntarily abdicated their responsibilities over the years. The mechanism had atrophied. It suddenly became important when their association stock became impaired and frozen and when there were threats of merger. Unfortunately, the farmer-members generally did not know what to do about it. For the most part, farmers acted in a clumsy, amateurish fashion. This was probably appropriate because they had never been through such a situation before. All they could seem to do was raise hell!

At the Denver Farm Forum in February 1986 the audience was given the opportunity "to dialogue with Farm Credit officials." On hand to field questions for Farm Credit was one of FCA's top economists, Ed Harshbarger, who had served earlier as an economist at the Federal Reserve Bank of Kansas City. Fortunately for Harshbarger, he is an affable and likable person, one at whom the Farm Forum audience found it difficult to direct their wrath. Even so, they fired questions like: "Has the Farm Credit System declared war on the American farmer?"

They were also angry over consolidation and merger decisions. The audience asked a number of questions such as: "Why is Farm Credit trying to ram mergers down our throats?" Because of the number of foreclosures, Farm Credit was accused of "trying to become the world's largest landowner!" One distraught borrower asked, "Is it not true that a farmer in trouble has only two options—turn his property over to his lender? Or face litigation?"

Even though Harshbarger patiently answered each in turn (for example, explaining why it made no sense at all for the System to become a gigantic landowner), it was obvious that the audience, although surprisingly restrained, was not there to listen, particularly on matters dealing with "our FC Credit System." They were there to complain and air their grievances.

What these farmers did not realize until the crisis emerged was that their control was limited to the credit side of the operation. Borrowers participate fully in the election of directors and maintain control over policy direction—the extension and servicing of credit, including serving on association loan committees, loan pricing, and cost control. They even have a vote on such matters as liquidation and merger. What they do not have control over is financial management—the association's balance sheet. This is in the hands of district bank management, which kept trying to make the point that "good financial management" dictates the need for merger or, in some cases, liquidation. So, although the members had votes in such decisions as mergers, by the time the opportunity arose to voice their protest there really was no viable alternative. Merger was crucial to the association's survival. Thus, the farmers felt that matters were out of their hands—things were being done to them on the district and national level. Moreover, coordination of capital appeared forced upon them at the national level, an even more difficult concept for the average stockholder to understand.

An added problem, particularly in the larger associations, was communications. It was not that being a small organization assured better communications; it was that being large increased the communications problem. An individual borrower, unless he is a director, often felt too far removed from where the decisions were being made. True, until things started coming apart, farmers made little effort to find out what was going on. They were just too busy making a living. So, who is to blame?

Often, the truth is elusive. It is not what *is* that counts, but how things are *perceived*. Farmer members often felt they had been betrayed by their credit cooperatives. Cooperatives, including Farm Credit co-ops, are considered to be a "family affair," particularly by the older members. Normally, such a feeling is considered an advantage in business. Not the case here. In co-ops, as in most families, although you may have the capacity to love more, there is the potential for hating with more intensity. Once distrust sets in, it's even more difficult to recover loyalty, something that became quite obvious when some association members deserted to other lenders, even when they could still get credit from their own organizations.

For example, System farm lending continued a steep decline during the first quarter of 1986. FLB loans outstanding peaked in the summer of 1984 at $52.4 billion, but had fallen dramatically since—by $6.3 billion to $46.1 billion on March 31, 1986, a 12 percent contraction in an eighteen-month period. Over the same period, commercial bank outstandings for agricultural loans rose from $10 billion to $11.8 billion, a 12 percent increase. The greatest percentage shift occurred in the Omaha Farm Credit District, where FLB loans declined 18.5 percent during the year ending March 31, 1986, while commercial banks increased their loans outstanding in the district by 37.5 percent.

Ironically, commercial banks for the most part have been spared the wrath that befell Farm Credit cooperatives, perhaps because of lower exposure. With commercial banks there is no single, nationwide target for the farmers' invective. This situation was almost the reverse of what occurred during the Great Depression when bankers suffered an immense public relations setback. Farmers in the depression tended to give up on the commercial banking industry and seized upon the opportunity to become their own bankers by developing their own system. Now, the situation seemed to have boomeranged; closeness to the farmer-borrower appears to be a distinct disadvantage.

There was an almost pathological urge on the part of some farmers to get even. Thus farmers vented their spleen publicly, joined protest groups and, if they had that option, thumbed their noses at Farm Credit and went elsewhere.

There was the case, for example, of the farm couple who had been member-borrowers of the Rushville, Indiana, PCA for eighteen years, working their corn/hog operation in close concert with the association. Although a number of the court cases during this period challenged the right to liquidate or consolidate associations (most of which were decided in Farm Credit's favor), sadly, others pitted member-borrowers against their associations. When this couple was unable to get their loan renewed, they took it to court on the basis that they had borrowed some $200,000 to build a hog facility on the advice of the PCA. While the case (in which the couple asked for a $6.5 million award) was in court, the farm wife exclaimed bitterly, "I hope someone will nail them [the PCA]." The circuit judge, however, ruled in favor of the PCA, noting that the farm couple, not the PCA, made all of the managerial decisions. In some areas, there were a great number of similar lawsuits.

There were many articles in newspapers and farm magazines that reported on this phenomenon. The March 1986 issue of *Farm Futures* magazine even ran an article on how to sue the PCA, which not only appeared to encourage lawsuits, but served as something of a primer on how to go about it. The article related how an Indiana farm couple, long-time PCA borrowers, had regarded their PCA as their "senior partner." Suddenly, as the couple's indebtedness ballooned to $400,000, the relationship soured when the couple was denied further credit. Although the association's credit decision may have been justified, apparently the manner in which it was handled was not. The couple became so enraged that they decided to go to court. The couple charged that they felt "betrayed" and "financially raped."

The *Farm Futures'* article carried a list of other "disgruntled farm borrowers who had filed [suit]." Among these cases was *"Graber* v. *Southwest Iowa PCA."* According to the article,

A Washington County, Iowa, jury last October (1985) awarded Peter and Wanda Graber damages of $1.5 million and declared the PCA could not foreclose on their 265-acre farm. The Grabers said that PCA encouraged them to expand unwisely in the late 1970s and then reneged on promises to renew their loan when the farm economy soured. However a state judge in January 1986 authorized a new trial. The Grabers had won 'excessive damages,' the judge said.

The claim that the local PCA had encouraged a borrower to borrow more money for expansion was one that often came up in lawsuits. There is no question that it often happened. Sometimes, when a farmer applied for a loan, the PCA might urge him to borrow more, to thereby gain greater economy of size and efficiency. PCAs for years had promoted their loan services on the basis of having credit specialists in a position to provide appropriate advice and counsel. When times were good, this was a great service, particularly for farmers in need of management counsel. Suddenly, this service also seemed to backfire.

It is not surprising that such plaintiffs made out better in the local, lower courts than at the appellate level. Most appeals in cases involving a bad advice charge came out in the lender's favor, the judges making the point that a lender cannot force a loan on a borrower. No matter what the result, the PCA was in a no-win situation; winning the battle, but losing the war. Although freed of culpability, the association had to take the blame, in any case. In such incidents, not only did the farmer involved become estranged from the PCA, but so did scores of other farmers who heard about it.

Even those Farm Credit banks and associations that were able to survive the early economic crisis—through merger, good management, or by whatever other means—were unable to celebrate their good fortune. A desperate "catch 22" situation existed due to loss of credibility (damage to their reputation in the money market), resulting in increased cost of money; loss of good credit business that cut deeply into their loan volume (profits); and the need to help shoulder the losses of those in financial trouble through loss-sharing.

When it came to public relations, it appeared that the FCA fared somewhat better than the System, if only because it does not actually make loans. It has less to defend on an individual basis and is a step removed from the farmers. Also, over the years, the agency had established solid press credentials. This contrasted with some Farm Credit districts that seemed to needlessly get themselves into deep public relations water when the bad news came. Perhaps because there had been little cause for criticism before, the System appeared ill-equipped and ill-prepared to handle adversity. When it came to public relations, a few of the Farm Credit districts were at best naive.

A favorite Farm Credit public relations story of yore concerned a young, newly hired PR man in one of the midwest districts. He was introduced to the district coordinating officer (then called the general agent), a crusty old curmudgeon who very likely thought public relations was having sexual intercourse in public. The new PR staffer, in an effort to make a good impression, asked the general agent, "What is your disaster policy?" Enraged at such youthful impertinence, the general agent banished the new PR man from his office, inviting him never to return!

In 1985 a Farm Credit district was loath to comment on any issue that involved other districts and did not want other districts speaking for it, either. It was to be a long time before the Farm Credit System came up with a national spokesperson, if, indeed, it really has. This was the role previously handled by the FCA, which by this time was saying things that the districts did not want to hear or want to have said publicly. When subjected to severe criticism, the System representatives tended to withdraw and remain silent, hoping the problem would go away. Worse yet, as was true in at least one midwest Farm Credit district, there was an attempt to suppress the facts, sometimes by intimidating employees against responding to any questions.

Clearly, as portions of this memo from a bank official (distributed to Farm Credit people nationally), indicates, there was an ill-advised attempt to manage the news:

> We're trying to get better control over the [news] situation. To do this, we plan to hold intermittent press conferences . . . giving a complete update on our operations in a number of areas, but then

> giving fewer individual interviews, and spending less time answering individual questions of reporters between press conferences. We held a press conference last Friday and have responded to subsequent press inquiries by saying we have nothing new to add. We need your help to better manage the flow of information.

This reaction was not atypical in Farm Credit at the time, nor in some other types of agricultural cooperatives, for that matter. When attacked there was a tendency to want to go underground! Or, as often was the case, to snatch the public relations function from the hands of the professionals who were being paid to handle it and to place it in the hands of management. Invariably, in co-ops when budgets get tight management often mandates a policy to "trim the fat." This often means to cut back on the public and member relations and advertising functions and at a time when inspired public and member relations or promotion is needed the most.

A flap between the Farm Credit Banks of Louisville and *Farm Journal* magazine provides an example of an unwise takeover of the public relations function by management. This incident also pointed up the greater vulnerability of the System when it no longer had a nationwide spokesman. The incident was triggered by an article in *Farm Journal*'s August 1983 issue, "Why You Pay Millions in Bad Farm Loans." It prompted the Louisville banks to distribute a critical memo to the other Farm Credit banks concerning the "inaccurate picture" the nation's largest farm magazine had painted of the System. Most of the other Farm Credit banks, not wanting to get tarred with the same brush, questioned Louisville's right to speak for them on loan policy. To this, Louisville responded acidly in another memo: "Loan policy decisions are made by each district's board of directors. Officials outside of this District are not afforded the opportunity to make our loan policy decisions." The Louisville reaction was a contradiction of the old PR axiom of not picking a fight with someone who buys ink by the barrel!

The Louisville banks also contributed to this checkered public relations image in another way. An announcement of widespread R-I-Fs (reductions-in-force; firings, in other words) was going to be made at the Louisville banks. Management, apparently upon advice of counsel, decided that those to be sacked would be asked to clear out immediately, for which purpose cardboard boxes were provided. Also, the police were present, just in case of violence. The whole action is referred to as the

"St. Valentine's Day Massacre of 1984," and shall be long remembered. Unfortunately for the Louisville banks, they also had been carrying on a running feud with the local daily, the *Louisville Courier-Journal,* for a number of years. The paper, of course, obliged by according the incident complete coverage.

Among other faulty public relations maneuvers was what is known as "the LaMoure Incident." This took place in LaMoure, North Dakota, in February 1985 when the president and the five-member board of the LaMoure FLBA were removed by the St. Paul district FLB. The announcement came without warning, resulting in "an emotionally charged meeting" being called at the LaMoure High School on a Saturday evening to enable the St. Paul officials to explain their actions. The meeting attracted some five hundred stockholders, undoubtedly the largest meeting ever held by the association. The gathering attracted, among others, North Dakota governor George Sinner and his state attorney general. According to press accounts at the time, Farm Credit district officials had locked the gym until the last minute, hired armed private police, and then called on the local sheriff to maintain order. Under the best case scenario, it was hard to convince anyone that the St. Paul FLB was acting on the side of right.

Altogether, the image of the Farm Credit System was not bright, nor were there immediate prospects for improvement. Intra-System cooperation and coordination appeared at times to be nonexistent. Yet, the System had its side of the story to tell—to its members and to the public. What was being communicated seemingly was being done in an incoherent, piecemeal fashion. At this point, it appeared that the System simply was not able to help itself and reacted in a manner that gave it the appearance of being its own worst enemy.

6

Fighting Back

"In any field of human endeavor,
anything that can possibly go wrong will go wrong,
and at the worst possible time."

Murphy's Law

 During 1985 most of those involved in the cooperative Farm Credit System must have felt like they were wintering at Valley Forge. They appeared aware of the Thomas Paine admonition that "these are times that try men's souls." The System could not have been more ill-equipped to face the battle of its life. We're talking survival here! was the warning and rallying cry that was being echoed across the land from the ever-so-few Paul Reveres in the System. Truth was, things were becoming unraveled; confusion reigned. The biggest roadblock to progress (or even to a proper defense) was the lack of national leadership.

Historically, national leadership was supplied in an ad hoc fashion by an informal, seemingly phantom group or invisible executive committee that came from God knows where and whose members communicated effectively, getting the "party line" around the System. For people at my level and below, it was one of those organizational mysteries, perhaps peculiar to Farm Credit, but more likely a part of most national farm organizations. It was not something one was elected to; rather, it was a post that one assumed by dint of his power and ability to command respect and get things done. You never really understood it unless you were part of it, but you were always aware of it.

Typically, the phantom group was composed of a representative or two from FCA or the Federal Farm Credit Board (always including the governor), key Farm Credit bank presidents and district board members, and perhaps a representative or two from a regional farm supply or marketing co-op who were closely identified with Farm Credit. This phantom group had an incredible, invisible grapevine, knowing who was doing what and who might be getting out of line. It was an uncanny purveyor of pertinent information. It could smoke you out and straighten you out at the same time. Normally, this phantom group would have been on top and out in front of this situation. However, it was not. Suddenly, it did not even exist, its members victims of attrition!

Men like Glenn E. Heitz, former FCA deputy governor of Cooperative Bank Service, and later CEO of the Farm Credit Banks of St. Louis Banks, had announced their retirement. Glenn Heitz came as close as anyone to deserving the title of "Mr. Farm Credit," having served in several phases of Farm Credit—Lafayette, Indiana, as manager of the PCA; director of the Cooperative Bank Service in the FCA; and president of the FLB, and then of all three St. Louis Farm Credit banks. Heitz was a very intense individual, dedicated to Farm Credit. He had an innate sense of knowing right from wrong, as well as an ability to remember those whom he felt did not. Heitz was a man of his word, which sometimes put him at odds with some politicians who occasionally complained about the rigidness of his positions. Yet, the politicians learned to be cautious about making any promises to him that they did not intend to keep. Heitz was not one of those presidents forced to retire; he did so entirely for personal reasons.

Among the highly astute district Farm Credit directors and co-op leaders was Armstead M. Feland, III, who normally relished challenges, but who was a bit weary and wary of Farm Credit battles by 1985 and who also chose to retire—first, as executive secretary of the Southern Farmers Association co-op in Little Rock and then from the St. Louis Farm Credit Board. Feland utilized his natural political instincts and other skills in Farm Credit; few national System issues or projects escaped his attention or moved ahead without his stamp of approval. He was almost a charter member of the phantom group.

Robert McDougal, a prime mover in putting together the System's new lobbying arm, the Farm Credit Council, and a viable candidate for secretary of agriculture at the time John R. Block was picked, suddenly dropped out for personal reasons, retiring from the Sacramento Farm

Credit Board. McDougal, too, was an astute farmer-director, often impatient and sometimes overly aggressive and too politically partisan for Farm Credit tastes. Still, he was a skilled politician, knowing all the political power points. Also, he represented the Sacramento district, always a force to be reckoned with in Farm Credit, although not always in a positive way. Like most Sacramento district directors, McDougal was an ardent Republican and often let it show, even in Farm Credit circles.

Terry Fredrickson, so active nationally as senior deputy governor of the FCA, was one of the latter-day rising stars of the phantom group. He was, however, recruited by Heitz to come to St. Louis, eventually to succeed him. He, thus, became occupied with matters of a more parochial nature and withdrew from national preeminence. Also by this time, Governor Wilkinson and the FCA were "at arm's length" with the System, while the Federal Board was busy just trying to stay alive.

Of course, there were others who were members of Farm Credit's phantom group. It was a dynamic, ever-changing body. The point to be made here is that when Farm Credit faced its ultimate crisis after September 1985, most of this leadership was either retired, otherwise occupied, or greatly out of position. Those, like Feland, who had gone through the grueling process of guiding the System to complete farmer-member ownership just didn't have the energy and drive to do it again.

True, there was a more formal national organization set up to perform the communications function within Farm Credit. It was called the System's Policy Coordination Committee (PCC), established originally by Governor Jaenke to garner support for the Farm Credit Act of 1971. The thirteen-member PCC was made up of a director from each Farm Credit district and the Central Bank boards to serve as "a much needed link among District banks and between District boards and the Federal Farm Credit Board." In view of the successful passage of the 1971 act, this Committee easily concluded that it was too important not to continue, and ordained itself to do so. The FCA governor who brought it into being was not inclined to exercise his power of abolishment, even if he thought he could do it. He probably felt the PCC might be useful again. For the most part after passage of the 1971 act, the PCC served primarily as a communications link between the FCA and the respective Farm Credit boards and, as a group, was not involved in influencing national policy, despite the fact it later took over the management of the annual National Conference of Farm Credit Directors from the FCA.

It should be noted that the Policy Coordinating Committee, to its everlasting credit, phased itself out voluntarily—a rarity in Farm Credit—and gave way to the new national organization (Farm Credit Corporation of America (FCC/A), whose responsibility was to coordinate and otherwise to provide leadership for the System. The "phantom group," however, at last accounting, has not been able to regroup, at least not in the form in which it once existed.

Top Farm Credit bank management was at a premium, particularly needed were those people who had a bent and zest for national leadership. Being involved in national matters could be hazardous to your health in your home base. Whereas a district Farm Credit board might be flattered at first blush by the status and esteem their staff members might enjoy nationally, that remained true only so long as they kept their fences mended back home. This situation was not unlike that of a senator or representative who seeks broader responsibilities and recognition in Congress. These people run the danger of being considered as "getting too big for their breeches," which might get them defeated at the next election for not paying due care and consideration to "the folks back home." During this period in Farm Credit, there were a number of career casualties that fell into this category.

As prime examples, both Arthur C. Buffington, president, FLB of Omaha, and Burgee Amdahl, CEO of Farm Credit Services, St. Paul, were held in high esteem by their colleagues around the country. For this reason, it seemed only natural for them to be plucked to serve on a number of national committees and task forces, including serving on the prestigious, four-member executive committee (called the Leadership Group) that ramrodded Project 1995. The other two members of the group were Terry Fredrickson, then FCA senior deputy governor (chief operating officer) and Thomas Farr, president of the Louisville Bank for Cooperatives. Both Buffington and Amdahl have taken early retirement, adding further validity to a business axiom that was gaining favor within the System—you are only as good as your last annual report. Service on the Leadership Group, although perhaps not the main cause, undoubtedly contributed to their downfall.

Buffington, who was discussed earlier, was at one time held in high esteem by his district board. Suddenly, he lost his charm. Amdahl, a quiet, soft-spoken but tough Norwegian, a dairy farmer and an honors graduate in agricultural economics from the University of Minnesota, had worked his way up the Farm Credit ladder via the Banks for

Cooperatives before being named to head all three St. Paul banks. Amdahl had to shoulder the added burden of having a United States senator—Rudy Boschwitz of Minnesota—criticizing him publicly about the St. Paul banks' lending policies. Public criticism of Farm Credit was something that neither Senator Boschwitz nor any other congressman would have dared to do in the St. Paul district even a few months earlier. The combination of these slings and arrows cost Amdahl his job. He took early retirement in June 1986 to avoid the inevitable. In Amdahl's case, faulty communications contributed to his demise.

Doubtless the most telling blow to the System was the abdication of the Farm Credit Administration from its traditional leadership position, a move that rankled the System for many months. The arm's length relationship, coming as it did, appeared to leave the System obliged to take all the lumps. One of the more bitter System spokesmen, who did not want to be identified because he remains in the System and feels he can still be reached (by even an arm's length regulator), explained it this way:

> Hell, it's a cop out! As soon as the FCA saw what was going on in the System around the country, it wanted out as fast as it could. FCA's reaction was typical of government—cover its own ass. Now, with all its new regulatory authorities [written into the 1985 act], it can sit back and do what it is now doing—being the world's greatest second guesser!

The FCA claimed that this just was not so, that it had to act quickly if it was going to have any credibility in its primary role of being able to vouch for the integrity of the System. This role was particularly crucial in its relations with buyers of Farm Credit securities. The FCA argued that, after all, it must first look after the public interest. The FCA could no longer afford to be perceived as an advocate of the Farm Credit System. As is usually the case, there was some truth on both sides. The problem was there was no time allowed for the orderly transition of the FCA from a System advocate to a hard-nosed government regulator. What was hoped to be a slow, evolutionary process turned out to be revolutionary because of the worsening crisis in the System. The System was probably right, however, in indicating that the FCA overcompensated, attempting to make up for past laxity.

Although the FCA staff had been discussing its new "emerging role as a financial institution regulator/examiner/supervisor," its regulatory function was now being emphasized; supervision was hardly mentioned at all, a fading memory. There again, the pressure was to determine what was wrong with the System and to try to right it again, as soon as possible. The FCA could do this better, it was argued, at a greater distance and without being so involved with the System's day-to-day operations. The first public announcement of the implementation of this change in agency policy was made by Governor Wilkinson at the National Conference of Farm Credit Directors in St. Louis in September 1984:

> We now believe that the FC System has reached a level of maturity where it must accept the challenge of being a fully independent network of financial institutions. This means the . . . System will be subject to the same tough supervision and examination by their regulatory agency as are their counterparts in other sectors of the financial community. . . . We do not want to be your [the System's] adversary, but we cannot [any longer] be your advocate.

Perhaps so the System would realize he meant business, Governor Wilkinson added this implied threat: "And if we need additional regulatory tools to take that stance — tools available to other financial regulators — we shall take them." The FCA did get those authorities in the Farm Credit Amendments Act of 1985.

Using the Farm Credit experience as an example, one would conclude that a government regulator must make a choice to be either an advocate or an adversary — that there is no in between. Not true. The Federal Reserve Board, for example, looks after the interests of the national banks on many occasions — tax legislation being a recent example. To be sure, the Fed can also be an adversary, and often is. However, it does not make a conscious effort to be so. However, relations between the FCA and the System began to drift apart in 1985, becoming more strained daily, as each sought separate goals. Later, relations degenerated into almost open warfare with the arrival of the new FCA board in 1986.

There were even some charges in the System of vindictiveness on the part of some FCA employees. *Inside FCA,* the agency's internal employee electronic newsletter, took these accusations seriously enough to run this editorial comment:

> Despite the new arm's length relationship between FCA and the
> Farm Credit System, their common objective of service to agricul-

ture remains the same. As set forth in the preamble to the Charter
Act, the Farm Credit Act of 1971, it is declared policy to provide a
System "to accomplish the objective of improving the income and
well-being of American farmers and ranchers by furnishing sound,
adequate, and constructive credit.

In retrospect, the editorial was more in the nature of wishful thinking. For some FCA employees, like myself, born with an affinity for the
soil, it was natural to embrace this concept; it was what had attracted
many to FCA in the first place. However, for some others that feeling
did not exist. In addition, personal rancor had developed with many
over the years and a get-even complex was not uncommon on both sides.

Although it took some time for the "divorce" to become final, there
were a number of things to which the System had to attend—the most
urgent being the need to get the new national entity (the Farm Credit
Corporation) rolling so it could attempt to coordinate System activities.
Fortunately a blueprint of needed action was essentially set forth in the
big research effort called Project 1995 that was released in June of 1984.
The study encompassed some six "various aspects of the Farm Credit
System and its environment," which were discussed and studied in depth
over a period of more than two years. Project 1995 recognized the
changing environment to which the System would need to adjust, such as
changes in technology, the farm economy, the financial markets, and
government policy.

In retrospect, undoubtedly the top benefit that came out of the
multimillion dollar research project was that it alerted and educated
many in the System to the urgent need for structural changes, but apparently too late. The study also indicated that a vehicle like the Farm
Credit Corporation would be needed to provide the leadership to implement such structural change. The study concluded that the System would
need more centralized operations.

Much of the language used in the study to describe the proposed
entity was incorporated in the resolution that advocated the establishment of the Farm Credit Corporation. The proposal was submitted to
the district Farm Credit boards for adoption at their March 1985 meetings. The resolution proposed specific authorities and/or responsibilities
for the central entity (which finally became known as the FCC/A):

1. Provide System leadership and strategic planning
2. Develop, monitor, and control standards for credit, financial

condition, financial disclosure, earnings, reserves and ratios, and
management information system
3. Act as a System spokesperson
4. Assume a self-regulatory role for the System
5. Develop and administer System loss-sharing agreements

Although gaining System acceptance of the concept of a central
entity did not pose much of a problem, putting it into practice did. The
difficulty started with getting the right person (believed to require a
combination of talents of Thomas Jefferson, Benjamin Franklin, An-
drew Mellon, Henry Clay, and Gen. Dwight Eisenhower) to head it.
Thus, the System opted to employ one of its time-honored dodges —
naming an interim manager. On May 15, 1985, the new FCC/A board
selected a battle-scarred Farm Credit veteran, Alton B. Cook, who had
spent his entire career in the System and who had recently retired and
was recovering from a stormy, two-year tour of duty as president of the
FICB of Louisville (a story unto itself). Upon accepting the reins and the
reign, Cook was told he would "be responsible for managing the start up
of FCC/A," a process that required a period of some nine months.

As if the System did not have enough internal trouble in picking the
proper person, it was also dogged by more unfavorable publicity. This
included the publishing of the salary range that would reputedly be paid
to the successful applicant to become the prospective "savior of the
System" — upwards of $300,000! In its recruiting, Farm Credit was in-
clined to think in terms of salary ranges, a practice that often attracted
applications. But the publication of the salary figure enraged some
farmer-members. This was particularly true in areas of farm loan stress.
Worse yet, it provoked similar sleuthing into the salaries of Farm Credit
bank officers and ultimately led to the insertion of salary restrictions for
bank officers in the 1985 Farm Credit bill.

On February 13, 1986, the Farm Credit System ended its agonizing
when the FCC/A board named H. Brent Beesley, a former director of
the Federal Savings & Loan Association Corporation (FSLIC) and CEO
of the First Charter Savings & Loan Association in his native Utah, as its
president. In making the appointment, the System displayed its new-
found political savvy by picking, as it did, a candidate with good Republican credentials, the better to get on with the Reagan administration. Beesley had been cochairman of the Ford for President campaign
in Utah during the 1976 election campaign.

However, before the System could get too serious about its central entity, it needed to make sure that there remained a Farm Credit System. Fortunately, the System had already put together a Farm Credit Council to handle its lobbying, a function that the FCA had also abandoned. The reason for this takeover was not solely from the new "arm's length" relationship. Following the passage of the 1980 act, during which time the FCA had gotten into the trenches and battled it out with the American Bankers Association and others, it was agreed informally by Congress, the System, and others that, as a government agency, the FCA would no longer be allowed to continue to perform in that manner — that "hard ball" lobbying, if deemed necessary, should be handled by the System itself.

So, with the concurrence of the FCA, the System incorporated its Farm Credit Council on November 24, 1982, after which Delmar K. Banner, senior vice president of the Farm Credit Banks of St. Louis, was installed as its first president. Banner, an attorney who had assisted in gaining passage of the 1980 act during its final stages and who had done the staff work in developing the constitution and bylaws for the Farm Credit Council, appeared to be a logical choice. Banner resigned after passage of the 1985 act, however. He was replaced by a political scientist, Dr. John Waits, who came to the council after a short stint with the FCA.

Without doubt, the esteem and tranquility that went with being a Farm Credit official has greatly diminished. In that transition, one was reminded of the drastic, sudden change in the lot of a university president, after the students "graduated" from the traditional panty raids syndrome into full-fledged campus riots during the Vietnam War. By 1985 a protest group could find its way to Farm Credit regional headquarters in St. Paul and Louisville almost as easily as to a PCA office in London, Ohio, or in Mankato, Minnesota. This being the case, one might assume that the compensation paid such a post would be in proportion to the degree of hassle involved.

Not necessarily so, as John St. John, citrus co-op official and long-time director of the Farm Credit Banks of Columbia and the Central Bank for Cooperatives, observed. In 1975 St. John had been named by the FCA governor to a systemwide study committee to determine what might be done about raising the salaries of FCA personnel, including the possibility of perhaps moving such personnel out from under the limitations imposed by the Civil Service Commission. Upon discovering that the FCA governor at that time was locked into a salary of $42,000, Chairman St. John exclaimed: "Man, that's a lot of guff to take at these prices!"

Doubtless, St. John is better known in Farm Credit for another feat. While chairman of the Columbia board, he managed, through advanced planning and mailouts, to cut the length of the monthly board meeting from 2½ days to 1. This did not endear St. John to some fellow FC directors around the country, those who relied on their per diem payment for board service as income. Not to worry. The idea did not catch on.

It was true that one did not become FCA governor in the early 1970s for the salary alone; another inducement was power and prestige. The salary situation had not improved much ten years later (late 1986) when the Level 3 (FCA governor's level) stood at $73,600 a year. Although this probably sounded like a healthy salary around the country, it was not comparable to salaries in private industry, including for the salary paid officials of the Farm Credit banks. On the other hand, government salaries seldom are comparable, and it was the perceived high salaries in some of the district Farm Credit banks that caused some credibility problems with their farmer-members.

Another early 1986 action by the Farm Credit System was to set up an organization to be in a position to purchase nonaccrual loans and acquired properties from the Farm Credit System and to determine whether to refinance or reamortize such loans or otherwise provide debt adjustment assistance to borrowers whose loans or property it had purchased. It was hoped that such could be done in a more orderly fashion. This also eliminated one of the awkward aspects of this process in the past, when hard decisions on Spokane and Omaha had to be made by a management committee of the System (namely the Finance Subcommittee of the thirty-seven Farm Credit banks). In times past, service on this and other Systemwide committees seldom worked a hardship on anyone individually, but, because of the frantic nature of the times, such interbank service was becoming a heavy burden. It was one of those jobs that had to be done now, even though at the same time the presence of a subcommittee member might be urgently required at the home bank.

Thus, the establishment of the "temporary" Farm Credit System Capital Corporation by the FCA was most fortunate; it took much of the pressure off district Farm Credit bank officers and allowed sensitive decisions on troubled banks to be made by the FCA. Also, the Capital Corporation was able to hire experienced people from those banks that were going through reduction-in-force situations. Ben Hauenstein, recently retired president of the FICB of Wichita, was named as the Cap Corporation's first president. Hauenstein started his Farm Credit career at a PCA in Missouri and at the FICB of St. Paul and later was in charge of farm loans at the First National Bank of Chicago. Hauenstein served as president until a permanent capital corporation was chartered under the 1985 act on February 24, 1986.

The Capital Corporation board then picked Hugh Macklin, an insurance loan executive who began his career with the FLB of Berkeley (now Sacramento), but later moved to the Northwestern Mutual Life Insurance Co., Milwaukee, to set up its farm loan department. During his seventeen years with Northwestern, Macklin caught the eye of one of its top executives—Francis E. Ferguson, now retired, who was serving as vice chairman of the Cap Corporation. Ferguson found Macklin in Visalia, California, where he was operating his own farm management and financial consulting firm.

When the time came to charter a permanent Cap Corporation, there was considerable jockeying by the System and the FCA over its control. Presumably, the System won. In any case, it was determined that three of the five members of the board were to be elected by the System; two were to be appointed by the FCA. However, as further specified in the 1985 act, the System must assure that one of its three directors be from a Farm Credit district that is "a net contributor of capital" to the Cap Corporation; conversely, one of the directors must come from a district that is a "net recipient of capital." The act goes on to specify that, if federal money ever was to be injected into the System, the secretary of agriculture was to appoint a sixth member, while a seventh at-large member would be chosen by the other six directors.

The FCA got some measure of satisfaction (or revenge) by insisting that the Cap Corporation headquarters be located in Kansas City, rather than be housed in Denver with or near the FCC/A, as was preferred by the Farm Credit System. FCA justified its choice of Kansas City on the basis that it be located at "a central and strategic location for servicing the loans and other assets likely to be purchased and administered by the Corporation, and from which the business operations and board meetings of the Corporation can be conveniently and efficiently conducted."

The corporation should not be located, the FCA insisted, in the FCC/A's area and its meetings held "not generally in conjunction with board meetings of other System institutions."

Poppycock! Just to prove its flexibility and generosity on such matters, the FCA went on to state that it "believes that the board should be able to hold occasional meetings outside that area." The conflict was not confined solely to the FCA and the Farm Credit System. There was also a controversy between the "have" and "have not" banks over the compulsory feature for "have not" representation on the board. The opposition, led by the Springfield banks, referred to this requirement as application of "the Robin Hood principle," taking from the rich banks to give to the poor. This analogy gained some support, but considerably more resentment from other banks in the System, who were anxious not to jeopardize passage of the Farm Credit bill in 1985. After the act was passed, however, and the healthier banks began to be assessed to assist their weaker sister institutions, the Springfield banks were joined in protest by the Farm Credit banks of Texas. A suit was filed in Federal Court in Springfield challenging the "Robin Hood principle," asking that FCA regulations be rewritten in this regard.

The year 1985 will go down as one in which the Farm Credit System tried mightily to fight back by trying to give up individual autonomy for the good of all. Adherence to such a philosophy had dogged the System down through the years because of its natural bent toward independence. A renewed effort at togetherness became mandatory in 1985 for the System to salvage what it could to keep itself a viable institution. A good start was made under severe difficulties and handicaps, but the effort fell short. Even at this writing, the Farm Credit System has not yet yielded sufficient sovereignty and authority to qualify the Farm Credit Council of America as a true central entity.

One of the System's failures that year was the fact that despite all the consolidations and mergers, it failed to accomplish much in the way of simplifying its operations. The net result of its efforts was to come up with an even more complicated setup. Not only was there reorganization, but a number of new organizations sprouted up in Farm Credit to add to the corporate confusion. Farm Credit Corporation of America, Farm Credit Capital Corporation, plus the still-new Farm Credit Council, although needed and useful, had been added to the System. The proliferation of new names to an already complicated organization reminded some people of the attempt at unification of the armed forces following World War II. After the smoke had cleared, the "unifiers" came forth in 1948 recommending yet another service—the Air Force!

During all the activity that dominated 1985, the System kept looking over its shoulder for a reading on whether it was going to have to ask for an infusion of government capital. System leadership hoped against hope that it would not be necessary but ultimately decided that there probably was no other way out. Ray Moss Tucker, member of the Louisville board and chairman of the board of the Farm Credit Council, described it this way when the decision was finally made to seek legislation: "Our request for federal assistance is one of the most difficult decisions which we have ever made as an organization."

Confederate General Robert E. Lee said it almost the same way over six score years earlier when the futility of the Civil War became painfully obvious: "Then there is nothing left for me but to go and see General Grant. I had rather die a thousand deaths."

7

Looking for Help

"Faithful friends are hard to find:
Every man will be thy friend
Whilst thou has wherewith to spend;
But if store of crowns be scant,
No man will supply thy want."

Richard Barnfield, *Passionate Pilgrim*

 By mid-1985 the FCA, the Farm Credit System and many of its borrowers were looking around for help. They were not necessarily all looking for the same things and in the same places; often they found themselves at odds. A spirit of cooperation was sadly lacking.

In past years the Farm Credit Administration would have taken hold of the problem, in tandem with the Farm Credit System, and would have proceeded in a fairly orderly fashion. If the situation demanded it, Farm Credit, as it always had done, would have turned to the farm organizations and its friends in Congress. Now, under the new "arm's length" relationship, the System was forced to fend for itself. As was explained in the April 1984 *Farm Credit Update,* the FCA's letter to the farm organizations and commodity groups:

> Although the FCA bears a statutory responsibility to protect the public trust, to be accountable to Congress, to recommend legislative changes to the Farm Credit Act directly to Congress, and to otherwise carry on an ongoing liaison with Congress, this is not an exclusive authority. Additionally, the FCA, as a federal agency, is

precluded from "hardball" lobbying. The actual lobbying is now to be carried on by the Farm Credit Council. As a federated trade association, the Council is the private industry representative of its member Farm Credit banks and associations in government affairs. The responsibility of the Farm Credit Council is to represent before Congress and the public the private interests of its membership.

It took quite some time for this change in philosophy and operations to really sink in with the System, partly because, as the FCA and the Federal Farm Credit Board freely admitted, "these institutions share the ultimate objective of service to agriculture." But, as the System soon realized, not only was the FCA not going to help the System out in this instance; it might even prove to be a hinderance as it pursued its prime responsibility of ensuring the safety and soundness of the System's institutions. To perform its regulatory job, the FCA would look first to strengthen its regulatory powers, the better to jerk the System's chain.

If it chose, the System would then have to go directly to the farm organizations for help. This included the general farm organizations—the American Farm Bureau Federation, the National Council of Farmer Cooperatives, the National Farmers Organization, the National Farmers Union, and the National Grange. Most of these farm groups also have state affiliates and, in some cases, even county organizations. Also, there are a number of commodity and cooperative groups in the agricultural community that have maintained a strong interest in Farm Credit, among them are the National Association of Wheat Growers, the National Cattlemen's Association, the National Cooperative Business Association (formerly the Cooperative League of the USA), the National Milk Producers Federation, and the National Rural Electric Cooperative Association (NRECA).

Appealing to these groups for assistance figured to be a delicate operation. Some of the farm organizations were upset over the System's setting up its own lobbying arm in the first place. The Farm Credit Council was not really needed in their view and further confused agricultural relations with Congress. After all, had not these farm groups handled such things well over the years? As one farm organization official protested privately—"Why go to the added expense to the farmer of setting up another lobbying organization?" And, once the Farm Credit Council was in place, there was a desire on the part of some farm organizations to "let the new kid on the block prove himself!" The farm organizations' cavalier attitude toward the Council may have mellowed some when faced with having to seek passage of both a farm bill and a credit bill in the same year. Both the farm groups and Farm Credit had their hands full and needed all the help they could get. Farm Credit likely would not have gotten legislation in 1985, 1986, and 1987 without acting in its own behalf; certainly they would not have gotten three bills.

Even so, the situation was complicated. The farm organizations and Farm Credit generally serve the same farmers—many of whom were in some degree of financial trouble and most of whom were concerned about having a continuing source of credit. It was also true that many of these farmers, if not directly involved in protests against their faltering credit cooperatives, knew people who were and felt they might be next to feel the credit pinch. In any case, farmers' sympathies, if they voiced their sentiments at all, were generally with those fellow farmers who were raising hell with their farm organizations, urging them to "do something about Farm Credit." Mainly, they were talking about high interest rates and the soaring number of farm foreclosures.

Farm organizations are known for their staying power. It goes without saying that they did not maintain this status by supporting the unpopular causes and issues of other organizations. Membership drives come around once a year, and to a farm organization employee it seems much oftener than that. During the 1983–1984 series of policy development annual meetings of the farm groups, which came at a time when the issue of merger and consolidation of PCAs and FLBAs had reared its head in earnest, the farm organizations stayed out of these bear traps and briar patches on the basis of not wanting to meddle in another organization's business. Also, when a merger hits a rural area, one town may gain, but others may lose business as a result, making it a no-win situation for a farm organization. They did not savor the prospect of being a party to it.

So, the farm organization resolutions on Farm Credit in 1983 and, for the most part, in 1984 did not change all that much. They re-emphasized the importance of credit to agriculture and reaffirmed their confidence in the cooperative Farm Credit's unique ability to handle the job, for which it would require "continued, unimpeded access" to the money market. Typical among these resolutions was one adopted by the National Rural Electric Cooperative Association (NRECA), considered to be one of the most powerful lobbying forces on Capitol Hill.

The 1984 NRECA resolution pointed out that "The credit provided by the Farm Credit System to the nation's agriculture and rural cooperatives is essential to the production of abundant food and fiber." Noting that the Office of Management and Budget (OMB) had directed the USDA to conduct a review of the Farm Credit System's techniques and methods of accessing the bond market, the NRECA specified that it "opposes any action by the Administration that would result in higher interest costs to the Farm Credit System and its members."

Among the many other similar resolutions from farm groups that year was one from the Cooperative League of the United States (CLUSA) that said much the same, but (at the insistence of its then executive head, E. Morgan Williams — never one to mince words) with even greater specificity in its opposition to some of the administration proposals in this regard. The resolution let it be known that "CLUSA opposes any type of penalty tax in the form of user fees and opposes the elimination of agency status of the Farm Credit System and pledges to work actively before Congress and appropriate government agencies to defeat such measures."

There were a number of other farm group resolutions that were highly supportive of Farm Credit. Even though the farm organizations' support had remained unwavering in regard to the concept of cooperative Farm Credit and in the manner in which it obtains its loanable funds, not all farm organizations were able to refrain from criticizing Farm Credit's operations in their press announcements and publications and in the halls of Congress, apparently because of pressure from their members. As the farm crisis continued to heat up in the latter part of 1985 and 1986, the American Farm Bureau Federation, under new leadership (Dean Kleckner of Iowa), typified the firmer type of criticism that was beginning to be leveled at the System by sponsoring legislation calling for the System to "adopt an attitude of forbearance, rather than foreclosure." The System, by the way, was not opposed to this policy; in fact, it had proclaimed it over the years. The argument, it appeared, came over the definition of forbearance.

On the other hand, the Ohio Farm Bureau Federation's executive secretary, C. William (Bill) Swank, went out of his way to explain the Farm Credit System's awkward, delicate situation. In the December 1986 issue of *Buckeye Farm News,* Swank pointed out that other lenders are not confined to lending only to farmers, noting that "there are a few banks in the Midwest . . . which have a very heavy portfolio of farm loans in their lending program. Most, however, have other kinds of loans and, if not, they have the opportunity." The Farm Credit System, on the other hand, "is dedicated to loaning to farmers in good times and bad. This happens to be a bad time and unless everyone looks alive, the times will get worse. It is clear the Farm Credit System is looking within for whatever help it can find, and not looking without as creatively as needs call for."

Swank's view, however, was highly unusual, probably not generally shared by most farm organization people. It appeared to fly in the face of the "farmers first, last, and always" philosophy that prevailed among most farm groups. However, you can bet that Swank's words were most welcomed by officials inside the System as they looked for ways to survive. However, most changes that would allow expansion of Farm Credit services would require congressional action, and the System knew it would need to save its congressional chips for matters of a more urgent nature.

In view of the stiffening attitudes by farm organizations toward the System, perhaps it was just as well that these groups were preoccupied with the farm bill in the fall of 1985 and could not spend an inordinate amount of time looking after Farm Credit. After all, price stabilization (net farm income) is the farm organizations' number one concern. With all the other momentous issues of national and world importance that faced the first session of the 99th Congress, it looked as though there would be precious little time to cope with the farm bill, particularly if it were to get mixed in with credit legislation. All of this legislative activity added to the difficulties of the Farm Credit System, which was attempting to make its way through the political morass pretty much on its own.

There was confusion enough caused by the myriad of proposals that were advanced to assist the ailing agricultural industry. Although the Farm Credit System found itself a little short of friends in mid-1985, there was no shortage of ideas or offers of help—that is, plans and proposals to "solve the credit crisis." Most often discussed were state moratoria on loans, a plan that offered more from an emotional standpoint than from substance. Loan moratorium plans proposed by states put a hold on loan payments. This would delay, rather than solve problems and the idea raised hob with lenders, particularly those like the System that relied on funds from investors. A loan moratorium could also prove counterproductive to a farmer who might otherwise pull out of the farm operation while he could still salvage some equity. Delay might make matters worse. Also, assistance to financially troubled farmers who took advantage of loan moratoria could be unfair to farmers who kept their loans current because it could result in increasing loan costs. A moratorium raised a lender's operating costs and put a chill on future investment in agriculture. Farm Credit institutions holding federal charters are exempt from such state acts, but resorting to the exemption in 1985 was considered an inhumane cop out and did nothing for the System's image with farmers.

Not surprisingly, there were a number of state plans. Perhaps the most notable among these was the Ohio Agricultural Revenue Bond (Aggie Bond) Program enacted by the Ohio General Assembly in late 1984. The bill (H.B. 826), a partial response to the financial difficulties of some of Ohio's farmers, established the Ohio Agricultural Financing Corporation (AFC) and gave the commission the authority to issue tax-exempt revenue bonds. The proceeds from the sale of the bonds were used to lend family farmers money for capital purposes at lower interest rates than those offered on the commercial market. The bonds were not an obligation of the AFC or the State of Ohio—the lender had to look to the farmer-borrower for repayment of the loan.

It worked this way. When an Aggie Bond was issued, lending institutions or other investors would buy the bond at a lower than usual interest rate because of tax benefits. The money was then loaned to farmers, allowing them to enjoy the same tax-free industrial revenue bond financing that only business and industry benefitted from in the past. (Ohio also had the Withrow Plan named after State Treasurer Mary Ellen Withrow, under which eligible small businesses could borrow at 3 percent below the market rate.) Lending institutions purchasing Aggie Bonds did not have to pay federal or state taxes on the interest earned.

It was estimated at that time (October 1985) that similar plans were available in fourteen other states. The Illinois State Legislature, for example, enacted a law to provide a grant or a loan of up to $2,000, or 2 percent (whichever was less) of the farmer-applicant's outstanding debt. In addition, the Illinois Farm Development Authority was authorized by the Farm Relief Bill to issue state guarantees totaling $30 million.

There were ideas that were utilized that did not require legislation. The Kentucky Farm Bureau Federation began what it called a match-making service to pair up people interested in entering and leaving farming—putting people who want to buy in touch with those who want to sell, an effort to make sure farms continue in production. On January 9, 1986, the *Omaha World-Herald* reported on a proposal being discussed in the Nebraska State Legislature to provide the state authority to purchase farmland from FmHA, the Farm Credit System, and other lenders in an effort "to stabilize the land market." The idea was that eventually the land would be sold to people who wanted to farm it.

The interest in such programs was understandable because farmers have always been adamant about keeping farmland in the hands of family farmers. At its annual convention in Phoenix in March 1985, the National Farmers Union adopted a resolution admonishing the System not to abandon family farmers and to strengthen its resolve against efforts to privatize Farm Credit. Despite the demand to stabilize farm land prices, an invasion of foreign investors was not welcome. The thought of farm land "buy ups" by the oil-rich Arabs and the Japanese was most repugnant to country people, providing intense "hot-stove" discussion material.

There were a number of sale-leaseback plans. The most publicized of these was a proposed plan of Farm Management of America, Chicago (under the name Consolidated Family Farms). This was a group of investors who hoped to acquire up to 300,000 acres of farmland in fourteen states. The plan was to set up a limited partnership with financially distressed farmers, under which the farmers would "contribute" their farms to a partnership in exchange for security interests in the partnership. According to the prospectus, which was issued at the time of registration with the Securities and Exchange Commission (SEC), the farmers would be entitled to rent their farms back and continue to operate them.

Sounded good. However, under questioning at a hearing held in August 1984 before the Senate Small Business Subcommittee on Family Farms, a Consolidated Family Farms representative explained that the leases would be for only one to five years with no guarantee that upon expiration of the lease the farmer would be allowed to remain on the farm. Furthermore, as a limited partner, the producer would have no input as to the management of the farm. NFO President DeVon Woodland testified that the plan was "nothing but a scheme to shelter the taxes of rich people," while his colleague—President Cy Carpenter of the National Farmers Union—said, "It's obvious to me that this is an attempt to take advantage of discount prices for farmland."

Woodland observed that the Consolidated Family Farm Plan was quite similar to those Congress examined during Agland Fund I hearings in 1977. That plan (Ag-Land Trust, proposed by the Continental Illinois

Bank in 1977) also created a storm of protest from farm groups, which were opposed to outside investors coming into the land market. The farm groups (NFO and NFU) generated congressional hearings, after which the idea was dropped. The 1977 plan, however, was offered during a strong land market. In 1984, except for a farmer who was faced with a last resort situation, there was not much enthusiasm for the Consolidated Family Farm proposition either, particularly after some of the fine print was brought to light in the congressional hearing. In fairness, however, the Ag-Land Trust concept did address a critical need at that time — channelling investment dollars into agriculture. It was one other possible way to keep people on the farm.

Not all save-the-farm ideas came from the outside; Farm Credit had some of its own. The Farm Credit System had its own agenda on how best to prevent the farmland market from being swamped. The System thought enough of one proposal to present it to a hearing of the Senate Agriculture Committee in April of 1985. The proposal was presented by Melvin J. Todd of Union, Nebraska. Todd is a livestock and grain farmer who at the time was a director of both the Farm Credit Council and of the Farm Credit Banks of Omaha. Todd proposed setting up the Agricultural Conservation Corporation (ACC) "as a limited-life, Federally-chartered corporation, which would be able to purchase farm assets of distressed farmers and their lenders."

Under the proposal, "Capital would be owned by users of ACC, including farmers, commercial banks, FC institutions, USDA, insurance companies, contract sellers and others. ACC would be a willing buyer of farm land during its first five years. Land would have to be sold in an orderly way prior to the end of the corporation's 10-year life."

In his testimony, Todd claimed that "the first and foremost beneficiaries of the plan would be farmers. The farmer who sells assets to ACC would have first right to lease the property back (he would be protected against sale of his property by ACC for three years), and he also would have right of first refusal, if the property were put up for sale." However, a more widespread feeling, even among farm organizations, was that the lender would benefit the most from the plan, not the farmer, and that conception carried the day. There were even some hallway insinuations that Farm Credit System officials were thinking first of the institution, secondly of the farmer-members.

Also, the fate of Farm Credit's ACC plan, like most other proposals at the time, turned pretty much on its cost, which was estimated to be

$1.5 billion over ten years. The amount seemed exorbitant to most people. One-and-a-half billion dollars was the proposer's estimate. Many other observers felt the cost would zoom much higher before it was over. The Farm Credit System did not get much support from the FCA or from the farm organizations or from other banking groups or insurance companies. Neither did the idea cause dancing in the streets on Capitol Hill. Reaction from the White House was that the Farm Credit System was going to have to do far more on its own before the government would consider stepping in to help.

Liquidation was not something farmers liked to talk about, but many were forced to consider it in the summer of 1985. They were

FIG. 7.1. *Dr. Neil E. Harl, Iowa State University. The farm crisis provided an opportunity for specialists of the nation's agriculture colleges to lend a hand, sometimes on a one-to-one basis with farmers. Dr. Neil E. Harl, Distinguished Professor of Economics at Iowa State University and an attorney, was particularly effective in explaining bankruptcy options available to farmers in trouble. He also authored most of the proposals embodied in the FmHA Debt Adjustment Program and contributed to ideas incorporated in Farm Credit legislation. Photo courtesy Neil E. Harl.*

provided some practical advice on the subject by a college professor —
Dr. Neil Harl, an Iowa State University agricultural economist — who
had been an early advocate of debt restructuring. Dr. Harl, having the
added advantage of being a lawyer, discussed and wrote about options
regarding partial and informal liquidation of farms for extremely hard-
pressed farmers. His views were transmitted nationwide by the wire services and by farm magazines and were sought by congressional committees, the FCA, the Farm Credit System, and others.

Dr. Harl advised farmers in financial trouble to consider scaling
back as a first logical alternative. This would be the best bet if by selling
a portion of the land or facilities the farmer could reduce debt and still
have a functional operation and could utilize the remaining operation to
provide the needed income and ability to service any remaining debt. Dr.
Harl also spoke of informal liquidation as a suitable alternative, when
assets could be sold or turned back to lenders, leaving the farmer with
some capital, or at least very little remaining debt. Dr. Harl had a word
of caution for farmers on using either of these methods — they must
consider all implications of their actions, such as the impact on the
amount of taxes they had to pay.

As for bankruptcy options, Dr. Harl outlined situations under
which farmers might want to consider Chapters 7, 11, and 13 of the
bankruptcy laws, and he listed the advantages and disadvantages of
each. In general, however, he admonished farmers to turn to bankruptcy
only as a last resort — only if the outlook was so dismal that there was no
other realistic way of working out of difficulty. Left unsaid was the idea
that the bankruptcy alternative was preferred over the grim prospect —
occasionally resorted to at the time — of suicide or of taking the law into
their own hands.

Passage of the Family Farmer Bankruptcy Act of 1986 on October
27, 1986, enabled farmers to file for relief under Chapter 12 of the
bankruptcy laws for the first time. It was felt that the provision would
give farmers a better chance to reorganize their finances, providing them
an opportunity to pay off debts over time rather than force them to
liquidate immediately. Among the qualifying requirements was that a
farmer needs to earn at least 50 percent of his gross income from farming and can attribute at least 80 percent of his debt to farming. Scores of
farmers did resort to bankruptcy. Dr. Harl reported that through January 31, 1987, there were some 571 Chapter 12 filings in the twelve north-

central region states alone, including 106 in South Dakota, 96 in Nebraska and 73 in Iowa.

Although there were a number of agricultural economists around the country who contributed mightily to helping solve the farm credit crisis, none have been more active than Dr. Neil Harl. It was primarily his proposals that were embodied in the FmHA Debt Adjustment Program (DAP). It was also Dr. Harl who drafted the options for developing a government agricultural credit corporation to help stabilize land prices and otherwise assist farmers in holding onto their land. Much of what he proposed was included in the Farm Credit Amendments Act of 1985.

In November 1986 the U.S. Department of Agriculture introduced a new program, "Business Management in Agriculture." This program consisted of five-day sessions conducted locally for farmers by the Agricultural Extension Service and the Farm Credit System, using video tapes and workbooks. Announcements for the program noted, "Declining asset values and commodity prices have put many producers in a severe financial bind. This management training program will help them develop the skills they need to manage their financial affairs."

Understandably, seminars of this sort were quite popular. About six thousand farmers from forty-two states converged on Des Moines in early December of 1986 to participate in "Adapt 100." Sponsored by *Successful Farming* magazine, the free, two-day conference was designed to help "save the farm." Guest speakers were farmers presenting one hundred ideas and innovations for hiking farm income. The main pitch seemed to be for farmers to lessen their dependence on traditional row crops by diversifying with such projects as breeding alligators, rabbits, or snails. These were extreme suggestions but tied in with *Successful Farming*'s Editor Richard Krumme's observation, "We can't continue to produce crops that are in surplus all over the world."

As for getting help from sympathetic consumers and the public in general, they too were provided opportunities to contribute to the farmers' cause. Easily the most publicized and dramatic opportunity was "Farm Aid," a telethon headed by country singer Willie Nelson. Nelson recruited the assistance of many of his country and rock star colleagues, most of whom also have rural backgrounds and who also donated their time and talent. The first and most successful of a series of three telethons was held on September 18, 1985, in the University of Illinois football stadium. On July 4, 1986, Farm Aid II was held in Manor, Texas (near Austin), while a Farm Aid III was held Saturday, September 19, 1987, before a near-capacity crowd at the University of Nebraska's 73,650-seat Memorial Stadium in Lincoln. Upwards of $20 million was raised.

Some objections were voiced at the outset—mainly by some politicians—as to how some of the early Farm Aid, Inc. money was spent. Most of the flak concerned a $250,000 grant to fund the United Farmers and Ranchers Congress in St. Louis in September 1986. The purpose of the Congress was to see what could be done about helping family farmers and to protest Reagan administration farm policies. Taking part in the Congress were the farm organizations more closely aligned to the Democratic party—the National Farmers Union, the National Farmers Organization, and the American Agriculture Movement. The American Farm Bureau Federation, for example, declined to participate.

However, opposition to Farm Aid began to evaporate as its good

FIG. 7.2. *Welcome and unexpected help came to farmers from a number of people, including popular country singer Willie Nelson, who staged three concert-telethons, called Farm Aid, through which he raised millions for farmers. Nelson is shown performing at the first concert, held on the University of Illinois campus at Champaign on September 18, 1985. Much more important than the money raised was the fact that Farm Aid helped bring the story of the farmers' plight to city people. Photo courtesy Nashville Network.*

works became better known. As of September 13, 1987, Farm Aid had helped fund the farm assistance programs of over one hundred organizations in forty states, ranging from the National Council of Churches and the Federation of Southern Cooperatives to West Area Young Farmers, Mt. Calm, Texas, to the Institute for Agriculture and Trade Policy. Most of the assistance was in the form of grants — for such things as food and emergency funds, hotline telephone hookups, outreach, education, and legal fees.

Those who doubt Nelson's commitment should have attended the press conference called in Lincoln in connection with Farm Aid III. Pressed about the farm problem, Nelson not only displayed his emotionalism but his populism as well:

> There are several big corporations, food processors, etc., that are spending hundreds of thousands of dollars lobbying in Washington right now to make sure that farm prices don't go up. And for every politician that gets talked to by one farmer there are hundreds of lobbyists talking to him about the same issue, slipping him a little bit on the side. So which one is he going to listen to?

There were those who belittled Farm Aid efforts as being too little too late. However, they overlooked the most important aspect of Farm Aid — communicating the farmers' message into metropolitan areas. Farm groups have experienced great difficulty over the years in getting their story to city people. Unfortunately, Farm Aid III, which received high marks from TV reviewers and viewers (but raised less money because it had less exposure), was expected to be the last. However, its founder — Willie Nelson — offered this comment: "Just because we won't have a Farm Aid IV doesn't mean that Farm Aid is going out of business. We're still out there. We're still gonna be letting the people know about the farm problems as long as they exist." And, as this is written, Farm Aid still had its national offices at 21 Erie Street, Cambridge, Massachusetts.

In looking for other ways to help farmers, there was even talk at one time, promoted mostly by former Oklahoma Senator Henry Bellmon about resurrecting the FCA's old Federal Farm Mortgage Corporation. FFMC was used in the depression of the 1930s to provide loan funds to farmers who could not qualify for land bank loans due to property risk. Such loans were used to supplement the FLB loans on a second mortgage basis. It was a great success story. FFMC was voluntarily liquidated in 1955 when its mission was completed. At the end, FFMC actually made money for the United States government.

Unfortunately, talking about the FFMC concept lends itself more to nostalgia than to anything else. As agricultural economists were quick to point out, "Things are different now." FFMC's success stemmed from a return to profitability in the farm sector during and after World War II, giving some credence to the claim that it takes a war to bring prosperity to the farm. Economists further observed that most of FFMC's features are available though existing government programs, namely those of the Farmers Home Administration. Others argued that the proportion of farmers facing difficulties in the mid-1980s was relatively small compared to the 1930s — that, in addition, funds are more readily available from commercial and government lenders. To this, the general response was, "Just wait a while!"

Farm Credit, like others in agriculture, did turn to FmHA for help. After all, a lot of bad Farm Credit loans, as well as those of commercial farm lenders, had been swept under the FmHA rug over the years. In his inimitable fashion, Charles F. McCoy observed this caustically and vividly in a *Wall Street Journal* article:

> The Farm Credit System is expected to shunt more than 100,000 of its debt-soaked farmers — roughly one in nine of its borrowers — toward the Government this year, fueling a credit crunch that will drive thousands of farmers out of agriculture and cost farm lenders billions of dollars.
>
> A Farm Credit System spokesman said the System doesn't know how many borrowers it will be forced to cut off, but he said "Obviously, we have a lot of nonaccrual loans, and it's difficult to imagine how farmers with nonaccrual loans could get financing at any institution."

Farmers did get help from FmHA, but in most farmers' minds, nowhere near enough to stem the tide. There seldom seemed to be enough money to go around, and certainly not during the current credit crisis. FmHA during this period was as beleaguered as the Farm Credit System, if not more so. Increasing incidents of violence were a matter of growing concern. In 1985 an amendment was inserted into the criminal statutes by the attorney general, listing certain types of federal employees to come under its protection. This was implemented by Department of Justice regulations in June 1986, in which field office employees making loans or providing loan services were protected, making it a federal criminal offense to injure or intimidate such personnel.

Although usually considered a last resort credit source for farmers, FmHA was often resorted to first during troubled times, and the agency seemingly developed a new plan with every nuance in the farm crisis. As a result, FmHA could well be one of the most overworked, understaffed agencies in government. At last count, it was administering upwards of thirty different programs with a staff thinly distributed throughout the country. Its legal staff was also severely taxed. In January 1986, for example, FmHA Administrator Vance Clark estimated the number of pending FmHA foreclosures at ninety thousand, among which mounds of lawsuits were pending.

During the FmHA fiscal year that ended on September 9, 1986, 5,723 farm borrowers filed for bankruptcy, up from 4,018 in 1984–1985, and 3,842 in 1983–1984. This did not include foreclosures involving other lenders, which numbered 850 cases in 1985–1986, according to USDA statistics. On September 30, 1986, there were 1,514 bankruptcy cases pending, compared with 89 in 1984–1985. Besides actual foreclosures, over 2,000 borrowers simply quit farming because of financial difficulties.

The "buydown" feature of the program appeared to create the most interest. This provided that a lender could request an FmHA interest rate buydown of up to 2 percent (matched equally by the lender) on any new or existing FmHA guaranteed farm loan. That was, provided that the loan could not show a positive cash flow without the buydown, but could with it. The buydown agreement between the lender and FmHA (executed on each note) provided for FmHA to compensate the lender for one-half of the total deduction in the interest rate to the borrower, thus providing the equal sharing of cost between the lender and FmHA.

As for the significance of such programs and an explanation of the sudden resurgence of debt reconstruction phenomena, perhaps the *Washington Weekly Report* of the Independent Bankers Association of America (IBAA) provided the best analysis:

> After a decade in which agricultural debt was often substituted for inadequate cash returns and equities in production agriculture, various proposals are now being launched in the opposite direction: of swapping debt for equities—or at least the appearance of equities, which are more or less substantive. At the extreme, the proposals are calling for outright debt forgiveness. All such schemes

purport to return the farming operations to a state of positive cash flow.

The various debt restructuring and forgiveness proposals are more similar at the "bottom line" than may appear on first glance — regardless of whether they are sponsored by the government or the private sector.

The administration's Debt Adjustment Program (DAP) program received mixed reviews. Launched with considerable fanfare by the Reagan administration, DAP was called "innovative" by some, helpful to debt-ridden farmers. Others said it was an election-year ploy that skirted the problems of high interest rates and low prices for farm goods. Mainly because of its purchase of stock requirement by Farm Credit borrowers, the Farm Credit System often had difficulty meshing with FmHA programs, and DAP was no exception. However, one would have to say that, perhaps because of the emergency situation, both parties tried harder this time to make it work.

One positive effect of the banking difficulties was that it placed farm lenders in a more cooperative mood. In January and February 1985, for example, FCA Governor Wilkinson called four regional meetings with FmHA around the country to discuss DAP. Similar joint programs were held by commercial bankers.

Even so, in March 1985, when FCA Governor Wilkinson was asked by Chairman Ed Jones during a hearing of the House Agricultural Credit Subcommittee to rate DAP on a scale of one to ten, he gave it only a "three to three-and-one-half." Wilkinson's low evaluation of DAP could not have endeared himself to Undersecretary of Agriculture Frank Naylor, who was also present to testify. Naylor, of course, was destined to succeed Wilkinson at the FCA.

So it was that DAP, too, enjoyed only limited success. This was in part because, as has been true with many government farm programs, it was too complicated for the average farmer to understand. The complexity of farm programs has been an enigma over the years. The smaller farmers, who generally need assistance the most, normally do not have someone handy to tell them what is available to them in the way of farm programs; neither do they seem to have the time or inclination to dig out the information for themselves. Also, while there was a certain amount of embarrassment involved in participating in a government program, there was even more embarrassment in not understanding it. Many farmers often would not bother to ask. However, this reluctance moderated somewhat when the full impact of the credit crisis hit and farmers had their backs against the wall.

Of course, there were many other ideas for assistance—various schemes and plans, government and otherwise, that were advanced during this period. It can be said of all plans that none were a panacea; most came under the heading of emergency, stopgap, or minimum, short-term benefit. There simply was not enough money available at the time to fully fund most proposals; and with some, there never would be.

Thus, it became increasingly obvious that the Farm Credit System was not going to be taken off the hook by FmHA or anyone else. It was back to the drawing board! The System was fortunate that it had something to put on its drawing board—the results of Project 1995, which was advertised as a blueprint for action. Historically, the System has not always gotten value received from its research studies; the dust has accumulated quite high on most of them. But Project 1995, despite its costs (or maybe because of them), was destined to be an exception. The timing, also, was right.

There appeared to be no question now but that legislation would be required. Project 1995 had outlined the structural changes required to obtain it. The issue now was time—which was rapidly ticking away! It looked like the System was going to need some direct assistance from Uncle Sam. Would it need legislation to get it? Yes, indeed, it would.

8

Going for Legislation

"When all else fails,
go for legislation."

Anon.

 On September 18, 1985 — just two weeks after the blockbuster announcement about its deep problems — the Farm Credit System decided to "go for it." The System would seek legislation that would provide government assistance, if needed. The decision was made by the boards of directors of all of the thirty seven Farm Credit banks at their annual conference held at Jackson Hole, Wyoming. However, there remained qualms among many of the Farm Credit directors as to whether there really was a need to appeal to the government for help. They wanted to make sure there was not another alternative for the Farm Credit System.

Historically, the National Conference of Farm Credit Directors had not been considered the proper place to make such decisions. Even though the national conference was the closest thing the Farm Credit System had to a national annual meeting, it was not set up as a policy-making body. Policy was a matter for the individual district Farm Credit boards to determine in the sanctity of their board rooms.

The National Directors' Conference was more of a "show and tell" exercise, set up for consultation and comparing notes. There also was a fair amount of time set aside for recreation. From its beginning, the meeting had been controlled by the FCA. But this changed as a result of the new "arm's length" relationship. Then, by mutual consent, the System took over sponsorship and control of the conference and, as relations became more strained, the FCA's participation was at the System's sufferance and by its invitation.

Farm Credit System leadership realized by the fall of 1985 that they were going to have to take what they could get in the way of legislation. If they were to get anything at all, they would need to press ahead with deliberate speed. To gain passage of a bill before Christmas—or by the end of the first session of the 99th Congress, only three months away— would be extremely difficult. In recognition of this deadline and of the fact that it was necessary to strike quickly before opponents to federal assistance had a chance to regroup, Alton Cook, the acting president of the Farm Credit Corporation of America, named a legislative committee "to act in behalf of System institutions."

The legislative committee was comprised of three System district directors (Armstead M. Feland, St.Louis District; Grant Lucas, Sacramento; and Ray Moss Tucker, Louisville); and three Farm Credit bank presidents (Gene Swackhamer, Baltimore District; Burgee Amdahl, St. Paul; and Douglas D. Sims, St. Louis). Serving as ex officio members on the legislative committee were Delmar K. Banner, president of the Farm Credit Council, and Alton Cook. Ray Moss Tucker, then president of the Farm Credit Council, chaired the committee. The legislative committee was provided a list of ten principles from the National Directors' Conference to serve as guidelines for the System's legislative efforts:

> 1. Assistance should be for the minimum amount necessary and of the shortest duration possible to enable the System to continue to perform its mandated mission
> 2. Levels of assistance must be sufficient to strengthen borrower confidence and assure full and timely payment of principal and interest to holders of System securities
> 3. Farmer/borrower control of the System should be maintained
> 4. Government involvement in the System decision-making process should be minimal
> 5. Extension and administration of credit should not be politicized
> 6. Except for ongoing supervision, the government's involvement with the System should end with the expiration of any assistance package
> 7. Expanded lending authorities are not contemplated
> 8. The System should not be mandated to assume any of the lending activities now held by government agencies

9. Significant structural changes for System institutions required as a condition for financial assistance must be approved by the FCC/A Board

10. The System recognizes the need for a strong and independent federal regulator and will support statutory changes to give the Farm Credit Administration powers similar to those held by other financial regulatory institutions, while also reducing the involvement of the FCA in the management of the banks.

The Farm Credit directors added these assurances:

While the 37 Banks recognize that federal financial assistance will likely be required if the present adverse trends in agriculture continue, they also acknowledge that the System currently has substantial financial resources. While the process of seeking federal financial assistance is underway, each institution of the System will continue to utilize such resources to deal resolutely with its financial problems in a businesslike manner.

The ten principles read more like a wish list or a political party platform than like something that one could realistically expect to get from Congress, given the seriousness of the situation and the loss of System clout. In all probability, it was written to placate the dissidents in the System. Or, as one System official explained with a wink: "You have to admit, there is plenty of room for compromise!"

Rather than directly declaring a need for government assistance, the Farm Credit directors' first principle seemed rather to speculate (or dictate) under what conditions it would accept it: "Assistance should be for the minimum amount necessary and of the shortest duration possible to enable the System to continue to perform its Congressionally mandated mission."

The Farm Credit directors adroitly got to the matter of utmost urgency (principle 2): regaining the confidence of the investors so order and tranquility could again return to the money market. There was a message there, too, for the administration to cease vacillating publicly on the matter, which caused the cost of System bonds to yo-yo in the money market.

You could not fault the System for trying to retain what independence it could, once it received government assistance; it wanted government help but not the controls that might go along with it. The System had been through the experience of government control when it accepted seed money from the government in the beginning. It did not yearn for a return to such a partnership because, having once gained its independence by paying off the government capital, it did not want to go through that process again, not knowing how it might turn out. These sentiments were expressed in principles 3 through 6.

To reduce the American Bankers Association's opposition to new legislation, the directors wisely inserted the promise that "Expanded lending authorities are not contemplated." This, also, was meant as a reassuring message to some farm organizations that feared the System would infringe further on their insurance business.

Also, in the System's continuing effort to remain a "pure" lender and to prevent involvement in the government (FmHA) lending process, the Farm Credit directors adopted principle 8—not "to assume any of the lending activities now held by government agencies." Over the years, there had been suggestions from administrations of both parties that the Farm Credit System consider taking over the subsidized lending now handled by the FmHA, setting up both "soft" (government subsidized) and "hard" (regular) credit windows for farmers. Up to that time at least, neither the System nor FCA had seriously considered the proposition. The intention was to keep the system and the FmHA separate at all costs.

In recognition of the internal strife over consolidations and mergers and the effect on member-borrowers' sense of loss of control, principle 9 was included: "Significant structural changes for System institutions required as a condition for financial assistance must be approved by the Farm Credit Corporation of America board." It is not certain what the purpose was in handing this hot potato to the fledgling FCC/A. Perhaps, there were some who hoped it would help FCC/A commit suicide. True, most System leaders were anxious for the new central entity to get its feet wet in exercising its leadership role over the System, but officiating over mergers and consolidations could result in its early drowning. Still, it was a job that needed to be done, and the FCC/A agreed to assert itself.

Then, there was the matter of dealing with the regulator (principle 10). FCA at the time was seeking more authorities that would allow it to deal with the System "at arm's length." Despite negative feelings and distrust of the "new FCA," the System knew, in view of its problems, that Congress would not go for reduced regulatory power and doubtless would be sympathetic to the FCA's request for more. So, it wisely decided to try to get something for going along with the FCA. The goal was to make it tougher for FCA to stick its nose into System management, a fair exchange.

Because of the high degree of confusion and indecisiveness within the System, the odds for gaining meaningful legislation before the end of the year were not high. The naming of a legislative committee and the presence of a central entity did not assure that this new leadership would be able on such short notice to carry the load. There was also the more basic question of whether or not the new organizations could even maintain the necessary discipline. In the past, the FCA had served both as the chairman of the board and sergeant of arms on legislative matters. FCA had not only voluntarily abdicated these roles, but might now, under certain circumstances, line up with the opposition.

On the other hand, the System had quite a bit going for it, not the least of which was much latent support for its cause. Chief among these allies was the chairman of the House Subcommittee on Conservation, Credit, and Rural Development, Rep. Ed Jones of Tennessee, and the ranking minority member of the counterpart Senate Subcommittee (Agricultural Credit and Rural Electrification), Sen. Ed Zorinsky of Nebraska, both veterans of Farm Credit legislation efforts of the recent past.

Farm Credit has been blessed over the years with a wealth of support in Congress. It has been watched over and looked after by a distinguished bipartisan list of senators and representatives who served on agriculture committees and watched (and took pride in) the growth and achievements of the System. Then, there was another category of elected officials who not only took pride in the System, but insisted that the System do everything precisely as they were told, lest they would come down on them harshly. Those in this group were referred to as "godfathers."

Representative Jones, on the other hand, was given to scolding the System like a naughty child but defended it to the hilt against all adversaries. Without Jones' leadership and support, Farm Credit probably would never have gotten much in the way of legislation after the 1971 act. Certainly, it could have kissed the 1985 act amendments goodbye.

Senator Zorinsky's shining Farm Credit hour came during the waning hours of the congressional session in December 1980. Defeated in his bid for reelection, Georgia's Herman Talmadge, longtime chairman of the Senate Agriculture Committee, was Representative Jones' Farm

FIG. 8.1. *Rep. Ed Jones, D–Tennessee. Rep. Ed Jones was a key factor in all Farm Credit legislation, beginning with the Farm Credit Act of 1971 through the Act of 1987. To be successful in the future, the Farm Credit System will need to develop new friends like Jones, who retired at the close of 1988. Photo courtesy Rep. Ed Jones.*

Credit counterpart on the Senate side. Senator Talmadge, understandably irked by his constituents, did not return to Washington for the December 1980 "lame duck" session. Senator Zorinsky, then chairman of the Senate Agriculture Credit Subcommittee, stepped into the breach and helped push through the 1980 Act Amendments in the eleventh hour.

Senator Talmadge, who shepherded the 1971 Farm Credit Act through the upper house of Congress and who otherwise duly qualified to be listed among the System's guardians, is deserving of further mention. He was a no-nonsense committee chairman who accomplished a great deal. He was an early riser and worked late, as did members of his staff. His committee was equally disciplined and efficient. Senator Talmadge could not abide verbose testifiers. On a number of occasions, after having admonished witnesses to be brief and having no apparent success, he would finally interrupt the witness with the warning, "You must understand, sir, that before this committee brevity is considered a virtue." A witness who continued to ignore the chairman's advice might get gaveled into silence.

Zorro (Senator Zorinsky) continued to be supportive of Farm Credit while serving on the minority side of the aisle after the 1980 elections. He did not, for example, succumb to the temptation to bad-mouth the Omaha Farm Credit banks during their time of trial, a practice that seemed to gain wide popularity. Instead, Senator Zorinsky, as he had done so skillfully during passage of the Farm Act Amendments of 1980, worked quietly and skillfully behind the scenes, trying to calm the waters. In mid-August 1984, the Nebraska senator sponsored a resolution right before the summer recess, that stated that it is in the

> best interest of the nation that the farmer-owned and farmer-controlled cooperative Farm Credit System be maintained as a strong and viable source of credit for agriculture and that the federal government stand ready to assert efforts by the System in maintaining the System's dialogue to perform its vital role in financing U.S. agriculture during this time of financial stress in the farming sector.

The Senate resolution, cosponsored by all the other members of the Senate Agriculture Committee, was adopted by the full Senate before it went home for its summer recess. The resolution did not put out the fire, but it did have a temporary calming effect. Unfortunately for Farm Credit, for Nebraska, and for agriculture, Sen. Edward Zorinsky died in office in March 1987.

Mention also should be made of the support provided by House Agriculture Committee chairman, Rep. E. (Kika) de la Garza of Texas, always a staunch supporter of cooperatives. Chairman de la Garza was hampered greatly in the 1985 session, however, by the fact that he is from Texas, where a local private Farm Credit civil war was being waged over the consolidation issue. In any event, Representative de la Garza continued to exercise some leadership on the credit issue. At a time when it appeared that the 1985 act hung in the balance, the chairman issued a public statement, enunciating his credo: "I believe the Farm Credit System is so important to American agriculture that Congress will not want to stand by and watch it, or large segments of it, collapse."

As luck (and wise selection) would have it, Representative Jones was one of the featured speakers at the 1985 National Conference of Farm Credit Directors, an assignment he was forced to perform by telephone from his office on Capitol Hill due to the press of congressional business. In a way, a telephone message from the longtime friend of Farm Credit was fortuitous because the Congressman at this point was almost out of patience with both the System and the FCA. Chairman Jones was irked at the System for its failure to get its act together sooner and for not confiding in him earlier on the seriousness of the System's financial situation. Jones was also peeved at the FCA, for he, like the System, was caught unawares when the *Wall Street Journal* article hit the streets. Like all congressmen, Jones does not like surprises, particularly from supposed friends.

In typical fashion, Chairman Jones laid out matters bluntly to the System directors. He did, however, partially relieve the directors of responsibility for the System's current problems (while getting in a plug for his pending farm bill) by reminding his audience: "Let's not lose sight of the central truth — until profit is restored to agriculture, you and all other farm lenders are in trouble."

Representative Jones indicated that he was pleased with the recent hearings his subcommittee had held on credit because they did not produce, as some had predicted, "a full scale assault on the Farm Credit System . . . instead, for the most part, we heard some very constructive and balanced testimony." He went on to remind the Farm Credit directors, however, that the twenty Congressmen who testified were from "Congressional Districts and states that are most affected by this agricultural depression . . . [and were not necessarily] expressing the will of all 535 members of the House and Senate."

Jones scolded System directors for some of their public and member relations failures:

> Let me assure you that if a Congressman ran his political campaign the way the System went about raising interest rates last year, he would be out of a job very quickly. Raising interest rates may have been good business in the short-run, but it was politically disastrous. The hearings clearly illustrated that the interest rate issue and the so-called "local control" issue are taking a real toll on System good will.

The matter of interest rates was one of the most frustrating and baffling problems facing the System, a real "catch 22." On one hand, the System was continually reminded by its regulator that it needed to set rates sufficient to cover losses and maintain itself. On the other hand, when it did, it often lost business, usually from the more solvent farmers, who did not feel obliged to carry their stumbling brethren. In one of his first public assertions as head of the Farm Credit Corporation of America, CEO H. Brent Beesley argued, "No financial institution can mount a recovery by charging noncompetitive interest rates." Beesley won his point later in gaining passage of the Farm Credit System Borrower Interest Rate Relief Act of 1986.

It was fortunate for the System, too, that it continued to have bipartisan support for its legislation, even though some of it may have stemmed from the instinctive desire of congressmen to survive the next election. Chairman Jones, for example, enjoyed considerable support from his Republican colleagues on the House Agriculture Committee, namely from Rep. Ed Madigan of Illinois and Rep. Tom Coleman of Missouri. Many other Republicans supported it, too, despite early administration opposition to the legislation on budget grounds.

Some Republicans, with an eye on the 1986 elections, skillfully put distance between themselves and the administration on this issue. This included a few senators, like Charles Grassley of Iowa, who was particularly candid and caustic in his remarks about both the System and the administration. Even though his actions and pronouncements created severe problems for the System, apparently Senator Grassley's strategy was sound because he survived the 1986 elections.

Other GOP leaders, like Senate Agriculture Committee Chairman Jesse Helms of North Carolina and Sen. Robert Dole of Kansas, attempted to strike a more conciliatory middle ground. For example, Senator Helms pointed out in a press release in September 1985:

> Certainly, the financial problems facing the Farm Credit System are serious, but it is a problem that can be managed and resolved if we first take time to gather all the facts. In any event, the worst thing we could do would be to allow the problem to become a political football. . . . If Congress were to treat this issue as [such], it would result in uncertainty in the bond market and increase the interest rates to farmers.

At the same time, Senator Dole, despite his demanding role as Senate majority leader, found time to evidence an interest in Farm Credit legislation throughout. During the hectic times of mid-September 1985, Senator Dole made this startling observation in an effort to gain his colleagues' attention and support for the Farm Credit bill: "There's no doubt in my mind that the Farm Credit System is in need of a major overhaul and possible restructuring. . . . We could be looking at up to $50 billion in nonperforming loans over the next year or two."

Even though the farm organizations were occupied with the farm bill and were not really much of a factor in the deliberations on credit when the legislation was in its final, crucial stages, they were helpful in two key areas—making sure Congress dealt with the issue in 1985 and keeping the issue separate from the farm bill. It was the view of the American Farm Bureau Federation that the System should not have to wait until it was down and out, its assets and reserves depleted, before it could qualify for federal assistance. AFBF, like the System itself, did not like the prospect of the System having to go hat in hand to the government, begging for help. In such a circumstance, the System would have no bargaining power left in its efforts to sustain some semblance of farmer ownership and control. Only two farm groups—the National Farmer Organization and the American Agricultural Movement—testified against the 1985 Farm Credit Bill.

Perhaps of most help to the System was the almost unanimous view in Congress that something needed to be done about agricultural credit—and before the Christmas break. And so, it can be truly said that the Farm Credit Amendments Act of 1985, signed into law on December 23, 1985, was something in the nature of a Christmas present. No one got everything they wanted. You rarely do in the legislative process. But on the whole and under the circumstances, the results, had to be considered satisfactory. Doubtless, the single most important aspect of the 1985 act is that it reaffirmed the commitment of the government to stand behind the Farm Credit System. Access to financial markets is something the System could never afford to take for granted. Before passage of the act, the System's cost of funds had reached unprecedented high levels—at one point more than 120 basis points over the cost of Treasury bonds.

The positive effect of the legislation was almost immediate. The bill authorized government assistance, albeit such assistance was by no means automatic. First, the FCA was required to certify that the System institution(s) truly needed assistance and had committed its own available capital surplus and reserves "to the point that any additional commitment would threaten its competitive viability." Following this certification, the Treasury Department (if it concurred with the FCA) could (until December 31, 1990) request Congress to appropriate funds. To say the least, there were a number of hoops to jump through. Government assistance to the Farm Credit System was not made available just for the asking.

To provide the necessary machinery, the bill permitted the rechartering of the Farm Credit System Capital Corporation, putting it on a more solid footing. The "Cap Corp" was designed to do three things: (1) mobilize System capital; (2) warehouse nonaccrual loans and acquired properties from System banks; and (3) serve as a channel for government assistance. In the process, the corporation was expected to provide necessary technical assistance and related services to the troubled System institutions.

One of the initial skirmishes between the FCA and the System involved control of the Capital Corporation. The System won this one, since it was granted authority to name the majority (three) of the members to the corporation's board, while FCA names only two. When federal money was actually to be injected into the System, the Capital Corporation would have a seven-member, rather than a five-member board. The sixth member would be appointed by the secretary of agriculture; the seventh appointed by the other six board members. The Capital Corporation board members were to serve three-year, staggered terms and annually elect their chairman. They also selected their CEO, subject to FCA approval. The System moved rather swiftly to install its new Capital Corporation.

The 1985 Act also provides the FCA with more enforcement authorities, making it more akin to other federal regulatory agencies such as the Comptroller of the Currency and the Federal Deposit Insurance Corporation. In general, these authorities officially placed it "at arm's length" from the System. Specifically, the bill directed FCA to conduct all regular examinations of all System institutions (the System had been doing them with FCA oversight). FCA also was given the power to issue cease-and-desist orders to Farm Credit banks and associations, remove officers and directors, merge like banks, and move capital among banks and associations. In addition, the Federal Farm Credit Board was abolished. So, too, was the Office of the Governor, supplanted by a three-member FCA Board, appointed by the president, with the consent of the Senate. In return for this, the FCA was directed to stay out of the day-to-day management of the Farm Credit System.

A significant portion of the act came as reaction and backlash to the local control issue. There were a number of technical amendments included that expand and clarify rights of borrowers and stockholders by providing a statutory basis for them to receive certain information and to ensure due process. For example, Farm Credit institutions are required to make "truth in lending" disclosures to borrowers and to announce the amount and frequency of possible changes in variable interest rates and to inform borrowers of the right to appeal an adverse loan decision.

Unfortunately, such changes also had the effect of adding more red tape to the loan process. Certainly, assuring borrowers' rights is important, but taken to an extreme, it can become a complicated, time-consuming process. A loan officer's time might be better spent helping troubled farmers restructure their loans. One section of the act, for example, requires each Farm Credit institution to establish a credit review committee that has some farmers as members and that otherwise is composed of "persons who were not involved in making the original loan decision." It requires that System institutions make annual financial reports, audited by an independent public accountant, another time-consuming process.

There are also a number of sections in the act that are something of a catchall, that stemmed from concerns of the moment and perhaps were not well conceived. For example, Congress inserted a freeze on the salaries of senior executive officers of System institutions (except for those in the local associations) for five years or until federal funds are repaid. This was an obvious retaliation for the System's stubborn refusal in a few instances to provide salary figures to individual congressmen upon request. When such a request was denied to Sen. James J. Exon of Nebraska, a feud erupted between the senator and the Omaha district, producing considerable animosity and adverse publicity.

When salary figures ultimately were released, the salaries appeared to be excessive in some instances, particularly to the farmer-members who read all about it in their newspapers. The salaries of CEOs of Farm Credit banks in 1985 ranged from a low of $105,930 in the Jackson (Mississippi) district to a high of $189,750 in the Columbia (South Carolina) district, while the salaries of the CEOs of the FCC/A and the Farm Credit Banks Funding Corporation were even higher—$250,000 and $205,900 respectively. Doubtless, many people, particularly farmers, felt that System funds could be better spent than on executive salaries.

The System's refusal to provide the salary figures was based on the contention that, as private institutions, they are not technically obliged to do so. Technically, they were correct. But one learns that you best not get too technical with Congress, particularly if your institutions are operating under a federal charter. Its competitive spirit once aroused, Congress will have the last word!

As a peace offering to those who expressed great concern about the future of the family farm, the 1985 act prohibits Farm Credit institutions from selling real property in tracts larger than "a normal family farm in the vicinity," and for less than the "fair market value" price available from the Capital Corporation. Maintenance of the family farm continues to be largely an emotional issue. Heretofore, attempts to legislate the family farm's continued existence have been unsuccessful. One of the problems is that a family farm is hard to define since it is not necessarily a matter of size. Best a definition be left to agricultural economists to argue about. Personally, I will stick with one that an old Ohio farmer gave me many years ago—"A family farm is one in which it takes the whole damn family to eke out a living!"

In any case, the Farm Credit Amendments Act of 1985 was passed and has since been integrated as amendments into the System's charter, the Farm Credit Act of 1971. The Monday morning quarterbacks have long since assessed the results and assigned the credit or blame. In this regard, one would have to say that, considering all the obstacles, the System deserves high marks, particularly its legislative wing—the Farm Credit Council. One of the wise things the Council did was hire consultants, the most effective of whom was probably E. A. Jaenke, former FCA governor and undisputed champion in gaining passage of the Farm Credit Act of 1971. Jaenke utilized the same strategy that had worked so well for him with the 1971 act, moving so swiftly that dissident elements within Farm Credit had great difficulty in keeping up, thus minimizing the threat of an internal discipline problem.

In addition to Jaenke, the Farm Credit Council used a number of other consultants during the 1985 legislative effort. At various times, the Council utilized the services of Dick Lyng, former under secretary and later to become secretary of agriculture in the Reagan Administration; James Lake, a former White House aide, but then a member of a Washington, D.C. law firm; the Carl Byoir public relations firm; and Bill DeBaghi, former lobbyist for the American Bankers Association. In addition to his own staff (which included John Waits, attorney and former aide to Rep. David Bowen of Mississippi, who had come to the Council from FCA; Ken Auer, long-time Senate Agricultural Appropriations Subcommittee staffer; and Joe Terrell, public relations specialist and author who had served as press secretary to Senator Helms on the Senate Agriculture Committee). Council President Banner made wide use of System personnel, as well.

Bringing some of these forces to bear, Banner came up with an elaborate organization chart (Farm Credit was particularly adept at devising organization charts). As he explained to his board as the legislation moved into its final stages in late 1985, "It is clear that as the workload on the Hill increases dramatically in the days ahead, we will need to add additional talent [over thirty names appeared on the organization chart] to our Washington force." Thus, Banner pulled in people from the System, like Jon F. Greeneisen, senior vice president of the Central Bank for Cooperatives and a deputy governor in FCA when the 1971 act was passed. A communications team made up of Farm Credit District public relations people—Monte Reese, Wichita district; Marsha Martin, Texas; and Rick McCarty of FCC/A—was added. Also, many district directors and bank officials were called in.

If there was any oversight, it was the underutilization of the district Farm Credit council heads, most of whom were true lobbying pros— people like John O'Day, St. Louis district, a political scientist who served for six years on the FCA Congressional Affairs staff; Roger Allbee, Springfield district, former aide to Rep. James Jeffords of Vermont; Evan Hale, Sacramento, former aide to Secretary of Agriculture Earl Butz and, before that, a Utah Farm Bureau official; Reider J. Bennett-White, Baltimore, former aide to Sen. Herman Talmadge; and Ron Wilson, formerly an aide to Sen. Nancy Kassebaum of Kansas, who had served on the Senate Agriculture Committee staff. In addition to working with their delegations on Capitol Hill, these professionals and their colleagues in other Farm Credit districts keep tabs on their state legislatures. None of these people were included in the Farm Credit Council's strategy group, however; that honor was reserved only for Farm Credit bank presidents, a real pity. Good internal politics, but not necessarily helpful to the 1985 legislative effort.

Even so, considering the Farm Credit Council's lineup of lobbyists caused a House Agriculture Credit Subcommittee staffer to comment: "Potentially, at least, the Farm Credit System has the best lobbying force on the Hill." In any case, the job got done, and it was time to take bows, a more pleasant experience than the situation a few months earlier, when the participants tended to stand around, disassociate themselves, and place the blame elsewhere. But before too many curtain calls were taken, it had to be recognized, at least privately, that in the end the group most responsible for the act's passage was the Reagan administration. True, the administration appeared to be an opponent throughout, but it adroitly became a proponent at the eleventh hour. When the administration felt it had exacted all it wanted from the System, it called off its hounds in Treasury, USDA, and elsewhere and permitted the rabbit (the Farm Credit System) to go free—that is, free within the administration's game reserve.

The administration made its move when it felt assured that the legislation would do these things: (1) save the System's money market; (2) silence the Farm Credit problem as an issue in the 1986 election campaign; and (3) get control of the Farm Credit System. In retrospect, it accomplished number one. In view of the 1986 senatorial elections, it was able to soften, but not silence the issue. Success also on number three, witness the demise of the FCA governor and the Federal Farm Credit Board—supplanted by a three-member FCA Board, appointed by the president.

However it came about, gaining passage of any kind of act in such a short time had to be a singular triumph for the System. In his *Food & Fiber* newsletter, Jim Webster tagged the passage of the Farm Bill "a Christmas miracle" and commented: "The president also will sign a farm credit bill that Congress approved in about one-sixth the time it took to report out a farm bill. The swift passage of the package, which abolishes the Federal Farm Credit Board and enables the U.S. Treasury purchase of FCS bonds necessary, also confounded skeptics who didn't think Congress could heed the System's September call for help by the end of this year."

Although the legislation was not considered a panacea, it did provide the Farm Credit System with one priceless ingredient—more time! Again, time appeared to be running out.

9

The Federal Farm Credit Board
. . . A Noble Constitutional Experiment

 When, on December 23, 1985, President Reagan signed the Farm Credit Act of 1985, the Federal Farm Credit Board became history! At the time, few wept because the federal board appeared powerless to stop the erosion of the Farm Credit empire. In fairness to this board, however, suffice it to say that the cooperative Farm Credit System fell upon hard times, and the federal board—like everyone else—could neither foresee it nor, once recognized, do anything about it. Thus, this board, along with the leaders of the FCA and the Farm Credit System, stood to take much of the blame.

But the Federal Farm Credit Board deserves a very special place not only in the Farm Credit legacy, but also in American constitutional history. It embodied the very essence of the new Farm Credit. This was the period that followed passage of the Farm Credit Act of 1953, which set a course for complete farmer-ownership and once again liberated the FCA from the USDA, making it an independent agency in the executive branch. This also got Farm Credit back on a bipartisan track, from which it never parted until it was derailed by the 1985 act. Although the Federal Farm Loan Act of 1916 (that set up the original part of the Farm Credit System, the Federal Land banks) was considered the "Magna Charta of the cooperative Farm Credit System," the Farm Credit Act of 1953 was its "Declaration of Independence." Farm Credit forefathers, particularly those in the 83d Congress, along with other farm leaders of the day, fashioned a neat little package that generated a credit system that went on to dominate the agricultural credit field for well over a quarter of a century.

FIG. 9.1. *President Dwight Eisenhower is shown signing the Farm Credit Act of 1953, considered the Declaration of Independence for Farm Credit. Farm Credit and farm organization officials witnessed the signing on August 3, 1953. Former Secretary of Agriculture Ezra Taft Benson is seated at President Eisenhower's left. The Act reorganized the Farm Credit Administration as an independent agency to be overseen by a newly formed Federal Farm Credit Board, and paved the way for farmer ownership and control of the Farm Credit System. With the crisis of the mid-1980s, most of these accomplishments were greatly diminished. White House photo.*

There had been considerable support in Congress for new Farm Credit legislation for several years prior to 1953. However, a bipartisan team of Agriculture Committee members—representatives Harold D. Cooley (Democrat of North Carolina) and Clifford R. Hope (Republican of Kansas) and senators George D. Aiken (Republican of Vermont) and Allen J. Ellender (Democrat of Louisiana) put the program together. So popular had the idea of a farmer-owned and farmer-controlled Farm Credit System become that it was picked up as a campaign issue by Gen. Dwight D. Eisenhower in his first bid for the presidency in 1952. In a speech at Omaha, candidate Eisenhower promised to "remove the federal domination now imposed on the Farm Credit System." Eisenhower said that "Employees of these farmer-owned, self-supporting institutions should not be federal appointees. A Federal Farm Credit Board, elected by farmer-members, should be established to form credit policies, select executive officers, and see that sound credit operations will not be endangered by partisan political influence."

Political candidates are often known by the promises they keep or do not keep. Chalk one up for President Eisenhower, who signed the Farm Credit Act of 1953 on August 3, 1953. He not only made good on his promises (except for those items that got edited out by constitutional lawyers), but he did so in near record time. The Federal Farm Credit Board was brought into being as an independent agency in the executive branch on December 4, 1953, and held its first meeting less than two weeks later on December 15.

The original language of the bill required the president to make his appointments to the Federal Farm Credit Board from the list of nominees advanced by the System. However, "this was thought to raise a serious constitutional law question as it might be considered as an unreasonable restriction on the President's constitutional appointive power. The amendment gives the President the required freedom of selection in making appointments."

Even so, Agriculture Committee Chairman Cooley, before agreeing to a change that would merely require the president to "consider" the System nominees, stated for the record that he was willing to go along with that language because he had confidence that the incumbent in the White House (and those who followed) would carry out the original intent of Congress. President Eisenhower did, as did presidents Kennedy, Johnson, and Nixon. Two presidents—Carter and Reagan—did not.

There are some other subtleties about the establishment of the federal board that deserve passing mention because the results achieved very probably exceeded even the fondest expectations of the legislation's architects. As part of its independence, this board, not the president, named its own governor, who served at the board's pleasure. It was the governor, not the president, who hired and fired the top FCA employees. Thus the FCA was less subject to the political gyrations and upheavals that most federal agencies experience every time there is a change in administration. Such independence also meant that FCA, unlike most other agencies, could ignore the inevitable list of names that an incoming administration would suggest be placed on the agency's employment rolls.

This freedom the FCA carried on with considerable aplomb—that is, until it had to revert to the regular set of government rules in 1986. FCA's independence and stability were further augmented by the terms and tenure of federal board members, each of whom served one six-year, staggered term. Ineligibility to be reappointed can, of course, contribute to independence, while the fact that only two new members could be appointed to the board in any year made it impossible for an incoming administration to gain an immediate working majority. It took a minimum of three years to achieve this, should the new administration entertain thoughts of a political massacre.

The odds of an upheaval happening were further diminished by the character of the board members themselves. Experience demonstrated over and over again that those chosen to serve on the federal board—most of whom were presumably of the same party as the administration in power at the time they were appointed—did not put a very high priority on partisan politics. Or, at least, in case of a conflict, they generally placed what they felt were the best interests of Farm Credit ahead of what appeared to be political expediency on the part of the administration.

Veteran Washington farm columnist Jay Richter captured this unique Farm Credit characteristic in a comment on the move to oust Governor Jaenke in 1973:

> Politics has never got a foothold in the Farm Credit System, but that's not because politicians haven't tried, Democrats and Republicans alike. According to underground rumblings through the System, another try is underway. Specifically, the talk involves an effort to oust Gov. Edwin A. Jaenke of the Farm Credit Administration (FCA) who is a Democrat, and award his job to a deserving Republican. Certain sources, United Press International reported, "said the Administration appeared to have been taking a hand in a politically-based effort to get the official (Jaenke) replaced by a Nixon Republican."

Richter also confirmed the federal board's penchant for putting Farm Credit first, ahead of partisan considerations. He noted that "Whatever their party, most [Federal Farm Credit] board members historically have opposed political meddling in farm credit. A current case in point is the board chairman, J. Homer Remsberg, Middletown, Maryland, a Republican appointed to the board by Johnson." Richter interviewed Remsberg at that time and was told that efforts to unseat Jaenke

> came as almost a complete surprise to me, and I think it is unfortunate. We have a fine, capable, young governor, and it is too bad this has come up when we've got so much to do. It's the caliber of the

man, not his politics that should prevail. Borrowers don't nominate candidates for the board on the basis of party . . . but on what they know about credit.

As indicated by Homer Remsberg's perception of a federal board member, administrations could not always count on the support of directors of their own party, not even from the federal board's thirteenth member—the one appointed by the secretary of agriculture. This was because most of the secretary's representatives also had a background steeped in Farm Credit, not unlike the other twelve directors. For example, the last of the secretary's representatives was George Steele, a Pennsylvania dairy farmer, who had served on the Farm Credit Board of Baltimore for eighteen years and who was a former chairman of the board and president of one of the nation's leading cooperatives, Agway, Inc., of Syracuse, New York. Steele's main obstacle during his tenure as secretary's representative was getting in to see the secretary because it entailed making it past one of the secretary's assistants, Frank W. Naylor, Jr., who was particularly officious in guarding access to the secretary's door on matters dealing with Farm Credit.

Farm Credit also benefitted from the fact most secretaries of agriculture were knowledgeable on and sympathetic to Farm Credit. For example, Secretary of Agriculture John R. Block, an Illinois hog farmer, was a land bank borrower. His immediate predecessor was Bob Bergland, who now heads the National Rural Electric Cooperative Association and is fond of recalling how the Federal Land Bank of St. Paul saved the family farm back in Minnesota during the depression of the 1930s. Ezra Taft Benson, secretary of agriculture under President Eisenhower, had been executive secretary of the National Council of Farmer Cooperatives and was knowledgeable about Farm Credit. There were others in leadership roles at USDA who were also very partial to Farm Credit, such as David Hammil, two-time administrator of the Rural Electric Administration. Hammil also tells of a family experience with the land bank similar to Bergland's.

Needless to say, independence on the part of the federal board and the FCA often rankled administrations, Republican and Democratic alike. Individual congressmen from both parties were equally irritated when the FCA and the federal board did not jump through a hoop quickly enough to suit them. Even worse, congressmen very often felt that Farm Credit jumped through the wrong hoop. Elected officials were often aggravated when Farm Credit did not do what they had hoped, like satisfying a constituent's loan request. However, if still around to observe, the program's founders doubtless would have applauded Farm Credit's performance, repeating the long-held Farm Credit contention that credit and politics do not mix. On the other hand, Farm Credit's autonomy probably explains why the federal board members found themselves floundering in the political waters in late 1985. Hardly anyone on Capitol Hill offered to throw them a life jacket. Everyone, it seems, enjoys witnessing an occasional comeuppance.

Another little known facet of Federal Farm Credit Board history is how its founders took care of a smoldering bit of internal politics. Although Farm Credit was itself bipartisan throughout the period following the formation of the federal board, this is not to say that there was not a considerable amount of internal politics going on. This primarily involved which part of the System—the FLBs, PCAs, or co-ops—could gain the upper hand. One way to do this was to get a majority of "your people" named to the federal board. To guard against this possibility, the following wording was included in the Farm Credit Act of 1953:

> In making appointments to the board, the President shall have due regard to a fair representation of the public interest, the welfare of all farmers, and the types of institutions constituting the Farm Credit System, with special consideration to persons who are experienced in cooperative agricultural credit, taking into consideration the lists of nominees proposed by the Farm Credit System.

What the new Farm Credit founders were really saying was "let's keep this thing in the family, with all members of the Farm Credit family taking part." Some believed this arrangement to be too cozy. Again, President Eisenhower, in naming his first federal board, observed these guidelines quite strictly, hoping to set the proper precedent for those who followed. Subsequent presidents did reasonably well, particularly when gaining fair representation would add weight to the rationale for selecting the person the administration had in mind in the first place.

To refresh the memory of each president at the time appointments to the board were being made, the FCA would attach pages of rather complicated background information and guidelines (which included the above paragraph) each time it sent the list of System nominees to the White House. The Farm Credit nomination process had to be a whole new world to any incoming administration. The package also contained a "History of Balanced Representation on the Federal Farm Credit Board," plus a roster of the current board and their Farm Credit affiliation. If such instructions did not enlighten the folks in the White House, it certainly would confuse them. In any case, this process was observed for the last time when President Reagan selected Larry DeVuyst, a farmer from Ithaca, Michigan, for a federal board appointment in September 1985, just weeks before the board's abolishment.

The FCA, which conducted the federal board nomination polls within the Farm Credit System, also sent explicit instructions to the local Farm Credit associations. This election notice also included much of the above information, along with explicit instructions, which noted that the associations were to vote first in a nomination poll and again later in a final ballot. At both stages, each association could cast the same number of votes as the number of stockholders on the voting list. A voting list was mailed with each election notice. The notice included all FLBAs (PCAs, cooperative associations) in the district, the name and address of each (association) chief elected officer, and the number of its stockholders. The chief administrative officer was instructed to keep this list in the office and make it available to members and potential candidates. The board of directors voted for their association at meetings of the board at which a majority of the directors was present. No person other than directors of the association were permitted to be present at the time of voting.

Despite all the benefits written into the Farm Credit Act of 1953, some System people would not be satisfied until they could gain full control of the federal board appointments. There were a few times when someone in the System attempted to have language inserted into the law that restricted the president's selection of federal board members to System nominees. Fortunately, wiser heads prevailed—pointing first to the advice of the constitutional lawyers and, failing to convince in this way, using common sense—don't mess around with a good thing! You might lose what you've got if you get greedy! Getting an undesirable change was always a hazard when possible amendments to the Farm Credit Act were considered.

Although partisan politics was a forbidden subject, not mentioned during the election polls conducted by the FCA in selecting federal board nominees, most Farm Credit districts were sophisticated enough to realize that they damn well better come up with at least one nominee from the party in power and at least one from both parties during a presidential election year. Even Farm Credit realized there are limits on how far bipartisanship can go. It was always assumed by the FCA that Republican presidents would select Republican federal board members, and Democrats would select Democrats.

As a matter of fact, the FCA made it a point not to know a nominee's politics; it only assumed that the districts would take care of the political part in a manner that would benefit the System. This was sometimes difficult, however, in a district like Springfield, Massachusetts, which takes in New England, New York, and New Jersey. Qualified, bona fide Democratic farmer leaders could be hard to find. A recurring political situation was averted because a moderate Republican or Independent in the Sen. George Aiken image could usually be found who was agreeable to the Democrats, who merely winked and turned their heads and remained silent during Senate confirmation hearings on such individuals. Such would have not been the case in most other parts of the country, however.

The presidents stuck to the nominee lists advanced by the System until Jimmy Carter's term. President Carter ignored the list his first year in office (1977) for the wrong reasons. In this one instance, in any case, President Carter could well have made the case that all three nominees advanced by the Berkeley (now Sacramento) district were all Republicans and extremely partisan ones, at that. This was a clear case of California arrogance. Either the Carter White House did not do its homework, or it did not care. Edgar C. Rutherford, an Imperial Valley, California, cattleman, was selected, not because he was a Democrat and a strong administration supporter or because the three nominees were all partisan Republicans, but because Assistant Agriculture Secretary Bob Myers insisted on Rutherford. Myers, like Rutherford, his Brawley, California neighbor, also had a proprietary interest in maintaining the Reclamation Act of 1902, the maintenance of which would ensure that low-cost irrigation waters in the California's Imperial Valley would continue to flow.

Ironically, the Rutherford appointment was also unsatisfactory to the then Berkeley Farm Credit District Board, since Rutherford was not one of their boys, either. Consequently, Rutherford's term (1977–1983) on the federal board was a rocky one for Farm Credit. Rutherford appeared only mildly interested and somewhat amused at the federal board's activities, and remained unmoved by the Berkeley district's overtures to win him over. For the most part, during his term Rutherford was able to ignore both the FCA agenda as well as the partisan and parochial gyrations of the Berkeley board.

Once there was a break in precedent it was easier for Ronald Reagan to follow suit and go off the nominee list to make his appointments. President Reagan jumped the list twice—selecting W. Proctor Scarboro, a North Carolina tobacco grower and a close friend and supporter of Senate Agriculture Committee Chairman Jesse Helms in 1981 and Crete B. Harvey of Sterling, Illinois, a horse raiser and member of the National Republican Women's Committee, in 1984. This is not to imply necessarily that an off-the-list federal board member was not competent and effective. As a matter of fact, Ms. Harvey, although labeled "extremely political," was considered, potentially, at least, to be one of the more competent directors to serve.

The appointment of Ms. Harvey provides the opportunity to mention the role of women in Farm Credit. As a matter of record, the cooperative Farm Credit System may not have been the most male chauvinist organization in the United States, but, like most rural organizations, it probably was in contention. When it came to electing women to Farm Credit boards, the borrowers have been particularly slow, possibly because farm women have been reluctant to serve. However, this did not stop FCA Governor Wilkinson from appointing Gloria Conant Daniels of Richmond, Vermont, as director at large on the Farm Credit Board of Springfield in 1982.

Trouble is, such an appointment is not going to happen again because there will not be the opportunity. Henceforth, as per the Farm Credit Amendment Act of 1985, the director-at-large, appointive positions on district Farm Credit boards became elective. This may be a giant leap forward for democracy, but it may be a backward step for women's rights and possibly for the quality of the district boards. As a rule, FCA governors took great care in making their director-at-large appointments. They saw to it that an appointee looked with equal favor on all three units of the System, had good agricultural and business acumen, would fit in with the current board, had great potential for the future, and could be elected on merit when the two at-large terms had expired. If a woman met these qualifications, so much the better. On that basis, Mrs. Daniels, a working farmer and a former member of the Vermont state legislature, was hard to pass up.

I do not want to imply in any way that being one of the "good old boys" assured a person's being a good board member because, the opposite was often true. Unfortunately, some Farm Credit districts appeared at times to advance a federal board nominee on that basis, apparently in an effort to make sure its point of view would be advanced in the FCA. Too often, a federal board member's first loyalty was to the Farm Credit district from whence he came. In a few cases, a federal board appointment was something of a "retirement gift" for long service on a district board, for which a member was no longer eligible because of age restrictions.

Generally, a federal board member preferred serving on a district Farm Credit board. This was manifested in the fact there were some federal board members who went so far as to use "we" in a federal board meeting situation in referring to their districts or sometimes to a specific bank within the district to which they were closely attached. There were many times, too, when an important or controversial issue came to a vote in the federal board room that a recess would be called to enable a director to consult with his home district in order to determine how to vote. This avoided the embarrassment of having to change a vote at the next federal board meeting, after getting a different set of instructions from the district. On the other hand, there appeared to be little that could be settled finally by a simple majority vote in Farm Credit. Almost every issue was subject to recall at a later date.

Generally speaking, the best federal board members were those who were not so closely tied to their district board—people who could truly take a national view and make a decision on a Systemwide basis, as they were supposed to do. Despite all the internal barriers, the Federal Farm Credit Board performed rather well at times, perhaps because it was often able to elect an effective chairman. Often, the chairman was a person who may well have been rather ineffective as a board member but who was able to rise to the occasion once vaulted into the head chair.

Undoubtedly the highwater mark for the Federal Farm Credit Board was the passage of the Farm Credit Act of 1971. A Commission on Agricultural Credit was named by the board in 1970. The commission was made up of some thirty persons from within and without Farm Credit—farmers, farm organization and commodity group leaders, college professors, two members of the farm press, a nationally known young farmer, and a member of the Board of Governors of the Federal Reserve System. Julian B. Thayer, of the Springfield district, federal board chairman, was appointed by Gov. E. A. Jaenke to serve as chairman of the commission, an assignment Thayer handled with great distinction.

FIG. 9.2. *The thirty-member Commission on Agricultural Credit developed the Farm Credit Act of 1971 and was available to support its passage through Congress. The photo above was taken at one of the sessions of the commission. FCA Governor E. A. (Ed) Jaenke, who named the commission, is shown at left. Julian B. Thayer, Connecticut farmer, chairman of the Federal Board and of the commission, is shown presiding. David G. Gault of Manor, Texas, vice chairman of the board and of the commission, is at right. FCA photo.*

The Commission on Agricultural Credit provided a pattern for cooperation within the agricultural community and produced a report, "The Farm Credit System in the 70's," which formed the basis for the Farm Credit Act of 1971. The beauty of the commission study was that it made it possible for the various segments of agriculture and credit to compromise their differences in advance of going to Congress for legislation, thereby providing a solid front. Strangely, this consultative process was not used again by Farm Credit. It probably should have been utilized when Farm Credit encountered more opposition within the agricultural community to its later legislative efforts, particularly the 1980 act.

Despite numerous opportunities to abandon its bipartisan status, the Federal Farm Credit Board was steadfast in maintaining it. This added mightily to its effectiveness throughout its tenure. Partisan politics, it always contended, almost as an oath of office, should not be involved in the extension of credit. Credit and politics do not mix. Such a policy, the board further pointed out, is essential to stability, noting that an organization involved in lending such huge sums of money really cannot afford the ravages and upheavals of periodic, political blood baths. The System needs to be able to recruit and retain competent personnel.

These sentiments were often stated in various federal board resolutions and by Farm Credit speakers everywhere. This, along with the policy of "sticking to our credit knitting" in legislative issues, proved very effective in holding the line. For the most part Farm Credit left the more controversial items like price stabilization to those organizations best suited to handle them — general farm organizations and commodity groups. It certainly made for better relations in the agricultural community, tending to make Farm Credit the source of expertise on credit matters and a neutral on all other issues. Such policies also helped Farm Credit avoid division within by not pitting one type of farmer-borrower against another.

As Dr. George D. Irwin, chief economist for the FCA for a number of years, often explained to the board and others: "Farm policy needs to focus on dealing with these economic forces directly, not by compromising the functioning of the credit delivery system. Thus, . . . credit legislation is best considered separately outside the context of general farm legislation and only after such legislation is in place." Following passage of the Farm Credit Amendments Act of 1985, it was felt that there would be less chance that credit legislation would be considered separately.

Although one could (and many did) register a number of complaints about the performance of the Federal Farm Credit Board, you would have to say that its members bowed out with considerable class. When push came to shove, most were willing to have the board abolished if it would enhance the passage of needed legislation and contribute to solving the innumerable problems that engulfed the System. It was easy to foresee the board's demise because it was written into the drafts of most credit bills introduced by Congress during the fall of 1985. It appeared that the board did not lift a hand to save itself and, in effect, signed its own death warrant, another rarity in the annals of government.

10

Cooperatives . . . Opportunities Lost?

 Throughout the many months of trauma and travail for Farm Credit during the mid-1980s, little press attention was accorded to the third wing of the Farm Credit System, the thirteen Banks for Cooperatives (BCs). Such attention was a dubious honor anyway, one that these banks were glad to forego. The inattention was not because the BCs did not share many of the same problems with the other banks. Perhaps the reason they were able to maintain a lower profile was that they do not deal directly with farmers, but with the farmers' cooperatives. Thus, their impact is less personal and dramatic and, so far as the press was concerned, less newsworthy. Action or animosity directed toward these banks usually takes place behind the closed board room doors of cooperatives, not on the farm or in the streets.

It is impossible to discuss the BCs without knowing more about the clientele (farmer cooperatives) they were set up to serve. Truly, they have grown up together. Just as farmers were able to prove themselves credit-worthy through participation in their PCAs and FLBs, so, too, have farmer cooperatives been provided a similar opportunity through their involvement with their BCs. In this regard, perhaps the co-ops had a more difficult time than individual farmers, since they not only had to prove themselves as businesses, but as a way of doing business. Cooperatives have always considered themselves a part of the private enterprise system, but have not always been accepted as such. Historically, cooperatives have been dogged by public relations problems. Cooperatives, it seems, mean many things to many people, ranging all the way from religious cults to a manifestation of socialism. The vast majority of co-ops in the United States fall somewhere in between. Many assert that co-ops represent the American free enterprise system at its finest. Cooperatives, which consist of people working together to meet a common need, are really democracy in action. Essentially, they are made up of people. As such, they often are unable to live up to the highest expectations of their members, but they come closer than whatever is in second place.

My favorite modern definition of farmer cooperatives in the United States is a simple one, supplied by editor Gene Ingalsbe of *Farmer Cooperatives* magazine: "A cooperative is a business owned and controlled by the people using its services." By this definition and in actual practice, all units of the Farm Credit System, not just the banks for cooperatives, qualify as co-ops and consider themselves as members in good standing of the family of agricultural cooperatives in the United States. One of the accomplishments that Giff Hoag was most proud of during his near forty-two-year tenure as chief public and member relations officer for the FCA, is the fact that he was able to install the word "cooperative" in the System's name — cooperative Farm Credit System. True, it is used only as an adjective, forever to be lower cased and, even then, for optional use, but it is there nonetheless. Or, at least it was in the publications and press releases over which Hoag had control.

FIG. 10.1. *W. G. (Giff) Hoag literally put the word "cooperative" in the cooperative Farm Credit System. Hoag is shown above autographing copies of his book,* The Farm Credit System . . . A History of Financial Self-Help. *Photo courtesy W. G. Hoag.*

Hoag sold the idea of inserting the cooperative designation to the then FCA governor Robert B. Tootell on the basis that it was a positive way of saying that the Farm Credit System was not government- but farmer-owned and controlled. This appealed to Tootell, whose passion was to pay off all the government capital in the System as soon as possible, a goal he saw accomplished on the eve of his retirement in 1969.

Cooperatives started blossoming in the United States as soon as farmers realized that they, as individuals, had little economic leverage in dealing with large buyers of farm products and large sellers of farm supplies. Before co-ops, farmers basically sold at wholesale and bought at retail. The record shows that farmers have made extensive use of their co-ops over the years, even though, many feel, their record should have been much better.

Farmer cooperatives were developed out of need. The banks for cooperatives were established to help nourish the co-ops while fulfilling the need. When the BCs were established in 1933, there was almost no outside capital available to co-ops through commercial banks and little prospect for it in the future. Actually, it was understandable why commercial banks were in no rush to finance co-ops during the early days. As explained in the BCs' silver anniversary circular:

> Cooperatives, like people, came in assorted shapes and sizes. On one day a new cooperative would rise with a burst of enthusiasm and oratory. Some co-ops kicked and sputtered; some died; others moved ahead to achieve distinct accomplishment. But, as a group, they did not present a composite of economic stability—the kind of promising enterprise into which investment naturally flows.

These were the hard facts that the BCs had to face when they were established along with the PCAs by the Farm Credit Act of 1933. However, the BCs had a number of things going for them. not the least of which was the legacy of the Federal Land Banks' good reputation. Also, there was the Clayton Act, enacted in 1914. Although considered labor legislation, the Clayton Act contains language that provided Americans a legal basis for organizing and belonging to "agricultural or horticultural organizations."

More importantly, there was the Cooperative Marketing Associations Act (Capper-Volstead Act) of 1922, considered by many to be the

FIG. 10.2. *President Warren G. Harding is shown signing the Capper-Volstead Act of 1922—the law that recognized the right of farmers to form and operate their own cooperatives. USDA photo.*

"Magna Charta of cooperatives in the United States." Capper-Volstead recognizes the right of farmers to form and to operate cooperatives and lays down the ground rules. According to the act, farmers may act together in marketing associations—corporate or otherwise—with or without capital stock, without being held in restraint of trade, so long as they are operated for the mutual benefit of their members as producers. To assure this mutuality of operations, Capper-Volstead provides that co-ops conform to one or both of the following: (1) that no member be allowed more than one vote, regardless of the amount of stock or membership capital held by an individual; or (2) that the association not pay dividends on stock or membership capital in excess of eight percent.

Having a legal foundation, as well as a social purpose for being, does not by any means guarantee success, something to which the BCs and co-ops can readily attest. Co-ops faced a myriad of other problems. For example, for a long time one negative side to co-op family affiliation was the widely held view that "co-ops don't pay taxes," a myth perpetrated and disseminated by organizations like the National Tax Equality Association (NTEA). Actually, co-ops pay the same taxes as all other businesses. The only difference—and this was a point that NTEA emphasized—co-ops, like proprietary businesses and partnerships, pay income taxes only at the ownership level, whereas the nation's very large corporations pay income taxes both at the corporate and stockholder levels.

Literally millions of dollars were raised for anti–co-op campaign purposes during the decades of the 1940s and 1950s—particularly from small businessmen, some of whom became convinced by NTEA that co-ops were tax dodgers, and, therefore, had a terrifically unfair advantage in getting the farmers' business. At the peak of the NTEA campaign, display ads were sponsored in papers across the country in an attempt to alert the public (and potential campaign contributors) to this imminent threat to the American way of life.

One memorable campaign involved the distribution by NTEA of a pamphlet, entitled "Sudden Death on Main Street," vividly describing how a family-owned grain elevator and farm supply store in Pataskala, Ohio, had been bought out by farmers in the area and converted into a farmer-owned cooperative. The pamphlet claimed that the proprietor was coerced into selling the elevator. The NTEA campaign was quite effective for a time, at least at raising funds. Although presumably seeking fair taxation, the more probable goal was the elimination of cooperatives altogether.

As often happens, the attack fostered unity among the accused. The NTEA campaign brought the farmers and their cooperatives together through their trade groups—the National Council of Farmer Cooperatives and the Cooperative League of the USA. The anti–co-op campaign also is given credit for putting the American Institute of Cooperation, the educational arm of farmer co-ops, on a full-time footing and supplied some impetus for launching such other professional enhancement correlative organizations as the Cooperative Editorial Association (now Cooperative Communicators Association) and the Advertising Council of Cooperatives, International (ACCI), all of which are examples of cooperatives working together.

Another parallel in the success of the BCs, as compared to the other parts of the Farm Credit System, is that their clientele (farmer cooperatives) have also enjoyed bipartisan support. This bipartisan support was brought to bear at the height of the anti–co-op campaign. Although the appeal of the NTEA campaign, for example, was aimed at gaining contributions from the business (generally Republican-oriented) community, some of the most devastating counterarguments also came from Republicans. Perhaps, the most effective of these was an endorsement from Sen. Robert A. Taft of Ohio, considered "Mr. Conservative," who was greatly admired by most of NTEA's constituency. At the height of

FIG. 10.3. *"Co-ops Are as American as Baseball," a testimonial ad in the March 1950 issue of the* Ohio Farm Bureau News. *Such ads helped provide credibility to the cooperative form of business. Courtesy Ohio Farm Bureau.*

NTEA's campaign, Senator Taft, at the request of the co-ops, issued a public statement that was used in a co-op ad campaign. The theme was "Co-ops are as American as Baseball." With Taft in the co-ops' corner, a number of other politicians from both sides of the congressional aisle jumped on the bandwagon. And so it has been ever since.

The cooperative community, including the Banks for Cooperatives, learned a very valuable lesson: Take nothing for granted and do not forever be on the defensive, sitting around waiting for someone to knock you off your perch. Go on the offensive instead. In this effort, cooperatives have not been averse to a bit of flag-waving of their own. United States cooperators, for example, have held up Ben Franklin as something of a patron saint, pointing out that Franklin developed the first formally organized co-op in the colonies in 1752. Franklin helped pioneer the use of the co-op approach as an answer to a number of pressing needs. He used it in organizing a volunteer fire department and in joining in the formation of the nation's first mutual insurance company—the Philadelphia Contributorship for the Loss of Homes by Fire. Although Mr. Franklin was obviously better at building co-ops than naming them, his mutual insurance company celebrated its 235th anniversary in 1987.

Although cooperatives were able to enlist Ben Franklin's help for free, they were also willing to invest funds in their image-building efforts. For example, there was an effort in the late 1970s to make statutory modifications in the Capper-Volstead Act. Cooperatives launched a public relations testimonial ad campaign, developed by Don Hanes of the National Council of Farmer Cooperatives, mainly to get their story across to Congress. One series of ads, which ran in the *Washington Post* during the 1975–82 period, utilized a bipartisan selection of government and congressional leaders including President Carter; Sen. Robert Dole, Republican of Kansas, member of the Agriculture and Finance committees; Rep. Tom Foley, Democrat of Washington, then chairman of the House Agriculture Committee; Sen. Russell Long, Democrat of Louisiana, then chairman of the Finance Committee; and Secretary of Agriculture Bob Bergland.

Although the anti–co-op wolves backed off on Capper-Volstead for a time, there have been renewed assaults since, as well as periodic forays in the area of co-op taxation. Doubtless, such assaults will continue. A given in Washington is that administrations come and go, but the anti–co-op elements within the Federal Trade Commission, Department of

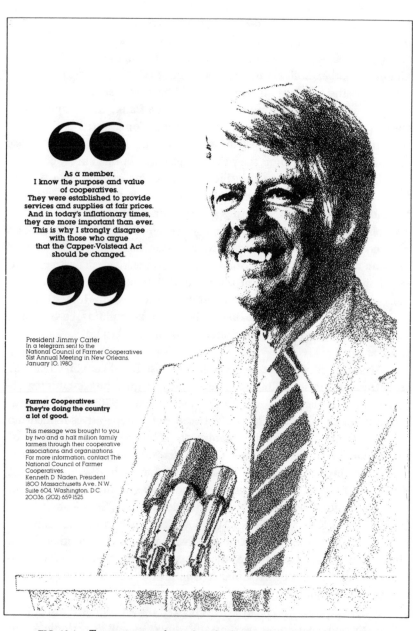

66

As a member,
I know the purpose and value
of cooperatives.
They were established to provide
services and supplies at fair prices.
And in today's inflationary times,
they are more important than ever.
This is why I strongly disagree
with those who argue
that the Capper-Volstead Act
should be changed.

99

President Jimmy Carter
In a telegram sent to the
National Council of Farmer Cooperatives
51st Annual Meeting in New Orleans.
January 10, 1980

**Farmer Cooperatives
They're doing the country
a lot of good.**

This message was brought to you
by two and a half million family
farmers through their cooperative
associations and organizations.
For more information, contact The
National Council of Farmer
Cooperatives.
Kenneth D. Naden, President
1800 Massachusetts Ave., N.W.
Suite 604, Washington, D.C.
20036, (202) 659-1525

FIG. 10.4.   *To counter assaults against the Capper-Volstead Act in the 1970s, cooperatives enlisted support in a series of testimonial ads from a bipartisan stable of politicians, headed by President Jimmy Carter, a co-op member himself. Illustration by Howard Miller, Miller Associates, Lancaster, PA.*

Justice, and even in the USDA will remain forever. Just as cooperatives attract their dedicated advocates, so do they seem to draw adamant detractors. For some reason cooperative attorneys have been reluctant to challenge bullying tactics from such government agencies—Donald E. Graham, former general Counsel of the National Council, being a notable exception.

Neither cooperatives nor any other businesses can long survive solely on public relations campaigns; there must be solid accomplishments to back the campaigns. Glenn E. Heitz, former FCA deputy governor of Cooperative Bank Service, often emphasized this aspect. He described to farm audiences around the country how co-ops had made an impact, pointing out that the three best bargains available to farmers were fertilizer, electricity, and credit—all areas of heavy co-op involvement. This catered to the long-held claim of co-op leaders that it is not only what co-ops do that counts, but also what they make others (private industry) do in order to compete. As many have observed over the years, one of the main contributions co-ops make is in being there—to provide the competition and set the standards of service.

Thus, the BCs' record of success is not surprising. Farmer cooperatives in the United States, particularly since World War II and until the 1980s, had enjoyed phenomenal success providing many agricultural commodities and services in many parts of the country. A few co-ops, in fact, have appeared in *Fortune Magazine*'s listings of the nation's "Top 500" corporations. The thirteen Banks for Cooperatives have played a key role in this growth, handling over 65 percent of the co-ops' credit business for many years. In recent years, as commercial banks started competing for this business, the BCs' percentage share has dropped. However, it is apparently turning upward again at this writing. With all the problems facing agriculture, it is possible that some commercial banks will become less aggressive in soliciting co-op credit business. Unlike the BCs, commercial bankers have the option of deciding whether or not to serve agriculture.

The BCs held about 51 percent of the total debt outstanding by co-ops during the early 1980s and were able to increase the proportion to 55.3 percent in 1984. The BCs reached their highwater mark in loan volume in April 1984 with $10.3 billion. BC loans outstanding were $7.4 billion on December 31, 1986, down 10 percent from the preceding year. However, this drop in loan volume was a reflection of the economic times in agriculture. BC earnings have held up well during this period.

And so it was that on September 4, 1985, when the big story on Farm Credit hit the front page of the *Wall Street Journal,* the Banks for Cooperatives could boast a record of service comparable to their sister banks of the Farm Credit System. They have been able to maintain a high level of financial strength ever since. What's more, the BCs feel worthy of this reputation. True, for a long time they faced little or no competition from the commercial banking sector. Even so, they had done much more than simply lend money to co-ops. They had provided co-ops with a wide variety of loans and services, assisting in the start-up of a number of co-ops and in nurturing them along through appropriate advice and counsel, much in the same manner as the PCAs and FLBAs had done for individual farmers.

Naturally, the financial well-being of the Banks for Cooperatives hinges greatly on the economic health of their member co-ops, which, in turn, are greatly affected by the status of individual farmers. Thus, the recession that gripped United States agriculture in the mid-1980s was felt by the BCs, but not as severely. Perhaps this was because the co-ops, a bit more accustomed to adversity over the years, recognized the situation earlier and cinched their belts a little sooner.

They also benefitted from taking seriously an article that had appeared in the July 23, 1984, issue of *Business Week,* which observed in its title that "The Golden Years Are Gone for Farm Co-ops." A subhead to the article fairly screamed: "Financial Setbacks Lead to Cost-Cutting, Sell-Offs, and Mergers." And, as the article explained further:

> During the 1970s—a golden decade for U.S. Agriculture—farmer-owned cooperatives seemed unstoppable. They were on the verge of capturing dominant shares of both ends of the farm market—the supplies the farmers bought and the crops they sold. Instead, falling revenues and soaring interest expenses have meant big operating losses for even the largest and healthiest co-ops. The downturn has touched off a scramble to slash overhead costs, sell off manufacturing assets, and merge operations.

For BC and other co-op officials, it was like reading their own obituaries. They admitted they had troubles but felt things were not nearly as bad as *Business Week* had painted them—that the reports of their demise were greatly exaggerated. However, the article did spur many co-op officials into action.

One of the major concerns was the threat of the BCs being pulled down by the other parts of the Farm Credit System. As stockholder-borrowers of the banks for cooperatives, the cooperatives moved to protect their investment in the BCs. They were hopeful this investment would not be wiped out by having to help bail out the troubled Federal Land Banks, FLBAs, Federal Intermediate Credit Banks and PCAs. Both BC and farmer cooperative leaders were instrumental in getting language inserted into the 1985 act that protected the "B" stock (that is, the stock investment of co-ops in their BCs) of cooperative borrowers of the BCs, as well as the banks' retained earnings. According to the 1985 act, these were not to be considered among those funds specified as "the System's full available resources" and, therefore, were not to be used by the other banks of the System. Prior to the legislation, the matter was unclear and it made BC stockholders extremely anxious.

Even so, the 1985 act did not insure the BCs' survival. For one thing, what Congress provideth, it can take away. It was not certain whether such a divorce from the rest of the Farm Credit System could ever become final. There were also a number of other problems to solve. For whatever consolation it was, there was the knowledge that just about all those involved in agribusiness had fallen on hard times. For proof, one need only turn to other segments of agribusiness, in financial distress for much the same reasons. There was International Harvester, for example, a company that can trace its roots back to the McCormick reaper. Its stockholders sold out to Tenneco in 1985.

One area of concern was the matter of leadership. Was sufficient leadership available, not only in the BCs, but in their member-cooperatives, as well? Some contend that the greatest problem facing co-ops, as well as the BCs, is the sorrowful lack of good leadership. In the early days, the real successes were leaders of the evangelistic, stem-winder variety. However, it should be noted that these men, although of an idealistic bent in their oratory, usually saw to it that they had hard-nosed, business-oriented staffers around to temper and mold their ideas into more realistic enterprises.

Among the most successful of the "co-op evangelists" was Murray D. Lincoln, the first executive secretary of the Ohio Farm Bureau Federation and founder of CARE (the worldwide relief agency) and of both the Farm Bureau Cooperative Association, Ohio (now called Countrymark) and Nationwide Insurance Companies. W. M. (Bill) Thatcher, organizer of the Farmers Union Central Exchange (now called CENEX), Grain Terminal Association (GTA, now called Harvest States); farm lobbyist Howard A. Cowden, founder of Consumers Cooperative Association (now Farmland Industries) and one of the organizers of the International Cooperative Petroleum Association; and D.W. Brooks, founder of the Cotton Producers Association (now Gold Kist) and co-op advisor to several U.S. presidents also worked hard in the cooperative cause.

The banks for cooperatives also could boast outstanding early leadership. Dr. William I. Myers, governor of FCA (1933–1938); Francis W. Peck, first cooperative bank commissioner (deputy governor) of the FCA and later the secretary of agriculture's representative on the Federal Farm Credit Board (1953–1961); J. D. Lawrence, deputy land bank commissioner under Peck and later (1948–1961) president of the Columbia BC; David M. Hardy, president (1934–1963), St. Louis BC; John E. Eidam, president (1955–1969), Omaha BC; and Ellis A. Stockdyk, first president (1933–1946) of the Berkeley BC should be mentioned as well.

When the evangelists passed from the co-op scene, they were usually replaced by more conservative types—people who were more inclined to consolidate the co-op's position than to launch out into new endeavors. These people were usually found within the organization. In any case, the replacement managers tended to be less imbued with "the co-op spirit," or were at least quieter about their enthusiasm. The theory was sometimes advanced that co-op evangelism and inefficient operations often went together, or that the former was often employed to substitute for the latter. In any case, this feeling sometimes prompted boards to seek new leadership elsewhere—in private industry, for example. Here, too, there were successes and failures. Those private industry recruits who were able to combine the co-op advantages with superior business acumen generally appeared to be the most successful—John St. John, of Citrus Central, Inc., as an example.

The BCs sometimes were heavily involved in recruiting management for their co-op stockholders. They did so usually by invitation and, as much as possible, operated behind the scene. Most co-op boards did not like it to be said that their banker picked their general manager for them. Obviously, those involved in recruiting top management have discovered there really is no pat formula in qualifications for a good co-op manager. Although it normally turned out that those managers who appeared to be the most imaginative and innovative were the most successful, that, too, was not always the case during the mid-1980s. It sometimes appeared, in looking at balance sheets of co-ops for those years, that the conservative, no-change style of some co-op managers came off better, or at least had the best chance for survival. They perhaps were not accomplishing all that much for their farmer-members — except keeping the co-op alive — and, during those days of economic stress, there was much to be said for that. As was true of farmers, many co-ops that had expanded greatly in the 1970s and early 1980s reaped a mixed harvest.

Part of the problem in obtaining and maintaining top management in co-ops must be laid at the doorstep of the farmer-boards. Although salaries in farmer co-ops have improved greatly in recent years, they have in general lagged behind their private industry counterparts. Co-ops over the years have sometimes taken advantage of the fact that many of their employees, imbued with cooperative philosophy and feeling they were contributing to the agricultural society in which they were reared, were willing to work for less.

Generally, Farm Credit was ahead of the rest of the co-op pack when it came to employee treatment, particularly in the area of salaries. Some Farm Credit banks were even criticized for alleged excesses in this regard when the going got tough in the mid-1980s and particularly during the legislative proceedings that produced the 1985 act. However, there were a few boards that favored a tight fist philosophy when it came to their human resources. As an extreme example of this in Farm Credit, one is reminded of the grand opening ceremonies in 1977 of the Farm Credit Banks of Sacramento (which had moved from Berkeley and changed its name). At the ribbon-cutting ceremonies, Snell Olson, a Utah sheepman and longtime director and chairman of the board, told his audience, "Anyone in Farm Credit who makes more than $1,000 a month is overpaid!"

Another hazard for cooperatives (and, perhaps, a deterrent to success) is that they sometimes get embroiled in side issues, often issues of a philosophical nature. There is still a lingering feeling on the part of some that co-ops are social organizations, rather than businesses. It was said once of a California consumer co-op that "It's the only co-op I know that has its own foreign policy." Co-op patrons can get sidetracked in a philosophical hassle — argue for years, for example, over whether each member should be served by its co-op "equally" or "equitably." The latter permits the co-op to give discounts for volume to the larger patrons (on the basis of cost in serving said patron); the former would make everyone pay the same, whether buying ten pounds or ten tons, regardless of the cost to serve. Inability to resolve this issue usually means the small member wins by default, and that the co-op, unable to compete for the business of the larger patron, loses out. Ultimately, both types of patrons lose because, over time, the policy can prove fatal to a co-op.

There was a close parallel to this in the Farm Credit System in regard to its money market operations. There is a long standing argument over whether the System and its member-borrowers might have been better served if the System had used marginal pricing in the sale of its securities rather than basing its interest rates on the average cost of money. Had the System followed the marginal pricing route, many argue, then it would have been able to build up its reserves, still been competitive, and passed along the savings, if any, to its members at the end of each year. As it was, the System was able for a short time to loan money at bargain rates (2 percent or more below competition). This average rate, one man–one price policy (a policy the System had followed for many years) made the System a hero in the short run, but a villain over the long pull as it tried desperately to cover its losses, build reserves, and yet remain competitive at the same time.

Regarding the one man–one vote or one man–one price philosophy, Terry Fredrickson, who in 1985 was still senior deputy governor of the FCA, did not make himself at all popular with some delegates when he pointed out what he felt to be a fallacy in existing co-op philosophy to delegates attending the annual meeting of the National Council of Farmer Cooperatives in San Antonio. "Cooperative leaders," Fredrickson said, "must recognize that cooperatives are of value to the owners only as long as they succeed as businesses—that is, so long as they make a profit." Cooperatives, Fredrickson claimed, are "economic instruments existing and operating to increase the profitability of their owners—nothing more, nothing less. They are not in existence to create or perpetuate any particular industry structure, neither do they have any particular role in promoting social values, movements, or structures, however desirable they may be."

Dr. Gary Schwendiman, Dean of the College of Business Administration, University of Nebraska, put much of this sort of philosophy in chart form, which he has used in seminars with Farm Credit and other cooperative groups throughout the country.

Outdated cooperative philosophies, values, ways of doing business	Up-to-date cooperatives philosophies, values, ways of doing business

Equal	Equitable
One man, one vote	Vote according to volume, economic impact
Many small cooperatives	Mergers forming larger cooperatives
Passive service	Aggressive marketing
Consensus—don't act; there is total agreement—don't offend anyone	Decision by majority and CEO delegated sufficient authority and support to make tough management decisions. Supported by board in doing so.
Decentralized policymaking	Centralized policymaking
Decentralized capital management	Centralized capital management

The chart covers nineteen separate areas. If nothing else, the chart stirred up considerable discussion and a fair amount of controversy at the seminars. For example, Dr. Schwendiman was challenged by Dr. Zita Cameron, who wrote in the September 1986 issue of *The Atlantic Cooperator,* member newsletter for CO-OP Atlantic, Halifax, Nova Scotia, that "Dr. Schwendiman betrays a complete lack of knowledge and understanding of the functions and purposes of a cooperative. He sees it as just another commercial venture that is not doing as well as it might because of an outdated commitment to democratic control, to members' (owners') rights and needs, and a silly old-fashioned notion that service takes priority over profit."

Dr. Cameron scolded Dr. Schwendiman, pointing out that "True democracy is cumbersome and a bother. Dictatorship is much more efficient. It sweeps out of the way all other troublesome little people, with their varying views and demands." In Dr. Cameron's view, co-ops are not founded for profit, but for service: "to give these ornery little people a voice in the disposition of the products of their toil and their incomes." She admonished those who agree with Dr. Schwendiman to "Go ahead and set up your monolithic commercial structure—run it from the top

and forget about the troublesome foundation of member-owners cling-
ing to the afterglow of Rochdale. Call it some equivalent to GM, ITT or
Hudson's Bay. There's nothing illegal about that. But never call it a
cooperative!"

And so such philosophical debates go.

Many co-ops, like some of their farmer-owners, appeared to have
decided that innovation is the real key to survival in agriculture. Perhaps
the innovation being watched most closely in the mid-1980s was the joint
venture between co-ops and private business. Chief among these is one
put together between GROWMARK, Inc., Bloomington, Illinois, and
Archer Daniels Midland (ADM), a Midwest agribusiness conglomerate.
In the arrangement, GROWMARK was permitted to buy into ADM by
exchanging grain terminals (which serve GROWMARK member grain
growers) for ADM stock, and agreeing to supply grain to ADM. ADM/
GROWMARK operates worldwide under a four-member board of directors (two from each organization) and currently is the world's largest
processor of grain and soybeans.

Some of the ADM/GROWMARK joint venture success is credited
to good chemistry, particularly because of the leadership of ADM's
Chairman and CEO Dwayne Andrus, who earned his co-op spurs under
Bill Thatcher at GTA. Although sentimentality may have nothing to do
with it, at least Andrus is aware of what co-ops can do. Bottom line for
GROWMARK is that the move put new life into its grain marketing
operations, and with its profit-sharing plan the organization is optimistic
to the point of talking about expansion. The joint venture also provides
GROWMARK access to ADM's worldwide trading company which, in
addition, works at developing new farm products. There has not, however, at this writing, been any apparent stampede on the part of other co-
ops to jump on the joint venture bandwagon with a noncooperative
organization.

There are, of course, some examples of successful joint ventures
involving only cooperatives. Among them is one involving Cenex, St.
Paul, Minnesota, and Mid-America Dairymen, Inc., Springfield, Missouri. This joint venture is largely an attempt to reduce costs by making
full use of plant capacity to develop a very low-cost system that will
make the maximum savings for members. Another similar joint venture
involves Cenex and Land O'Lakes, about which Land O'Lakes President
Ralph Hofstad reported: "This is a phenomenal joint venture. It only
started January 1 (1987), and it's going to exceed our expectations by

about 10 percent." The anticipated savings to members of both co-ops was set at $10 million, but it appears that savings, just at the operational level, would total $11 million.

Although there appears to be movement among cooperatives in the joint venture area, there is still considerable room for improvement in the cooperation area. Another perennial problem with cooperatives, ironically, is their lack of cooperation with each other. One should realize that the words "cooperative" and "cooperation," although often used interchangeably, are not necessarily the same. A cooperative business is not by definition obliged to cooperate with a sister organization. Very likely, it will not, particularly if it means merger or even the slightest loss of sovereignty. Cooperation among cooperatives in the United States, it would seem, has advanced about as far as peace in the Middle East, and the similarities do not end there. Banks for cooperatives, of course, have been heavily involved in merger of their stockholder co-ops, not often with much success.

Unfortunately, in most mergers, a "bird" and a "worm" are involved—that is, a "merger" and a "mergee." No organization likes to be considered the latter. Farmer directors get involved, often in a negative way, right along with the co-op officials whose jobs are on the line. Often, when you hear of a co-op merger, you can figure that one or both co-ops were at a point where there was no choice but to merge—and little or nothing left to merge.

Of course, there have been notable exceptions in mergers, the most important and bloodless of which was the merger several years ago of Cooperative GLF of Ithaca, New York; Eastern States Cooperative Exchange of West Springfield, Massachusetts; and, later, the Pennsylvania Farm Bureau Cooperative Association of Harrisburg into Agway, Inc. There also have been a number of highly successful and enlightened mergers of dairy co-ops around the country.

If both parties in a merger are more or less on an equal footing, it can help facilitate matters, but this often leaves the merged institution top heavy with leadership positions. This apparently was the case in the 1985 merger of Landmark (formerly Farm Bureau Co-op Association, Columbus, Ohio) and the Ohio Farmers Grain & Supply Association of Fostoria, Ohio. When merged, it became known as Countrymark, Inc., the state's largest agricultural cooperative. The president of one was made CEO of the newly-merged co-op, while the president of the other was installed in the number two spot—chief operating officer. There was a further meshing of directors and staffs of the two organizations in an effort to achieve parity and unity. On paper, it may have appeared to be a natural solution to a sticky situation, but obviously it was not.

The August 16, 1986 *Columbus (OH) Dispatch* reported the resignation of several of these officials (including the president and the chief operating officer) in the face of huge losses in fiscal 1985 and contemplated losses in 1986. As one on-the-scene observer — Dr. Charles Ingraham, formerly a co-op specialist and professor of agricultural economics at Ohio State University — analyzed it: "When you put together . . . organizations and keep the top man from each company, pretty soon you have to get just one boss; this isn't an unusual move in any type of business. It's going to be a big extra cost to the co-op to pay these people off and bring in a new management."

At least the Ohio merger went through. There are many more that did not, or had not at this writing. A most unfortunate failure of co-op cooperation occurred in 1985. At that time there was great excitement in co-op circles, particularly at the Central Bank for Cooperatives, over the possibility of four grain co-ops going together on a contract with a foreign country, which would have brought a higher return to the growers. The deal fell through as the co-ops quibbled over the terms of the contract. Meanwhile, Cargill, definitely not a co-op, ended up buying the grain from these four co-ops and selling it, presumably at a handsome profit.

Cooperation among cooperatives for the common good is an elusive thing, but not because the theory has not been expounded long, hard, and often from the speaker's rostrum in recent years. For example, Ralph Hofstad, Land O'Lakes president and then chairman of the National Council of Farmer Cooperatives, made an impassioned plea in his address to the NCFC's 1982 annual meeting about "a growing need for farmers and ranchers to unite their strengths and voices, so that they act and speak as one on critical issues that affect all agriculture." Hofstad made the offer for this effort to be done under the aegis of the National Council. Noble sentiments, these, but not much came of it. Most organizations are in favor of cooperation, understand, but only so long as they are the one to take the leadership role.

Hofstad, by the way, later had a golden opportunity to affect some cooperation closer to home when there was considerable discussion about Land O'Lakes working an arrangement with Farmland Industries of Kansas City, another of the nation's largest co-ops. Nothing came of this working arrangement nor a later, more comprehensive plan to merge Land O'Lakes, Farmland, and CENEX. However, Hofstad continued to espouse greater cooperation among cooperatives. Reporting on the fifty-ninth annual National Institute of Cooperative Education at the University of Tennessee in August 1986, *Farmer Cooperatives* magazine later noted that Hofstad had suggested "one structural method of bringing cooperatives together under what Land O'Lakes calls its umbrella concept." Hofstad visualized the structure as having "individual governance boards providing policy direction for specific areas of cooperative activity." He felt that such would offer great flexibility for consolidations and joint ventures to take place on either side of the business."

FIG. 10.5. *Ralph Hofstad and friends. An early advocate of greater cooperation among cooperatives was Ralph Hofstad, president of Land O'Lakes cooperative and former chairman of the board of the National Council of Farmer Cooperatives. Often regarded as "the last of the co-op visionaries," Hofstad enjoyed limited success in this effort. He is shown at a briefing for the NCFC board in June of 1981. Several cabinet officials were called in, including Vice President George Bush. Awaiting her turn in the background is Elizabeth Dole, then Secretary of Transportation. Photo courtesy National Council of Farmer Cooperatives.*

The above is not meant to be critical of Ralph Hofstad, very likely one of the last of the "co-op visionaries." At least he has made the effort to bring about mergers and consolidations and continues to do so. It should be noted further that he was not without success in this regard, having been a prime mover in bringing about a merger of the regional FELCO co-op, Ft. Dodge, Iowa, with Land O'Lakes in 1970. This was considered a master stroke at the time.

Although the banks for cooperatives naturally have been involved in affecting co-op mergers, they have suffered mightily from their own "do as I say, not as I do" image. When it came to mergers, the BCs had not set a very good example. These banks have indulged in various discussions about merging themselves (and continue to do so at this writing). In 1986, for example, two committees were working on proposals. One committee was made up of CEOs from six large, regional cooperatives: Ralph Hofstad, Land O'Lakes; Gene James, Southern States; Kenneth Baer, GROWMARK; William Gaston, Gold Kist; Russell Hanlin, Sunkist; and Bill Hiller, Agway. This effort was doomed to failure because one is reluctant to tell one's banker bad news.

The Farm Credit System Planning Committee was also studying a possible merger. John Harling (since resigned), CEO of the Farm Credit Banks of Omaha was chairman of this Committee; while W. Malcolm Harding, president of the Central Bank for Cooperatives, represented the BCs on this committee. Unfortunately, no final decisions were made throughout 1986. They could only agree on generalities, not specifics.

There was another attempt at BC merger in 1987. This time, the BCs followed a tried-and-true formula—paying an outside consultant to tell them what they already knew. This study was done under the overall direction of the BC Restructuring Project Steering Committee, made up of a mixed group of BC chief executive officers and directors, representing all twelve district banks and the Central Bank for Cooperatives. The steering committee commissioned Hopkins and Associates of College Station, Texas, to produce a research study. The findings indicated the need for a merger because of business trends and greater competition.

The consultants recommended a full merger of all twelve BCs and the CBC into a new bank. However, being realistic, the Steering Committee provided some possible alternatives, admitting "It is possible that not all of the BCs will choose to merge into New Bank. Consequently, the business consultants considered it minimum efficient size for consolidation of less than thirteen of the BCs." The study indicated that, as a minimum requirement, at least seven of the existing twelve district banks and the Central Bank should get together to make a merger feasible and that this grouping have at least 75 percent of the total gross volume of the BC system and a combined equity of at least $700 million.

Based on past experience one had to doubt whether this effort to merge would ever be successful. Although the member–co-op stock-holders could exert considerable pressure on their BCs to get on with a merger, the feeling was that it very probably would take some coercion, such as an act of Congress, to bring merger about. That is precisely what happened in the Agricultural Credit Act of 1987, which paved the way for a merged National Bank for Cooperatives (CoBank).

Historically, the banks for cooperatives, unlike the PCAs and FLBAs, have never had to be too concerned about borrower loyalty to their banks. The banks must, however, be concerned about the farmers' loyalty to their co-ops. It is an ever-present challenge to co-ops because they are dealing with a new generation of farmers. Old-timers used to revel in telling about what happened when cooperatives first entered the fertilizer field. Prices dropped. This phenomenon made a large impact on the farmers involved. Succeeding generations were less impressed, however. Somehow, such stories told to children and grandchildren lose much in the translation. The attitude is: "Yes, but what have co-ops done for me, lately?"

This attitude becomes understandable as one observes the farmers' current fight for survival. Unfortunately many of today's young farmers, unfamiliar with the past, generally cannot contemplate what is best for them in long-range terms. They seem to have great difficulty seeing past the next growing season. They seek the best deal they can get—for the moment.

But to indicate that all young farmers are apathetic about the future of their co-ops would be an injustice. Dr. Cameron and other ardent cooperators can take some hope for the future in some of the activities of youth around the country. For example, Brian Severts, graduating senior at Moorhead State University, Moorhead, Minnesota, in a prize-winning essay in a contest sponsored by the CENEX regional coopera-tive, wrote: "Amidst the unavoidable changes that lie ahead, not every-thing will disappear in the past. There are some age-old concepts that need to be maintained, especially now in these less than favorable times for agriculture. These concepts are far from new. In fact, they have been passed down from generation to generation in farming for centuries.

They include self reliance, self discipline, determination, dedication, and, above all, good old common sense."

Other entries in the CENEX contest were equally as positive and resolute, leading one to conclude that today's farm youth are made of pretty good stuff. In any case, the jury on whether the Banks for Cooperatives will succeed is still out. Their fate is entwined not only with the fate of the other banks of the Farm Credit System, but also with the future of farmer cooperatives generally. If cooperatives are allowed to fail, farmers of the future will be obliged one day to build them all over again! Or, as in the words of George Santayana, "Those who cannot remember the past are condemned to repeat it."

11

Politics, As Usual

"The professional politician is one of the mysteries of American life, a bundle of paradoxes, shrewd as a fox, naive as a school boy. He has great respect for the people yet treats them like boobs, and is constitutionally unable to keep his mouth shut."

James Reston, *Book of Political Quotes*

 There really was no way that Farm Credit Administration employees could understand or prepare themselves for what was to come, so sheltered had they been for so many years from the hard realities of partisan politics! By 1986 most FCA employees were so isolated from other government agencies that they had no opportunity to witness what goes on during a change of administrations. Even previous switches in FCA governors had not affected the rank and file of the agency. Only those employees who had been with the FCA while it was still housed in the USDA had any idea of the trauma involved. They had observed the fate of friends in other USDA agencies.

Over time, FCA employees had tended to take their unique working conditions for granted. They not only enjoyed the job protection afforded by Civil Service, but they also were shielded from changeovers of top management. The latter protection was extremely important, as FCA employees were to learn in 1986. Even with the Civil Service shield, a highly partisan administrator can find ways to exert his will.

FCA employees had been blessed in other ways also. As a government agency, the FCA was obliged to follow the Civil Service pay schedule, but the FCA positions tended to be evaluated and equated to those salaries being paid by the Farm Credit banks for similar positions. It was almost a necessity for the FCA to attempt to meet the competition because there was considerable interchange of personnel, something of a revolving door. Without comparable salaries, the FCA would lose its better employees to the System. It was partly this revolving door situation that led to the charges of conflict of interest in Farm Credit. Some claim this was one of the contributors to Farm Credit's downfall.

There were other, more subtle advantages to employment in FCA when compared to work in most other government agencies. Perhaps most important among these was the fact that FCA employees could identify with the System and all it was doing for agriculture and the American public. You were not just another government clerk in the vast Washington bureaucratic jungle. Traditionally, the FCA took better care of its employees, continually searching for special benefits such as extended medical services and staggered working hours to ease the crush of traffic during commuting hours. This enlightened philosophy probably started with the late H. T. (Bill) Mason, who served the agency in the late 1950s and early 1960s as deputy governor for administration. Mason rode herd on employee service departments of the agency. As a consequence FCA employees normally did not have to wait for weeks to be reimbursed for travel and were often granted advances upon request, and would receive them in a timely fashion. When federal employees received a pay raise, FCA employees were always among the first to have it appear in their paychecks. Mostly it was a matter of attitude. It was Mason's view that you were not in the FCA to work to the rule, but to serve. In return FCA employees were given the benefit, within the law, of any doubt. Such benefits may appear trivial, but not if you work for the government, where little is taken for granted. No one likes to be treated like a whipping boy, a number, or a dog!

To FCA employees USDA was not much more than a past benevolent landlord, although there are those who would tell you that being located in the drab, dingy South Agriculture Building was no favor at all. Until passage of the Farm Credit Act of 1971, the FCA, at congressional insistence, and particularly at the insistence of Rep. Jamie L. Whitten of Mississippi, was housed rent free in the USDA. Whitten was not only chairman of the full House Committee on Appropriations but the House Agricultural Appropriations Subcommittee, as well. The independence that stemmed from the 1971 act made it possible for the FCA to move into new rented quarters in the L'Enfant Plaza. The distance was only a couple of blocks, but it was really light years removed from the standpoint of office lifestyle. This move made FCA employees very happy, but Chairman Whitten, a System "godfather," never forgave the FCA and vented his wrath about the plushiness of the new quarters whenever FCA officials had to appear before his subcommittee. Representative Whitten was very supportive of Farm Credit over the years, but it was always on his own terms. Authorization for the FCA to build its own building in suburban Virginia came shortly thereafter with the Farm Credit Act Amendments of 1980, a development that did not further endear the agency to Representative Whitten nor to many other congressmen.

One really must experience a political changeover firsthand to fully comprehend it. It is a phenomenon that only real estate people can enjoy and profit from. A political changeover, like a death in the family, brings out the best and worst in people, but mostly the latter. There are those who argue that a new administration must be free to bring in its own people to move its own programs. Within bounds, there can be little disagreement with this premise. Certainly it is common practice throughout government. Farm Credit spokesmen over the years, however, pleaded an exception on the grounds that partisan politics should not be involved in the extension of credit—that an organization involved in lending such huge sums of money could not afford such drastic upheavals. The FCA was having difficulty enough in recruiting competent personnel from the field, it was argued, without the added handicap of job instability created by partisan politics.

This stance had not been seriously challenged since the first change in administration after the passage of the act of 1953, which had launched the bipartisan approach in the first place. In 1961 Orville Freeman, secretary of agriculture for the incoming Kennedy administration, started to treat FCA like any USDA agency, looking for spots to place his people. He was quickly instructed by officials of two farm organizations to observe a hands-off policy toward the FCA. Months later Secretary Freeman, by then duly educated on the matter, related this story to the Federal Farm Credit Board: "I never realized until then that Farm Credit is such a sacred cow." But in late 1985 neither Congress nor anyone else was in the mood to debate the issue. In the midst of a credit crisis, the feeling was that something drastic needed to be done, and bipartisanship simply got lost in the shuffle. Mistakes had been made; heads had to roll!

Even so, FCA employees were slow to grasp the situation. Their lack of early reaction was similar to that experienced by their Farm Credit System counterparts after the announcement of the new "arm's length" relationship arrangement. Interestingly, many FCA employees still held out hope for a time that ex-Governor Wilkinson might have sufficient GOP or bipartisan credentials to hang on and become the first FCA Board chairman. Wilkinson had been brought to Washington under a Republican Administration to be administrator of the Agricultural Marketing Service in the USDA, to be named later as FCA Governor during a Democratic administration. There was precedence for such a move. Ed Jaenke, a Democrat, had been named FCA governor in the face of an incoming Republican administration. The Federal Farm Credit Board's philosophy in both cases was why not take advantage of the available talent.

FIG. 11.1. *FCA governor Donald E. Wilkinson took the brunt of the criticism over the fall of Farm Credit. It was his interview with Charles F. McCoy of the* Wall Street Journal *that gave credence to the rumors about trouble in the System. Photo by Diana H. Walker.*

Also, in Wilkinson's case, the Federal Board could argue that prior to coming to Washington, he had served both a Democratic and a Republican governor as secretary of agriculture in Wisconsin. Also, he had, as late as the preceding October, survived a coup perpetrated by some members of his own Federal Board, who, responding to the dictates of their home districts, had become irked about the governor's "letting the cat out of the bag" on the extent of financial stress in the System. According to farm columnist Jim Webster, Governor Wilkinson "came within a whisker" of being axed. If the vote had been taken at Jackson, Wyoming, at the National Conference of Farm Credit Directors, one insider said, "he would have been out of there." Webster made this further evaluation: "Ironically, what may have saved Wilkinson's job was a lobbying effort by the System's bank presidents—a few of whom would be delighted, under other circumstances, to see him out, but who felt it would be the wrong signal to send to Wall Street and Congress."

Although a few Federal Board members groused for a time about Wilkinson's decision regarding the "arm's length" stance, the relationship between the governor and his board actually improved during the period prior to his ouster on December 23, 1985. Suddenly the board and the governor were without portfolio. The main reason for this renewed "era of good feeling" was the naming by the governor of a board subcommittee for liaison with the board. Governor Wilkinson stayed in daily contact with the subcommittee until the board's demise. If nothing else, this renewed communication allowed the governor and the board to share the blame and to hold a collective vigil while awaiting their fate.

As for the Reagan administration, the unvarnished truth was that it was also incensed over the September 4 press announcement that indicated the System would need federal help. White House staffers were caught short and felt Governor Wilkinson was trying to back them into a corner. The immediate reaction of the administration was to rap the knuckles of those USDA officials who had even hinted publicly that the government would act in the System's behalf should it need financial help. Such talk on the part of USDA ceased; the department became noncommittal, at "arm's length" with the FCA.

Even so, Donald E. Wilkinson assumed his role as acting chairman of the new FCA Board with aplomb, immediately calling a meeting of his management group (executive committee members and department heads) and urged them, despite all the uncertainties, to continue their good work in order to make the transition as smooth as possible. Wilkinson's exhortations resembled a locker-room pep talk at halftime of a football game. Whatever he was feeling underneath, Wilkinson was always very positive, sometimes to the point of being syrupy. The incentive and the enthusiasm of some of the players was somewhat lacking, however, because the feeling was that the coach was going to be fired in any case, and when that happened a number of key players would be demoted or thrown off the team. This probably accounted for the fact that the loyalty of some of his staff appeared to waver during the waning days of his tenure at the FCA, not an uncommon occurrence in Washington, D.C.

The acting chairman told FCA employees about a Transition Task Force, appointed by the Reagan administration, that would be appearing on the FCA scene momentarily and conferring with him and with others in FCA management. He urged employees to give the task force their fullest cooperation. The first Transition Task Force was composed of two people from Treasury (Robert Zellick, attorney, and Jill Ouseley, Office of Government Finance & Market Analysis) and Kathleen W. Lawrence, deputy under secretary to Frank Naylor in the USDA. It was significant that two representatives were from Treasury, a first indication of the major role the agency would assume in the future of Farm Credit. Even though the USDA member was made chairman of the task force, it soon became obvious that Treasury was in command, calling most of the shots in behalf of the administration.

The task force made its first appearance at FCA on January 17, 1986, and continued its surveillance up until the two Republican members of the FCA Board were named. Even the task force seemed impressed with the manner in which FCA employees performed during the transition period. Working efficiently was probably a wise move on the part of the employees, realizing that one of the top assignments of the task force was to gather intelligence on employees that would be useful in the upcoming upheaval. On the other hand, it was well for the task force to treat FCA employees in a humane manner. As is true during the implementation of any new legislation, there was much to do, and during this period most of the work at the FCA had to be carried out without the assistance of the new boss.

True, one of the leading contenders for the new chairmanship was

Marvin Duncan, a former FCA senior deputy governor who was still on the scene and in the administration's good graces (if only because he was a Republican and had not been with the FCA early enough to catch any of the blame for what had happened). Duncan's presence provided some guidance, but he did not seem to be a person who would act on any issue of consequence without first checking for orders from above, however long it may take such instructions to appear!

As it turned out, Duncan had to settle for the number two spot on the FCA Board, under the circumstances not a very enviable position. In retrospect, one would have to question the wisdom of Duncan's move from a position as a noted agricultural economist with the Federal Reserve Bank of Kansas City to the Farm Credit can of worms. In less than a year Duncan saw his job as senior deputy governor at FCA abolished and found himself in the fight of his life to salvage something from this venture. He could have hoped for a better fate than runner-up. The nature of this position was to be a virtual rubber stamp to the chairman, important only in the sense that he supplied a majority vote.

Up until the naming of the new chairman, FCA employees were comforted by the fact that Governor Wilkinson was not acting like a lame duck. On the other hand, they could read the newspapers and the newsletters. The articles were replete with names (over fifty at one stage) of possible candidates to become members of the FCA Board. Governor Wilkinson's name did not appear among them. It was assumed he was on his way out. The sense of nervousness and anxiety intensified as the name of Frank W. Naylor, Jr., surfaced with increasing regularity. Naylor was well known in Farm Credit. He had held a number of government posts during the Nixon administration, including positions in the USDA with the Federal Crop Insurance Corporation and the Farmers Home Administration. As senior vice president of the Farm Credit Banks of Sacramento during the Carter years, Naylor had kept in close communication with Washington, apparently with the consent and encouragement of the Sacramento Farm Credit Board. With the Reagan election, Naylor was rewarded with a USDA post for his loyalty and service to the Republican party.

Naylor, therefore, was considered a natural to speak to the 1981 annual Conference of Farm Credit Directors at Houston. However, when he ascended to the speaker's rostrum, Naylor proceeded to scare the hell out of the directors by weaving a tale of how the administration planned to privatize the cooperative Farm Credit System. It was explained by Naylor that the proposed privatization of the System called for "radical changes" in its funding, namely by restricting the System's ability to raise funds in the money and capital markets by removing key characteristics of the System's securities. Naylor's warning rang true. There were some in the audience who were aware that such an idea had been proposed by the Office of Management and Budget and later picked up by the Grace Commission (the President's Private Sector Survey on Cost Control). There was knowledge, too, of the plan to impose a user's fee.

After sufficient shock had set in, Naylor jerked his audience back adroitly by urging them "not to worry." He assured them that he had direct access to the all-powerful Cabinet Council on Economic Policy at the White House. Naylor indicated that he would take care of matters in the System's behalf. The not-to-worry, Frank Naylor-will-take-care-of-you approach had, at times, backfired and severely damaged his credibility with the Farm Credit System when he failed to deliver. There was a feeling, too, on the part of many of the delegates at the Houston meeting, that, if he truly had been a friend to the System, he would have warned them sooner.

For weeks prior to Naylor's appointment to FCA chairman, his candidacy was pooh-poohed for different reasons. Naylor, himself, appeared to be headed for more lucrative and prestigious job opportunities. For example, it was assumed by many that Naylor, since he had retained ownership of his Sacramento home when returning to Washington to join the Reagan administration, would be in line to succeed George (Bus) Anderson as president of the Farm Credit Banks of Sacramento. At the time that position carried a salary well over $150,000 a year.

Naylor also was considered a prime candidate by a few for CEO of Farm Credit's new central entity—the Farm Credit Corporation of America—on the basis of his connections with the Reagan administration. Rumors at the time were that this job was to pay from $200,000 to $500,000 a year. Failing there, he might turn to the emerging new Farm Credit System Capital Corporation, which reportedly paid in the neighborhood of $200,000. In addition, the position of secretary of agriculture suddenly became open when John R. Block resigned in early 1986 to become president of the National American Wholesale Grocers Association. A cabinet position paid only $86,200 a year, but what it lacks in salary, it more than makes up in prestige. The post can help launch one higher into politics or into a six-figure salaried position in private industry. Block chose the latter, becoming president of the National American Wholesale Grocers Association.

But the fortunes of a career in the nation's capital can be fickle. What looked like a grab bag of opportunities from which Naylor could choose suddenly disappeared into thin air. The administration picked Dick Lyng, former deputy secretary, as its secretary of agriculture, a move that made it doubtful whether Naylor would even be asked to stay on as under secretary in USDA. Meanwhile, the Farm Credit System opted for H. Brent Beesley for its central entity CEO, and it began to look certain that Naylor would not be considered for the Farm Credit System Capital Corporation spot. In truth, Naylor, despite his experience in Sacramento and with the FmHA and Federal Crop Insurance Corporation, was not considered a credit man. The sentiment among leaders in the System was that if they had to contend with Frank Naylor, they preferred him at the FCA, an agency that had become an adversary, anyway.

Suddenly, the chairmanship of FCA—even at only $73,600 a year— may not only have looked inviting to Frank Naylor but essential to salvaging a government career. It was time for Frank Naylor to call in his political chips, which he did in an all-out campaign with the White House, Congress, and the farm organizations, to garner the FCA post. The last chance for Donald E. Wilkinson to be retained as FCA chairman was a forlorn hope that the agency would maintain its bipartisan format. When it became obvious that Naylor was to be appointed to the FCA chair, Wilkinson announced his resignation in a letter to the White House on March 3, 1986, in which he projected a date of March 28, 1986, for his departure.

In this letter, Governor Wilkinson noted that

> It has been my privilege to serve as the Chief Executive Officer of this regulatory agency for nine years, a period of extraordinary change within the agricultural credit sector. The new authorities granted the agency in the Amendments of 1985 provide the new board and the agency's very competent staff the opportunity to examine and regulate the borrower-owned Farm Credit System in a manner designed to ensure safe and sound financial practices to

stockholders and investors as well at the public interest." Wilkinson
concluded by pledging "my continuing cooperation to achieving a
smooth change of leadership within this agency.

These were perhaps the last noble words to be delivered by an official of FCA for a long, long time. Wilkinson was true to his word. He
left FCA for good on Friday, March 28, 1986.

It was at this point that uneasiness set in at FCA, as "horror stories"
of Frank Naylor started making the rounds. Employees who earlier had
mentioned Naylor as an FCA chairman in jest were now walking around
the office looking like they had just swallowed a live polliwog. Old-
timers recalling the old rumor, for example, that Frank Naylor had been
a "CREEP"—member of the Committee to Re-elect the President—
during the second-term campaign of President Richard Nixon said he
"had never learned a damn thing from the whole experience!" This alleged background information about CREEP was offered in the context
of being the main reason why Naylor, one of the four finalists for FCA
governor, was passed over by the Federal Farm Credit Board when it
selected Donald E. Wilkinson for the post in 1977. In truth the Federal
Board had turned him down as being too political. Naylor never seems
to try to deny this image; at times, he appears to encourage it.

In any case, the Naylor appointment was something that was not
easy for Farm Credit people to fathom in the spring of 1986. The wait
for Naylor's arrival at the agency was so disturbing to some FCA employees that the director of human resources, Charley Row, was
prompted to reassure employees through an item in the employee's house
organ, *Inside FCA:* "The new Farm Credit legislation does nothing to
change the status of current or future employees of FCA. We are and
will continue to be fully competitive Civil Service. The procedures and
requirements of the competitive service will continue to apply for hiring
and other purposes. Enough said!" Not really. The reassurance only
seemed to heighten the anxiety.

The vigil for Naylor's arrival was rather eerie, perhaps akin to a
vanquished country waiting for the occupation troops to arrive. You
heard employees being grateful for the fact that they held a low-grade
position for the first time in their careers. They felt it was probably safe.
The advance arrival of a cadre of short-term appointees, assigned the
task of paving the way for Naylor's arrival, added to the uncertainty.

As columnist Jim Webster described it, "Past and present USDA staff taking at least temporary residence at the Farm Credit Hyatt are Sylvester B. Pranger, retired assistant director of the Office of Personnel Management and former USDA personnel chief; Phyllis Mowery, personnel officer well known to USDA politicos of both parties; Mike Bronson of Federal Crop Insurance Corporation and rumored successor to Bacon [Larry Bacon, mentioned below]. The role of Pranger, who once was deputy FmHA administrator for administration, and Mowery make clear Naylor's intention to continue the shakeup: they're skilled implementors of personnel rules to make the changes an executive wants." Webster had once served as assistant secretary of agriculture and, therefore, was not unfamiliar with such situations.

For FCA employees, the activities of Pranger and Mowery were new and interesting, to say the least. Despite their benign smiles, it soon became apparent that they were at the FCA to do a hatchet job; they were under instructions to move or remove as many employees as they could within the letter, if not the spirit, of Civil Service law. Nothing personal. Thus the sordid side of a political takeover unfolded before the eyes of FCA employees. The dismantling of the old governor's staff was carried out by Larry H. Bacon, head of the Office of Administration. He was asked to find spots elsewhere in the organization (at lower levels, of course) for two of the governor's assistants. Only one veteran secretary, who was highly competent and the only one left who knew where things were in the files, was asked to remain.

Another survivor was the resilient Kenneth J. Auberger, who served as acting chairman in the interim between Wilkinson's departure and Naylor's arrival. Auberger had served the agency as chief examiner from 1966 until mid-1982 and was deputy governor and chief of staff to Governor Wilkinson, during which time he was also secretary to the Federal Farm Credit Board. On the face of it, one would assume that Auberger would be a prime candidate for an early ouster. Strangely, Auburger continued for a time to serve as secretary of the new FCA Board and handled other duties, "as assigned," by the new FCA chairman. Obviously, Auberger found a way to make himself useful to the new administration.

Ironically, for his efforts in arranging transfers, Bacon later was rewarded by being given the ax. He had earlier made the mistake of permitting himself to be put on noncareer status in order to ascend to deputy governor status more quickly than he otherwise would have been able to qualify for it. It was one of those decisions that seemed the right thing to do at the time. The FCA was not political when Bacon accepted the promotion. Now it meant that he was bereft of Civil Service protection and could be fired with no reason required and with no recourse. Suddenly Larry H. Bacon, a thirteen-year professional with the organization, was given sixty days to get out. As the sixtieth day approached, it appeared that Bacon was not exerting sufficient effort to remove himself from the premises. He received this further reminder from the new FCA chairman on July 28, 1986:

> This is to notify you that your service as Deputy Governor, Office of Administration, ES-5, will be terminated effective at close of business, July 28, 1986.
> This action is not due to lack of confidence in your ability to carry out the programs and policies of the current leadership of this agency, and should not be construed in any way as a reflection on you personally.

Nothing personal! Undoubtedly, this is a hard thing for one outside government to comprehend. But it happens often. Very likely, if Bacon had asked for assistance from the FCA in gaining a position elsewhere, he would have been accorded it, just so long as it was elsewhere. At least, nothing would have been done to scuttle his chances. In the nation's capitol, such a courtesy is not scoffed at.

As a matter of fact, Bacon received tender treatment compared to that extended to the director of Congressional and Public Affairs (C&PA), Kim C. Bowersox. Bowersox had come to Washington, D.C., as a law student and as an aide to Rep. Leon Panetta, Democrat of California. He accepted his FCA position as a noncareerist partly for the same reason as Bacon—because his experience did not qualify him for the grade at which he was hired. The separation of Bowersox was among the first acts the new chairman performed upon his arrival at FCA. He gave Bowersox forty-eight hours to get out and promptly dispatched Francis Boyd, a lobbyist he had worked with at USDA, to take his place. Congressional affairs is such a sensitive and essential function (even more so in the new highly political setting) that the surprise over Bowersox's ouster was only because of the speed and flourish with which it was handled. Such personnel actions did not create a ripple on Capitol Hill where everyone lives and dies by the same rules of the political jungle. Events like this are taken for granted.

Three other employees in the congressional and public affairs division were found lacking, mostly lacking the three years' service necessary to gain Civil Service career status. Among these was Roger Stromberg, who epitomized the young but experienced talent that was recruited by the FCA from the Farm Credit System. Stromberg had been in communications work with both the FICBs of Wichita and Sacramento. Despite his good works and ten-point veteran's preference, Stromberg was axed.

The three C&PA staffers were given their thirty days' notice. Not surprisingly, a spot was created elsewhere in the FCA for a fourth member of the C&PA staff, even though she had the least amount of experience and government tenure. The fact that she had solid Republican credentials, having worked for a time in the office of Senator Nancy Kassebaum of her home state of Kansas and had other connections in the party, may have had something to do with her favored treatment. Political antics such as this do not go unnoticed by the opposition party, which will likely seek retribution once it regains the White House. On the other hand, this knowledge is of little consolation to those who remember the FCA as it once was.

Normally another most vulnerable spot in an agency during a changeover of this sort is that of general counsel. Here Fred R. Medero had reigned supreme for six years, much to the disdain and chagrin of many other Farm Credit employees—FCA and System alike—who, anticipating his early removal, were prompted to rationalize: "Well, some good does come out of such things as political takeovers!" But they underestimated Medero's resilience. He was able to number among the survivors for a time. His experience in the Comptroller of the Currency Office had to have helped because, with all the System's problems, past service with other bank regulators had suddenly become tantamount to the new FCA chairman's seal of approval—almost, but not quite, equal to political connections.

Medero was adroit at recognizing the seat of power in an organization and positioning himself in close proximity. He also was adept at employing the old lawyer intimidation tactic of "let me protect you from harm's way," a very effective ploy, particularly in government where blind-siders and second-guessers are prevalent. In government a person wants to have all the protection he can muster. Much to the chagrin of other FCA employees, Medero also seemed to take delight in ridiculing the past performance of the agency. Some of this criticism was justified, but not in such large and frequent dosages. For a time at least, Medero seemed to amuse the new FCA chairman, who was known to indulge in the practice himself. But perhaps most importantly, the general counsel displayed a Reagan/Bush bumper sticker on his car. Outward identification with any political candidate was something FCA employees had never before indulged in. It had never been necessary to obtain or maintain employment, and no one had been anxious to make it so. In any case, the relationship between the FCA chairman and his general counsel must have cooled in time because the chairman installed his own general counsel and Medero joined the office of junior Senator David Karnes of Nebraska as an agricultural credit specialist.

The new FCA chairman's modus operandi had become quite clear. Unless an FCA staffer (particularly one at division director level or higher) could make it politically with the new chairman, he or she would be replaced or neutralized. It was the usual scenario that follows a change of administration. Those in high positions who were eligible to retire did so; those who could find employment elsewhere abandoned ship. The unlucky ones were those who had no place else to go and yet had considerable time invested in government service. They could not afford to get out. They would grin and bear it and hope for the best. Often, this is difficult because a person may be placed in an intolerable assignment or get shipped to the field. There are many ways to encourage one's early departure from government service.

In government situations when an administrator is unable to remove some key people in order to bring in new people, another solution is to layer over them. That is, you bring somebody in and have the retainee report to him. This happened in the FCA. It became readily obvious that FCA's management staff would be made up of these new political appointees. In addition, each member of the FCA Board would be permitted an executive assistant, as well as a "confidential secretary." From this group, "the inner circle" would be formed. As for the rest, they would be the troops, to respond only when called upon. This, too, was a radical departure from the old FCA—known for its openness and broad involvement of employees, an approach that was assumed to be helpful for morale.

Long-time observers of Naylor's management style were not surprised to learn of his narrow policy on distribution of public and internal information. This, too, is not unusual among government officials, particularly those who feel they have been burned by the press. Naylor's distrust of information programs not under his direct control was well known. While USDA under secretary, for example, he had put a lid on Farmers Home Administration public information activities. A Washington-based staffer of the *St. Louis Post Dispatch* noted that FmHA public information officers refused to talk to callers, because they were told to do so. They were told to "refer all calls to Frank W. Naylor, Jr., Under Secretary of the Agriculture Department."

The article went on to explain that "Others in the agency shed some light on the deafening silence. Naylor apparently suspected people in the PI [Public Information] office of being the unidentified sources in a newspaper story that depicted the agency in less than glowing terms. So Naylor, a hard-core supporter of President Ronald Reagan with a reputation as a tough administrator, angrily decreed that the PI office employees were forbidden to do any talking—even as sanctioned spokesman for the agency."

The *Post Dispatch* pointed out further that the FmHA PI office "has fallen on times nearly as hard as the farmers." The staff, the article observed, "has been pared down to four in recent years—about a third of its former size." As Naylor's secretary explained to the *Post Dispatch,* " 'Mr. Naylor likes to talk about some of these matters himself.' " However, the *Post Dispatch* writer did not buy that explanation, noting "Apparently, though, he's reluctant to talk about them too much—he left town shortly after silencing the public information office."

Naylor's secretary was quite correct. He not only liked to do the talking himself but, whenever possible, to pick the reporters he talked to. He made himself accessible to the press, at his convenience, particularly to those who had been proven to be reasonably friendly. Again, such a practice is not uncommon in government. Ed Curran, long-time USDA office on information staffer, noted in February of 1988 that moves by the Reagan administration had "brought information at USDA to a grinding halt (and has) all but killed off the information civil servant in the department." Curran explained, "It's done it by picking its targets . . . whittling away a limb (or even a twig) at a time." The administration, according to Curran, has all but eliminated the so-called "Sunshine" freedom of information law under which the government operates by "cutting back on the number of press releases it issues and by eliminating free distribution of press releases to many via its so-called user fee system." Again, Curran admitted that what the Reagan administration had done to government information programs was not new, but that it "has more or less refined the art."

One of Frank Naylor's favorite publications was the *American Banker,* which devoted a half-page feature on him in its August 12, 1985, issue. Headlined, "Farm Lending's Chairman Eyes Credit Crisis," the article quoted an American Bankers Association official as saying: "Frank is very accessible to bankers. He has a lot of willingness to listen. If we ask him to attend a meeting, he's there."

Many Farm Credit people could not have agreed more with such an assessment, often complaining privately that Frank Naylor is a lot more friendly and helpful to commercial lenders than to the Farm Credit System. The feeling among these observers was that with other routes of enhanced career opportunities closed to him, Naylor's next move would be into the commercial banking industry.

Later, in the October 6, 1986 issue, Naylor used the *American Banker* to get in some licks against the System's efforts to get more legislation, describing the situation as one in which Naylor "is working to blunt a legislative assault on his power to discipline ailing System lenders." Another of Naylor's apparent pet publications was ABA's monthly *Banking Journal,* which in its November 1986 issue ran an article based on an interview with Naylor, entitled "Tough Talk from Farm Credit Regulator." Failing to head off 1986 Farm Credit legislation, Naylor used the *Journal* article to stir up the commercial bankers to rally behind him against the Farm Credit System by indicating that FCA's inability to set System interest rates would "cost another $1.2 billion a year in operating losses (for the System) and that "a very large, unregulated, nonbank would be created" as a result.

Upon arrival at the FCA, Naylor carried censorship matters a few steps further. Traditionally, the FCA had been very open and above-board with its employees—some in management argued that it was too open. Among the early acts of the new FCA chairman was to abolish the agency's award-winning weekly internal electronic house organ—*Inside FCA*—which kept FCA employees informed about Farm Credit activities and the agricultural community environment in which Farm Credit functioned. *FCA This Week* was also effectively discontinued for a time through the dismissal of its editor, Roger Stromberg. This publication was a well-read, morale-boosting, weekly newsletter that concentrated on personnel and personal items about, or affecting, FCA employees and their families. Suddenly such items became unimportant to the agency's operations.

In their place, the FCA launched a new publication, designed primarily for Farm Credit System distribution but distributed externally as well, called *FCA Bulletin.* It was a very bureaucratic looking and sounding monthly of pre–World War II style. It carried little but identification of official actions of the agency, such as new or changed regulations and a summary of court cases involving Farm Credit. At the outset, it was edited by a congressional and public affairs staffer whose name did not appear on the masthead, such space being reserved for higher officials of the agency. The real editor was obliged to use only that material that had been sanitized, either by the office of general counsel or others of sufficient authority.

Later another publication "to serve as a communication link with FLBAs and PCAs" was added. It was called *FCA Report to Farm Credit System Associations* and was about as exciting as its title. It rivaled the *FCA Bulletin* in drabness and dryness. On the other hand, the publications did accomplish their intended purpose – they made the agency look like an old-line government financial regulator.

Another agency publication that felt the Naylor ax was the *FCA Alumni Quarterly,* aimed at keeping FCA retirees (many of whom were regular buyers of FC securities and who attended the annual agency picnic and Christmas party) informed. Naylor's action was another indication of his desire to sever all ties with the past.

Early FCA employee reaction to the no-news policy was bitter and widespread, but was confined to griping in the halls of the agency; later the situation was accepted as part of the changes taking place. By this time a certain amount of fear, intimidation, and distrust had permeated the agency. It was considered wise to remain silent or at least know to whom you were voicing your sentiments. At best, the new atmosphere made one appreciate what had been, as there was but a faint hope that those days would ever return again. Censorship was not something over which a good family person at FCA would risk losing his job.

One assistant chief, however, did become so incensed with the deterioration of communications within the agency that he drafted the following memo of protest to his chief: "Internal communications in FCA have deteriorated to lousy. From an environment of perhaps over-informing, we have seen the pendulum swing to the point that most staff rely on the grapevine to know what the agency is doing. Need-to-know management runs the grave risk of having inferior staff work, due to oversights in failing to inform people. The alternative is a careful program of review of nearly everything by each office director before it goes out."

Before sending the memo, the writer shared a copy of the draft with the author. However valid his case, the memo drafter was counseled that, unless he contemplated employment elsewhere, he should not send it—that he would accomplish nothing other than being identified as a dissident. No one else cared, or at least not enough to risk their jobs. Wisely he concurred and did not send the memo.

Frank Naylor's first appearance as chairman before FCA employees was in the atrium of the FCA office building on the day after he was sworn in—May 28, 1986. The address was a vintage Naylor production. He can be unusually disarming and was on that day, saying the right things in the right way. He vowed that accepting the challenge of the FCA chairmanship was like "rejoining the Farm Credit family," a reference to his days in Sacramento. In an informal yet dramatic manner, he quickly set forth the agency's mission: "to do whatever is necessary, within the bounds of the Farm Credit Amendments Act of 1985, to reestablish the Farm Credit System to its rightful role as the pre-eminent lender serving U.S. Agriculture."

Considering "the depth of the problems facing U.S. Agriculture and the Farm Credit System," he observed it would not be easy, "It can't be done overnight." He expressed confidence that the mission was not impossible and invited FCA employees "to join in what for most will be the most important challenge of your career."

Externally, however, his tone was considerably different, not unusual for politicians, even after the age of television. Many Washington politicians, Naylor among them, appear to believe federal employees in the nation's capital live in a vacuum. Either they do not know or do not care what federal employees think. Externally Naylor talked of the need to convert FCA into a "lean and hungry" organization. This would require considerable restructuring of the agency, he indicated, in order for it "to resemble the Comptroller of the Currency." Naylor underscored the need for the FCA as an institution "to stay out of System operations that do not come under its regulatory authority." This would require establishing quickly the competence of FCA's examination force, he said.

While these austerity statements were being made, Naylor, a physical fitness addict, was having an exercise room installed in FCA's McLean, Virginia, headquarters. The Washington press picked up on this. Under the heading of "Lean and Hungry," Marjorie Williams wrote in the August 5, 1986, *Washington Post:* "[Naylor] wasn't kidding when he promised to get the fat out of his agency and to run a lean operation. . . . Well, they've just opened a new exercise room at the FCA's capacious digs in McLean and Paul C. Redmer, chief of records and projects division, has five pages of policy and procedure for using the mini-spa (which includes an explanation of its purpose): 'To enhance the continued physical and mental well-being of the employees of FCA.' "

Actually, in fairness to Naylor, the FCA exercise room was extremely modest by private industry — or even other government agency — standards. It was just that his timing was bad.

To enhance his own well-being and life-style, however, Naylor added some other perks, such as upgrading the agency's limo to a Mercury Grand Marquis in early 1987, and added a seven-passenger Ford Aerostar XL wagon to the stable. At last count the agency had three limos — two Mercury Grand Marquis and the Ford Aerostar XL wagon. Also, the agency instituted something new for FCA, albeit not for most other government agencies, reserved parking spaces for members of the inner circle, a further reminder that power has its privileges.

In addition to the installation of a politically acceptable staff, there were other indications that the agency would be run in tandem with the White House. This was made clear in no uncertain terms by Naylor at his first staff planning conference on July 27–29, 1986, in Elkridge, Maryland. At the conference, assembled division directors were told flatly: "FCA is now a political animal, run from the White House. I am the White House lead representative on the job. We (Office of the Chairman) shall handle the politics; you will handle examination and regulation." Between being told this and having to sit quietly while General Counsel Medero berated them in front of the new chairman for their past sins and errors, most of the FCA employees returned home from the conference in an advanced stage of shock.

For any FCA employees who still harbored doubts, the agency's new attitude was further confirmed in a personal profile of Naylor penned by Ward Sinclair in the December 8, 1986, *Washington Post* entitled "Frank W. Naylor, Jr., Sandpapery 'President's Man' On the Farm Credit Front," in which Naylor was quoted as saying: "I've always been identified as a partisan person, very hard on policy. I'm the President's man. My philosophy is that I will argue like hell for what I believe is the right course, but if the boss says I'm wrong, you'll never know that what I support publicly is not my own view."

One had to admire Naylor for his frankness, but later it became apparent that he sometimes got so wrapped up in what he was doing that he did not always bother to catch or discern the changing winds within the administration. Sinclair noted this in his column via a quote from an unnamed Capitol Hill observer: " 'He [Naylor] was really cut out of the game in 1985 because we couldn't get cooperation from him. . . . We did our dealing on the legislation with Treasury. His stock is way down in the administration partly because of this.' "

One would think that the rationale of having a "loyal opposition" member on the new FCA Board would be to maintain some semblance of bipartisanship in the agency. Apparently, that is not to be, at least with the first board. The Democratic appointee, James Billington, did not get appointed until September 1986, long after key new policies were in place and the spoils system at FCA had nearly run its course. As an added insult, Billington was provided an office around the corner from the offices of the other two board members and other members of the inner circle. With this arrangement Billington did not inhibit the day-to-day chatter, scuttlebutt, and internal strategizing that goes on in the chairman's office.

However, Billington had a few weapons of his own. First, there was a Farm Credit background, as well as commercial bank experience in his native Oklahoma. Billington, a farmer-rancher, had been president of the Woodward (Oklahoma) PCA and was president and CEO of the First National Bank of Beaver, Oklahoma, for three years. A former president of the Oklahoma Wheat Growers Association, Billington was president of the National Association of Wheat Growers in 1981. Unfortunately Billington also had some scars from the PCA/FLBA wars in the Wichita Farm Credit District, as well as from skirmishes with the FICB of Wichita. This did not necessarily bode well regarding his future relationships with the Farm Credit System because he did not let bygones be bygones when he took office.

Jim Billington also had many friends in Congress, the most important of whom was Sen. David L. Boren of Oklahoma, who was to become chairman of the Senate Agricultural Credit Subcommittee. Billington, in fact, hired Barbara Webb, Senator Boren's press secretary, as his administrative assistant. Although a minority member of the board, Billington was in a position to at least make some mischief for the majority. His presence on the FCA Board, along with Frank Naylor's reaction to him, did not make the board bipartisan but, rather, adversarial. The "arm's length" relationship was not merely between the FCA and the Farm Credit System but within FCA as well.

Traditionally, or at least since the Farm Credit Act of 1953, FCA had scrupulously maintained its independence from administrations — Republican and Democratic. As evidence of this, one did not see the usual color photo of the president of the United States smiling down upon you as you walked through the halls of the agency. Nor did you find such photos in the offices of agency officials. There would be only one such portrait of the president and that was nestled in the Federal Farm Credit Board Room or in the main conference room, along side photos of previous presidents who had served since passage of the 1953 act. FCA made no use of the presidential photo allotment that usually comes to an agency uninvited every four years. The agency's bipartisan policy also took the onus off FCA employees who, unlike their counterparts in some other federal agencies, did not have go through the hypocritical process of taking down the photo of the outgoing president in their offices, replacing it with the new one.

Obviously, a dearth of presidential photos will no longer be the case in the FCA. Upon his arrival in the agency, Bill Hendrix, deputy director of the Office of Congressional Affairs, sent a letter to the White House noting that "It has been brought to the attention of Frank W. Naylor, Jr., Chairman of the Board of the Farm Credit Administration, an independent Federal agency, that there are no suitable pictures of the President in our new building. Because we are a division of the executive branch of government, we would like to prominently display pictures of our President."

Hendrix wanted to know if "it be possible to obtain two pictures of President Reagan, in large format (14 × 22 or larger) to display? If so, please send the photos, which we will frame, to Chairman Naylor of the Farm Credit Administration, 1501 Farm Credit Drive, McLean, VA 22102–5000."

Hendrix wanted it to be made clear that, "We are proud to be a part of the Reagan team and would like to let those who visit our agency know for whom we are working."

Soon, 15 × 19 color photos of President Reagan graced the walls of FCA/McLean, a constant reminder that things would never be the same again. Obviously, from this point forward, it would be politics as usual in FCA! The die had been recast!

12

Back to the Future

With the passage of the Farm Credit Act Amendments of 1985, it was inevitable that the Farm Credit Administration and the Farm Credit System were headed for a showdown. Not only were the notables "at arm's length," but the situation became almost totally adversarial with the implementation of each step of the 1985 act. The main bone of contention was interest rates, specifically who set them for the System. FCA maintained it did not have that right and did not want it. Yet it did have the authority to approve the rates set by the System, which it was doing with great vigor. The System maintained that such a distinction was meaningless, that the authority to *approve* interest rates was in effect the authority to *set* interest rates. The System felt for its own survival that it damn well should be able to set its own rates or it surely would go down by default.

The principals in the skirmish—at the outset, at least—were H. Brent Beesley, CEO of the Farm Credit Corporation of America (for the System), and FCA Board Chairman Frank W. Naylor. As the issues started splashing over into Congress, there were many observers who considered the confrontation a mismatch and winced in Beesley's behalf. They were mistaken. As a matter of fact, it turned out to be quite a bout, with the first round going to Beesley, a young, aggressive, risk-taking Ivy Leaguer (Harvard Business School and Harvard Law School) from Utah.

Unable to get much satisfaction from the FCA on the interest rate issue, Beesley decided to go on the offensive, carrying his message on the plight of the System far and wide. He emphasized the "catch-22" the System found itself in—on the one hand having to keep interest rates high to satisfy the FCA's demands for maintaining capital adequacy, while losing good credit customers on the other by being unable to compete with commercial bankers. Former FCA Governor Ed Jaenke, serving at the time as a consultant to the Farm Credit Council, characterized compliance with the FCA directives as "trying to make the FC System blow and suck at the same time."

In his pronouncements, Beesley argued for "much needed interest rate relief [so that] System loan officers will be able to match local competition in many areas." In addition he pointed out that "under the law, FCA, the System's regulator, must approve interest rate changes and reductions. No other lender is required to seek interest-rate approval from its regulator." If, indeed, the System is to go down, Beesley seemed to be saying, then it should not be without a fight.

It should be noted at this juncture, however, that, despite the logic

FIG. 12.1. *Most of 1986 featured a running battle between Frank W. Naylor, Jr. (left), chairman of the FCA Board, and H. Brent Beesley (right), chief executive officer of the Farm Credit Corporation of America, shown testifying before a congressional committee. The result was passage by Congress of the Farm Credit Act Amendments of 1986, indicating at least partial victory for the Farm Credit System. Photos by William E. Carnahan.*

of Beesley's stance, all the hypocrisy was not on Naylor's side. Both men were guilty of grandstanding and glossing over some pertinent facts. For example, while Beesley was making his pronouncements and accusations, some of his Farm Credit System units were very swiftly depleting their reserves. Besides, the System, as was its custom, was not presenting a consistent nationwide picture. In some cases interest rates were sometimes too high to meet local competition; in others rates were too low to meet reserve requirements. As a result, some good borrowers left the System because they could get lower rates elsewhere and would not have to carry the "bad" borrower who was a major cause for the high rates. The Farm Credit System, on the other hand, needed to preserve its share of the market and was fearful that the FCA, a government bureaucracy, would not be able to move swiftly enough in local situations to approve interest rate adjustments in a timely fashion. Both sides appeared to be taking advantage of the fact that no one wants high interest rates, whether they can be justified or not.

Meanwhile Naylor pursued his course with great relish, attempting to turn Beesley's arguments to his own advantage, even though the wisdom of his strategy appeared to most to be shortsighted. Depending upon his audience, Naylor would alternately insist that FCA must maintain the power to prevent Farm Credit System banks from setting interest rates so low that they would undermine the System's maintenance of capital adequacy or demand that the System lower its rates to be more competitive and provide farmers credit at the lowest possible rate. Naylor tagged the erosion of capital adequacy as "an unsafe and unsound practice" but at the same time encouraged cutting interest rates in an effort "to improve the System's image."

The dichotomy of Naylor's argument was demonstrated in a July 1, 1986, press release put out by the FCA. The release was headlined: "Regulator Calls On Farm Credit System To Lower Interest Rates And Improve Image With Borrowers." Many System borrowers (farmers) must have thought that it was about time the government stepped in! If a newspaper using the release had printed it in its entirety, however, it would have noted some of the fine print in the way of FCA guidelines, which pointed out that "each FC System bank or district can offer a wide choice of lower loan rates with more attractive terms to qualified borrowers, as long as their weighted average rate to all borrowers does not drop more than one-half of one percent from their current loan rate."

Perhaps the guideline sounded reasonable enough, but in reality it did not provide the System much leeway.

What farmers would understand and concur with was this portion of the press release: "Frank W. Naylor, Jr., FCA Chairman, cited the need for System leaders to improve borrower relations by adequately informing borrowers of their policies on loan restructuring and on eligibility requirements for different rates." No one could be against this protection written into the 1985 act, except a person who had to carry it out. It could, for example, provide false hopes to already "busted" farmers who might think they could be bailed out, causing them to line up at the FCA association office door. One of the compounding problems of periods of economic stress is that a loan officer's workload multiplies many fold. A loan officer's time could be better spent restructuring loans for farmers who had a chance of making it. Many loan officers during this period were put under as much stress as some of the financially troubled farmers they were attempting to serve.

To make sure that the message got out to the System, this FCA release was sent to all Farm Credit banks and local associations. This was something that in the olden days the FCA would not have done without the Farm Credit banks' permission. This concession was perhaps uncalled for by a government regulator, symptomatic of some of the problems involved in being a System advocate. In retrospect the FCA should have maintained its open access to the associations. In any case, this release must have caused a considerable amount of gnashing of teeth at all levels of the System, particularly the portion having to do with keeping members informed. One retired former FICB official happened to be visiting at the PCA from whence he'd gotten his career start many years ago. When shown a copy of the release, he snorted and scoffed, "You know, we used to give away cash and refrigerators and put on ox roasts just to entice our farmer-members to come out to their annual meeting—to vote for their directors and to find out what was going on in their association in general. Not many came, and most of those seldom read anything we sent out during the year. They just weren't interested." The old-timer's voice tailed off—"until now."

Even so the retiree expressed grudging admiration for Naylor. "An amazing guy. He can say one thing one day and do a 180 degree turn on it the next, without even batting an eye. Kinda runs the FCA like a political campaign." The old-timer expressed relief that he was retired and was not going to have to deal with the myriad of problems facing the System. This feeling was expressed by many others in a similar enviable position.

Although careful not to name names, Naylor seemed to enjoy regaling his audiences with stories about how the FCA was run prior to his arrival at the helm. He described the agency as "sort of a cheerleader and lobbyist for the System." This rhetoric probably irked older System borrowers and employees because they felt that was what the agency ought to be doing now in view of current events. But there was more than an element of truth in the statement, and the System had provided over time the FCA chairman with plenty of material to draw upon.

In an interview printed in the November 20, 1986, issue of *Drovers Journal,* Naylor described "a lack of good common sense" in Farm Credit and its past way of doing business as "highly decentralized with few real checks. Local officials had a lot of discretion. Things were lightly directed—the store wasn't being watched." Among sins of the past that Farm Credit had committed, Naylor cited, "Poor management; poor credit operations and control; deteriorating relations with farmer-borrowers; lack of attention to borrower rights in such areas as loan restructuring; lack of full disclosure about interest rates, financial conditions, insider loans to officers, directors, relatives; and high costs and overhead." It was hard for the System to argue with that.

Because the conditions Naylor described could be found in some places in Farm Credit, it looked for a time as though he was getting the better of things with the System, making believers in Congress and with the public. However, Naylor's pronouncements and revelations about the System became irrelevant. Although what Naylor said continued to have some validity, there was nothing positive in his criticism; it did little or nothing to correct the situation, which Congress, among others, was earnestly striving to do. Seizing upon this opening, the System decided it was time again to seek new legislation.

In its renewed legislative effort, the System was delighted to discover a new champion willing to espouse its views—Sen. Thad Cochran of Mississippi, a Republican Senate leader and, at the time, chairman of the Senate Agricultural Credit Subcommittee. Much credit for the Mississippi senator's insight into the farm credit situation is given to Wayne Boutwell, his former top aide, who now heads the National Council of Farmer Cooperatives. Senator Cochran was willing to combine forces

with his counterpart subcommittee chairman in the House, Rep. Ed
Jones of Tennessee. One simply could not ask for a more potent bipartisan agricultural combination.

Upon introducing his bill in the Senate on August 15, 1986, Senator
Cochran commented:

> The need for this legislation is underscored by the fact that today's
> interest rates charged by the FC System are often as much as three
> percent higher than other agricultural lending institutions. . . . This
> wide differential in interest rates encourages the System's most
> financially secure borrowers to seek credit elsewhere. Flight from
> the System is already happening and, to the extent it continues or
> accelerates, will reduce both the size and quality of the System's loan
> portfolio. This trend must be reversed. Enactment of this legisla-
> tion, allowing the FC System's farmer-elected boards of directors to
> expeditiously establish competitive interest rates, is the best way to
> reverse this trend.

Since the Reagan administration was by no means entertaining
thoughts of another farm credit bill at that time — or any legislation that
would impact negatively on the budget — there was some surprise that
Senator Cochran made his push. It should be remembered, however,
that Senator Cochran is not alone among congressmen from farm states
who are prepared to abandon the administration loyalists when it comes
to significant issues affecting rural America.

Chairman Ed Jones said much the same in introducing his compan-
ion bill less than a month later (September 10, 1986). However, he was a
bit more pointed in his analysis of the situation:

> Many System institutions have been seeking to lower their interest
> rates, but the System's regulator has consistently rejected, delayed
> or limited any rate reductions. This needs to stop. My bill would
> simply allow the FC System to determine its own interest rates
> without prior approval of Government regulators. Commercial
> banks are not required to seek prior approvals for their interest rates
> from the Federal Reserve, the FDIC or the Comptroller of the Cur-
> rency.

One had to admire Chairman Jones, too, for his editorial creativity in
titling a bill. His H.R. 5494 was duly christened the "Farm Credit System
Borrower Interest Rate *Relief* Bill."

Although Naylor obviously was caught off-stride by Senator Cochran's apparent desertion from the administration's position on Farm Credit, he felt he still had much running in his favor. For starters, there was the ill-timed announcement by the System of its projected losses for 1986: $1.7 billion, with expected continued losses of $1.1 billion projected for 1987, followed by an additional $600 million in 1988. Losses were also projected as a result of drops in System loan volume—from $66 billion on December 31, 1985, down to $49 billion by the end of 1988. The announcement also put everyone on notice that government capital might be needed soon.

Although concurring on most of the projected loss figures, Naylor hedged on the need for government capital "in the foreseeable future." At this point in the Beesley/Naylor battle, one was inclined to give a slight edge to Naylor—that is, until he got blindsided by another GAO report, "Farm Credit System, Analysis of Financial Condition," which was released at the congressional hearings in September 1986. The report from the congressional investigative agency estimated the System's projected losses for 1986 at $2.9 billion, nearly double that indicated by the System. If true, this would be the largest loss ever by a financial institution in the United States. In his testimony, William Anderson, a GAO assistant comptroller, noted that these huge losses would wipe out the System's capital by early 1987 and would require an injection of government capital to save it.

The GAO revelations, however, appeared at the time to be a clear case of overkill, ironically turning the momentum over to the System's side by enhancing the need for legislation. The statistics added a greater sense of urgency to the situation and, hence, a recognition of the need for legislation. It was at this point that Beesley performed at his finest, unveiling a new System business plan to the congressional committees, in which he also reviewed and updated the committees on the System's efforts to solve their own problems through the provisions of the 1985 act. At the same time, Beesley was able to refute some of Naylor's arguments and innuendos by pointing out: "Notwithstanding comments to the contrary made by Chairman Naylor and others, the System has the self-discipline necessary to administer a responsible rate-lending program. The issue (as stated earlier by Representative Jones) is whether farmer-directors and their management or the regulator determines what rates are competitive." Suddenly, it became clear to most that because of the changing environment, it made sense that the System should set its own rates and have a hand in determining its own destiny.

Beesley was also able to criticize effectively FCA's stance on control of the Farm Credit Capital Corporation, which included a prohibition of the corporation to recruit from the System. "We are concerned about the FCA's actions to separate the Capital Corporation from the remainder of the Farm Credit System," Beesley told Congress. "By issuing arbitrary regulations, without any statutory basis, FCA is prohibiting many of the most able and dedicated System leaders from serving on the Capital Corporation Board, as well as prohibiting the Capital Corporation from drawing on the talented and capable personnel in the Farm Credit System. Through these regulations, the FCA has made this important institution much less effective."

There probably should have been Congressional debate over the wisdom and propriety of a System employee transferring to another unit in the System or transferring from the System to the FCA on the basis of a possible conflict of interest. There simply was not time for it. The stark truth was that a huge reservoir of such people was available, largely because of the reductions-in-force taking place throughout the System. The preponderance of evidence, as well as the human element (there were a lot of System people out of work), argued for utilizing these people. The prevailing feeling was these people were qualified and available and, after all, would be superior to political appointments that the FCA chairman might select.

Although matters seemed to be emerging well for Beesley and the System, a question was raised over what the System would really gain with legislation that would only permit it to set its own interest rates. Only half a loaf was the thoughtful conclusion. It would only be a matter of time before government capital would be required. The System was also reminded of the grim prospect of having to go, hat in hand, through the chairman of the FCA Board who (as things then stood by virtue of the 1985 act) would be the one to determine whether conditions were serious enough to warrant the infusion of government funds. The conclusion was that in his present mood the incumbent FCA chairman might not be a very willing, compassionate individual with whom to deal. No, the System needed to seek more than the right to set interest rates in its legislation.

What resulted was another spectacular ninth-inning rally by the System. Just prior to adjournment on October 17, 1986, Congress included in its Farm Credit Act Amendments a provision that granted the System some further freedom from its regulator, permitting it to adopt lower interest rates and, with FCA approval, to apply a twenty-year amortization to losses ordinarily absorbed over a three-year period. The amendments would also permit the System to incur new debt for the purpose of purchasing an estimated $30 billion of high-priced, long-term obligations until December 31, 1988, and would allow System banks to capitalize the provisions from July 1, 1986, to December 31, 1988.

The latter part of the amendment was something of an accounting maneuver, setting aside historically abnormal losses from treatment accorded under GAAP (Generally Accepted Accounting Practices), a procedure the System was required to adopt under the 1985 act. GAAP would not permit amortization over a twenty-year period, while another accounting procedure—RAP (Regulatory Accounting Procedures)—did. Noting the GAO's warning that the Farm Credit System might be losing money at the rate of $1 billion a year, the House Agriculture Committee was looking for ways to prevent the exhaustion of the System's reserves and hoped it had found such a way through the use of RAP.

Although the GAAP-for-RAP maneuver did not amuse the FCA, the press had a lot of fun with it, referring to it as "an accounting gimmick." The October 12, 1986, *Washington Post* headlined an article: "Farm Credit Ready To Paper Over Its Red Ink," noting: "With the quiet acquiescence of the Reagan Administration, Congress is on the verge of authorizing the FC System to pretend that it is making money instead of chalking up the largest losses of any financial institution in history." Earlier (October 3, 1986), an equally unkind article appeared in the *Wall Street Journal,* headlined, "Plan Speeding Through Congress To Let Farm Credit System Mask Huge Losses." It told much the same story.

In her October 10, 1986, wire story, headed "Creative Accounting," UPI Washington Farm Editor Sonja Hillgren also referred to the plan as "a gimmick," but said that it would "provide emergency help needed for smooth operation of the System in coming months." The new plan, she said, "would let the nation's largest farm lender pay off high-interest debt incurred in previous years by borrowing at current low-interest rates and then spread resulting losses over 20 years."

Not surprisingly, the representative of the System's rival commercial banks—the American Bankers Association—was incensed. For one thing, the ABA had attempted to make it possible for commercial bankers to utilize RAP and were denied. In an editorial in its *ABA*

Bankers Weekly, "RAP Replaces GAAP," ABA noted caustically: "The Farm Credit System is at it again! Wheeling and dealing in the halls of Congress . . . engineering new accounting rules and some fancy security swaps, as well as a total exemption from usury laws." ABA claimed that the legislation did not solve Farm Credit's problems; it merely delayed the day of reckoning. ABA's ire regarding RAP subsided, however, with passage of the Competitive Banking Act of 1987, which granted to small, commercial agricultural banks a similar plan of amortization of loan privileges as contained in the 1987 Farm Credit act.

The GAO also appeared somewhat skeptical, making these observations in a letter to Chairman Ed Jones in response to his request to GAO for "an overview of the important issues confronting the Farm Credit System." The GAO response pointed out:

> As you know, the Act allows the System to capitalize and amortize over 20 years resulting from its poorly performing loan portfolio and the high current cost of its debt. This legislation could have the effect of hiding the serious financial problems that the System will experience in the future. Of more importance, this legislation does not address the System's underlying problems and could impede the needed reforms to its management practices and operations.

No matter how you sliced it, the Farm Credit System had racked up another piece of legislation—the Farm Credit Act Amendments of 1986—its second legislative success in as many years. It provided the System with a good one-two punch. As summarized in the November/December issue of Farm Credit Corporation's newsletter, *The Farm Credit Letter,* the act:

> 1. Gives institutions of the Farm Credit System the authority to set interest rates without approval of the Farm Credit Administration; and
> 2. Authorizes the FCA to allow System banks to use regulatory accounting procedures to capitalize and amortize excessive interest costs and extraordinary loan losses over a period of up to 20 years.

The Farm Credit System was particularly anxious to do something to help buoy its member stock. Since the System is a cooperative, member-borrowers are required to purchase stock as part of their loan. Traditionally, as a member of PCA, a farmer would leave his stock in the association to be used again when requiring another loan the following year or growing season. A farmer tended to look at this stock as a compensating balance that was not at risk. Now, with tough times for their associations, it looked as though some farmers were going to lose their stock. Needless to say, salvaging stock value presented a problem for both sides. The association could not afford the loss of volume when a disgusted borrower pulled out because it raised the association's per-unit costs. There not only was the loss of business for the association but the denial of use of the member's stock. And who paid for this loss? The farmers who remain loyal to the association through higher interest costs, that's who!

Par value on the stock normally was $5 a share. A provision in the 1986 act made it possible for the System to make good on a $5 book value in the event the association was liquidated. This, it was felt, would have a soothing effect on member morale and loyalty to the association, even though it had the appearance of farmers being bought off.

Most of the celebration over the passage of the Farm Credit Act Amendments of 1986 was confined to the System. The reaction of most of the other supporters of the legislation was simply relief. Perhaps Agricultural Credit Subcommittee Chairman Jones put the best face on the legislation when he commented, "It buys time at a critical period and gives the System and its regulator the tools to deal with a potentially explosive situation. At best, this bill is a short-term solution aimed at relieving the pressure until a permanent answer can be found and it does so without any cost to the taxpayer."

As was his custom Chairman Jones was generous in sharing credit with others on both sides of the congressional aisle. Jones proclaimed good bipartisan support and singled out in particular his comrade of many years, the ranking minority member of his subcommittee, Rep. Edward R. Madigan, Republican of Illinois. Madigan described the legislation as "a compromise effort to give the FC System, under the supervision of Federal regulators, a chance to help itself out of the serious problem it is now facing."

House Agriculture Committee Chairman Kika de la Garza also stamped the legislation as "a very necessary step," while Rep. Thomas Coleman, Republican, Missouri, commented that the bill "provides a tool for the FC System to continue to operate into early next year. The fear is there may be some problems develop in the System if we don't act."

A most succinct analysis of the 1986 Act was provided by David Freshwater, Senior Economist, Joint Economic Committee, in his paper, "The Political Economy of Farm Credit Reform": "The 1986 amendments were a classic example of government 'smoke and mirrors.' . . . the various parts of the System thought they were getting what they wanted, and Congress was able to defer a hard decision."

Perhaps the most disappointed and disillusioned over passage of the 1986 act was Frank W. Naylor, Jr., who had the rug jerked out from under him for the second time in two years by the administration. Once again, as it had done right before passage of the 1985 act, the administration at the last moment jumped out of the way of the Farm Credit bandwagon. The administration let its support for the Farm Credit legislation be known after having most of its concerns about the bill satisfied. In the end the administration, as it had done earlier, turned to Treasury for direction. Assistant Secretary Charles O. Sethness was the messenger for the White House to Capitol Hill on the Farm Credit issue.

As one veteran Capitol Hill observer commented, "At no time did the 1986 Farm Credit legislation get out of the administration's hands and control." When the critical hour approached, Senators Cochran and Helms were able to convince the administration of the correctness of their position, whereupon Naylor was commanded to back off.

Ever the good Republican soldier, Naylor refrained from further lobbying against the bill. He could not resist delivering a few jabs later, however. Most of these were aimed at Senator Cochran. In an interview published in the November 1986 issue of *ABA Banking Journal,* Naylor described Senator Cochran as "well intentioned," but that "his legislation goes far beyond regulation of interest rates. It effectively deregulates — even does away with — much of what Congress put in place last fall when setting up the FCA board. . . . To deregulate — to say, in effect, that unsound pricing is a safe banking practice — just isn't good legislation."

In any case, FCA went into action. The regulatory agency shot off an official memo on October 28, 1986, signed by Michael J. Powers, the agency's new director of the Office of Analysis and Supervision (and another recruit from the Comptroller's Office) to the CEO of each System institution regarding interest rate reductions: "The establishment of rates that result in a return insufficient to cover expenses will be considered an unsafe and unsound practice and will require FCA to initiate corrective action. I bring this to your attention only as a word of caution as the financial position of the FC System is precarious; therefore, improper pricing could result in damage from which the System may not be able to recover." This probably brought a sigh of relief to some of the "well" Farm Credit banks who were getting nervous about how some of the other banks were slashing interest rates in the name of remaining competitive.

Apparently not wanting to appear a spoilsport, Powers nonetheless put the System on notice that hostilities may not be over. The memo concluded: "The FCA wishes you well in this endeavor, but nevertheless stands ready to quickly address any action that demonstrates a lack of responsibility or propriety in the implementation of your new authority."

It is part of the record that FCA implemented the 1986 legislation in a timely fashion, albeit not necessarily in a manner to the liking of the System. As a matter of fact, its regulations for the 1986 act were issued after a special meeting of the three-member FCA Board on December 18, 1986. The FCA conformed to the letter of the 1986 act, but perhaps not to the spirit. The FCA's regulations permitted the System to use the 1986 act, but made it as difficult as possible. The FCA claimed in its December 1986 issue of the *FCA Bulletin,* that its regulations "give reasonable latitude for implementation of RAP and leave business decisions with the System institution." However, there appeared to be strings attached:

> Other provisions of the RAP regulations require System institutions to issue financial statements to borrower/stockholders in accordance with GAAP and disclose use of Regulatory Accounting Practices (RAP) in footnotes that reconcile the differences between the two accounting systems.
>
> The regulations allow System institutions to defer money set aside for anticipated loan losses. However, to use this provision, institutions must sign an agreement with the FC System Capital Corporation to correct operating deficiencies, control the management of high-risk assets and improve management efficiency.

The System for the most part was furious about what it considered unnecessary delay on the part of its regulator. But perhaps what irked it the most was a quote from Frank Naylor in the FCA press release of December 18, 1986, announcing and explaining its "Regulations for Regulatory Accounting." Claimed Naylor, "It was the intention of Congress with the 1986 Amendments to enhance the ability of the System to provide competitive interest rates. However, Congress clearly did not want to create unfair competition for other lenders." Although such was stated in the 1986 act, there were some System officials who claimed privately, that Naylor "continues to be the voice of commercial lenders."

In any case, the release forced the System into the open in its behind-the-scenes efforts to get the FCA to issue what the System felt to be "realistic and workable" regulations. What resulted was described as a Farm Credit System bank presidents' blitz of Capitol Hill to complain to their congressmen. The two-day blitz was successful, resulting in the FCA easing its restrictions on use of FC System authority for long-term amortization of losses. After the blitz, System sources said the FCA modified its rules so that abnormal loan losses, as well as expense in redeeming old high-interest FC System bonds, could be deferred more extensively than was possible under original regulations. The System also felt that the danger of preempting farmer-borrowers' stock in System cooperatives to cover System losses of the past year or an early call for federal funds to avert an FC System financial collapse had been alleviated.

Meanwhile, the Farm Credit System had other nagging problems. For one, the System continued to be dogged by internal dissention, making one wonder if it could claim to be called a system at all. Much has always been made of the fact that Farm Credit was a nationwide system, implying an all-for-one and one-for-all spirit. Historically, when the Farm Credit banks went to Wall Street for funds, they went as one bank and this technique paid off in lower cost funds. However, in most other ways the banks and FC districts acted independently. Now whatever unity there was seemed to have disappeared. The so-called "well banks" of the System were being pitted against the "sick" ones.

For example, in the Texas and Springfield Districts two of the well banks filed suit in September, 1986, challenging the capital-sharing mechanism that forces solvent banks to come to the financial aid of their financially disabled brethren. The plaintiffs charged that the mechanism "effectively deprives all the banks of the ability to serve their farm borrowers." The suit named both the FCA and the Farm Credit System Capital Corporation (the body which administers the cost-sharing).

It was hoped by the System leadership that passage of the 1986 act would reduce the lawsuit to moot through the protection of member stock. Such was not the case, but the 1987 act did the job. In any case, Farm Credit people agreed that, even so, internal lawsuits are not something that cements family relationships—that the whole matter would open some wounds that would fester for a long time.

Even those who were not concerned about the Texas/Springfield court action could not ignore the similar association discontent that appeared to be going on nationwide. Local associations (PCAs and FLBAs) had filed suit in Wichita, Kansas; Albuquerque, New Mexico; Oklahoma City, Oklahoma; Denver, Colorado; Cape Girardo, Missouri; and Springfield, Massachusetts. The FCA was named in many suits. In most cases a single association was involved in the suit, but in others several associations joined together.

The bone of contention in most of the suits was the portion of the 1986 Farm Credit Amendments that provided for the Farm Credit System Capital Corporation to use the unallocated retained earnings of the System's healthier institutions in a transfer to the more troubled banks. However, since each local association is considered a private corporation owned by its stockholder-borrowers, many of those being assessed claimed that neither the Congress nor the Farm Credit System has any right to take their money.

Further complicating the System's problems was the fact that many of the same divisive issues that caused the grassroots elements of the System to rebel—namely mergers and consolidations—were still in dispute. As a matter of fact, mergers and consolidations were an integral part of any System survival plan that sought greater efficiency of operations. Again, at a very bad time, the System was faced with massive restructuring. The situation promised not to be confined entirely to an internal affair because to merge unlike System institutions—PCAs with FLBAs, for example—would require legislation, a very public endeavor, indeed. In addition to internal opposition, the System could count on opposition from the commercial banking sector, which manifests a certain paranoia at the mere hint of the Farm Credit System becoming a full service bank.

Perhaps the American Bankers Association's research study, "Transition in Agriculture: A Strategic Assessment of Agriculture and Banking", which was released in the fall of 1986, provided the clarion call to its members to be on the alert for such a legislative move. The study warned that the Farm Credit System "may be down but it's not out . . . [that it] will ultimately emerge from its present difficulties with its advantages still largely intact, and with changes in structure and procedures which should strengthen its competitive position in total lending."

For the most part the ABA study was considerably more optimistic than System people had any reason to hope for. As its "worst case" scenario the ABA study projected that FLBs would increase their market share from the then current 42 percent to 55 percent by 1995. Even in its "best case" scenario, the ABA study had the FLBs increasing their market share by 46 to 48 percent, even in the face of increasing competition from life insurance companies (13 to 15 percent) and commercial banks (15 to 17 percent).

In the non–real estate farm debt market, the ABA study had as its worst case scenario, the commercial banks decreasing their share from 36 percent to 26 to 28 percent by 1995, while PCAs by contrast would increase their market share from 15 percent to 28 to 30 percent. Under the best case scenario, PCAs would gain only a 22 to 25 percent increase, while the commercial banks' share would jump to 43 to 47 percent.

In any case, it was difficult for anyone to conceive of merger of unlike banks in the System when progress in the merger of like banks and associations was proceeding at a snail's pace in the face of continued internal opposition. Even the Banks for Cooperatives, which had been talking merger for so many years, appeared to be making little progress. The Farm Credit System needed to face the fact that mergers never come easy but need be done, a truth that was later forced upon it by Congress as a condition for passage of the 1987 act.

Despite all the negatives it faced, the System produced and released its "1986 Strategic and Business Plans" in which it pointed out the rapid strides it had made and set forth its near-future plans, the key elements of which called for:

1. establishing a Systemwide data system to allow the Farm Credit Corporation of America to monitor compliance with loan restructuring and acquired property guidelines;

2. initiating programs to identify and personally contact potential high quality customers;

3. establishing programs to identify and personally contact potential high quality customers; and

4. encouraging each bank to review and evaluate existing human resources programs.

Of the four sections to the System's plan, doubtless number three was the most important to the System's future. Would the System be able reconcile relationships with estranged borrowers? In view of all that had happened, it would not be easy. On the other hand, there would be times, as in the past, when farmers would have no alternative source of funds. Such a forced marriage might not be a good foundation on which to rebuild loyalty and support. But it was a start.

For what it was worth, the System got a boost from GAO, which applauded the System's "1986 Strategic and Business Plans" in its own report: "Farm Credit: Actions Needed on Major Issues." GAO did note, however, that "the System lacks central and accounting management (and) it may not be able to ensure that its entities implement the Systemwide objectives." GAO also pointed out ominously that the System needed to accomplish much more to complete its strategic and business plans.

As the System moved into 1987, the consensus was that its central entity—FCC/A—was carrying a heavy burden, that the System's future turned on the performance of this entity as a unifying force. There was general agreement that the extent of FCC/A's success was in direct proportion to the cooperation and support it would receive from its component parts. Again the history of the System in this regard did not lend itself to optimism. Judging it on this basis, the FCC/A could not really qualify as the System's central entity and has not at this writing. Meanwhile the clock for the need for infusion of Government capital kept ticking.

13

One More Time

"History is past politics,
and politics present history."

Sir John Seeley, *The Growth of British Policy*

 After several years of doom and gloom, one might have expected complete despair to have gripped American agriculturists by the end of 1986. However, negativism, while evident, was not all-consuming. Farm organizations, like the farmers they serve, tend to look at each new year with renewed optimism. As 1987 approached, there was the feeling among the agricultural groups—at least those stationed in the nation's capital—that things had "bottomed out" and were now looking up. As they looked at the new year, you heard people say that the worst was over—that those farmers who had survived thus far had weathered the storm. All the clichés were optimistic.

A new Congress was in session. The main change was that the Democrats had regained control of the Senate, which resulted in Sen. Patrick J. Leahy of Vermont replacing Sen. Jesse Helms as chairman of the Agriculture Committee. Overall, this change did not concern Farm Credit. Both men were considered friends of the System. However, it would give the well banks in the System some advantage, as Senator Leahy was close to the Springfield (Massachusetts) Farm Credit Banks, one of the districts that still operated in the black. The Springfield banks also had wisely employed the services of Roger Allbee, former aide to Rep. James M. Jeffords of Vermont, a key member of the House Agriculture Committee, as its congressional liaison. The relationship between Chairman Leahy and the Springfield banks proved mutually beneficial and greatly enhanced the chances for passage of the Agricultural Credit Act of 1987.

Another interesting switch was the replacement of Republican Sen. Paula Hawkins of Florida with Democratic Sen. David L. Boren as chairman of the Senate Agriculture Credit Subcommittee. Although the loss of Senator Hawkins was not considered a tragedy in Farm Credit, Senator Boren had always been viewed as a maverick—unpredictable and sometimes vindictive as far as Farm Credit was concerned. Farm Credit never seemed to know just how he would react to any given situation or which Oklahoma faction or cause he would champion. Also, there was the matter of Senator Boren's new FCA connection—Board Member Jim Billington, a fellow Oklahoman who had been named as the Democratic representative on the FCA Board.

It was not difficult to imagine some of the tableaus that unfolded at FCA Board meetings at the time. "It's like a three-ring circus or a Chinese fire drill," was one assessment by an FCA employee. Invariably, Chairman of the Board Naylor would make a proposal and Billington would dissent, or vice versa. Debate would range from whether the FCA should apply formally to the U.S. Treasury for assistance to the Farm Credit System (by far the most crucial issue of the moment) to whether the agency should hire the services of a clinical psychologist to assist with the stress problems within the agency. Unfavorable publicity was getting out about the FCA Board's performance, and it was hurting its credibility.

Billington bore down on the clinical psychologist issue as an indication of Chairman Naylor's insensitivity to proper use of available government funds. Billington voted against rehiring Dr. Craig Wasserman (who had been employed earlier by Governor Wilkinson), charging it was "an extravagant nonsense . . . that comes out of the farmer's pocket. We don't need a psychologist to inform us that stress exists." Naylor, on the other hand, called the process "an accepted management practice."

Nor did the third member of the FCA Board, Marvin Duncan, escape such criticism. The House Agriculture Appropriations Subcommittee, in reviewing the agency's annual budget, picked up on the fact that Duncan had spent over $11,000 on trips to Sweden in September 1986; to Japan, China, Indonesia, and Thailand in July 1987; and to

FIG. 13.1. *The FCA Board. Early meetings of the new FCA Board (which replaced the Federal Farm Credit Board) were described as being like a political "three ring circus." Chairman Frank Naylor is shown in front center, with board members Jim Billington (left) and Marvin Duncan. Photo by Mike Sprague.*

Turkey in September 1987. Duncan explained that such trips were required for the interchange of information for those who purchase Farm Credit System securities, both foreign and domestic, but a subcommittee spokesman maintained that "the farmer can ill afford to have his money used for $100-per-hour psychologists, receptions, foreign travel and unnecessary personnel."

Regarding the question of certification for financial assistance, Naylor argued that the technical preconditions (such as commitment of all reserve capital in the Farm Credit System to help shore up financially troubled institutions prescribed by the Federal Credit Act amendments of 1985) had not been met. They (Naylor and Duncan) preferred to mark time while Congress worked up a new rescue plan for the System in 1987, or better yet, delay until it could come under the auspices of another administration. Billington made another run at certification at the May 1987 FCA Board meeting, only to have it die for lack of a second to his motion, a procedure that was repeated at the June board meeting.

The arguing and back-biting that went on inside the FCA board-room would have been considered amusing were it not for the fact that "Rome was burning." Precious little help could be expected to come out of a government agency thus preoccupied. One could argue that the FCA Board had a majority view that could prevail, but this view was usually suspect on the basis of political partisanship and personal ani-mosities. Duncan would concur with Naylor on matters of major sub-stance. He seemed to disagree only on form. The FCA Board resembled the Italian cabinet, torn asunder by virtue of having to have representa-tion from three major political parties.

It was not surprising, therefore, that in 1987 government leadership in Farm Credit in 1987 emanated more from the Treasury than from the FCA, and gave rise to a recurring rumor that the agency would one day end up in the Treasury. After all, the FCA was an independent agency, too independent in the eyes of most administrations and many members of Congress. Ultimately, expenditure of taxpayers' money is a Treasury affair—why delegate certification authority to an independent interme-diary? Later, the question was rendered moot because, in any case, the Treasury will call the shots at the FCA, at least the big ones.

As for other changes in Congress that affected Farm Credit, perhaps the most notable casualty on the Senate Agriculture Committee was Republican Sen. Mark Andrews of North Dakota, a long-time sup-porter of cooperatives and a populist in the best North Dakota tradition. Senator Andrews was also a member of the Senate Agriculture Appro-priations Subcommittee. An indication of Andrews' strong bipartisan support in farm and co-op circles was that in his reelection campaign bid he had the backing of Bob Bergland, former Democratic congressman and secretary of agriculture under President Carter and then general manager of the National Rural Electric Cooperative Association. The blow of Andrews' loss was lessened by the fact he was being replaced by Kent Conrad (both in the Senate and on the agriculture committee) whose credentials were imposing insofar as Farm Credit was concerned.

The House Agriculture Committee had its usual turnover, but main-tained its leadership—Representative de la Garza as chairman and Ed Jones as chairman of the Agricultural Credit Subcommittee. Thus, there was little about the One Hundredth Congress that concerned Farm Credit beyond the usual anxieties. But these anxieties were quite enough. Some problems the System faced at the onset of 1987 were:

1. of the Federal Land Banks' $45 billion in debt maturing between then and 1991, the average interest rate, counting the stock purchase requirements on land bank loans averaged two percent higher than other loans in the industry;

2. nonperforming (considered high risk) loans represented almost one-fourth of the FLB loan portfolio;

3. out of $13 billion in nonperforming loans, about $7 billion were considered nonaccrual (uncollectible); and

4. System loan volume had dropped from a high of around $82 billion to $55 billion and was continuing its downward trend.

It was obvious that the Farm Credit System was not going to be able to affect enough efficiencies in operation in 1987 to offset this price differential. For example, even with the high number of reductions-in-force (it was reported that the number of System employees had dropped by 3,100 during 1985–1986) the savings in salary cuts had not kept pace with the losses due to the drop in loan volume. Although FCC/A's Brent Beesley claimed that a 17 percent decrease in employees had resulted in savings of upwards of $90 million, it was not commensurate with the volume decline. Perhaps worst of all there were growing whispers that Farm Credit System management was not ready to come to grips with the needed structural changes in the System.

One concern that the System did not have in 1987 was whether or not Congress might abandon it. The Farm Credit System was, after all, the nation's largest institutional agricultural lender. The question was not whether to rescue it, but how. The System had become increasingly integrated and complex. The hope was to revise the laws governing banking in the United States in a way that would increase competition, yet in a way that would allow the System to meet the competition and maintain its social mission. It was felt that a balance had to be maintained between the social mission of the Farm Credit System (a cooperative dedicated to enhancing farmers' control over their supply of credit) and its commercial imperative (the need to be profitable). This, it was conceded, would take a neat bit of tightrope walking on the part of Congress.

Hardly had the ink dried on the Farm Credit Amendments Act of 1986 than there was talk of a 1987 act. Such talk was prompted by the release of the Farm Credit System's report that it had sustained over $1.9 billion in losses in 1986. This, in turn, triggered the One Hundredth Congress to action. For example, Senate Minority Leader Robert Dole of Kansas told the National Governors' Association meeting on February 24, 1987, that it looked like a bailout of the System would be required, but that there would be strings attached. "They [the System] would just like the money with no change, but I think there are going to have to be changes," Senator Dole said. This was an early clue that a 1987 legislative initiative might be taken out of Farm Credit's hands.

Senate Agriculture Credit Subcommittee Chairman David Boren began his hearings in late February, wading into a myriad of System issues including such things as borrower rights, borrower flight, and whether the System should continue with its cooperative structure or with a decentralized one with each entity "rising or falling on its own." These hearings brought a wide range of people to the witness chair and very likely produced the most fireworks.

The hearings provided an opportunity for the three members of the FCA Board to testify independently. Each was asked his opinion regarding the imminence of the need for government assistance. Predictably, Republicans Naylor and Duncan indicated that they "did not favor certifying the System's need for financial assistance at this time." Just as predictably, Democrat Billington told the Boren subcommittee that he did not think "the System was all that far from meeting the legal requirements for federal dollars"—that the System had only $1.4 billion left in reserve. Billington observed that "they are losing $400 million-plus each quarter. There are not all that many quarters to play with."

Not surprisingly Senator Boren agreed with Billington and expressed his exasperation with Naylor and others who wanted to delay federal help as long as possible. "I've not talked with a single person who hasn't felt a capital infusion isn't necessary," Senator Boren snapped. There followed, as reported by Washington correspondent Jay Richter, a snappy dialogue between the senator and Naylor, in which the senator attempted to get a commitment from Naylor on how soon federal help would be forthcoming. Despite intermittent table-pounding and an admonition that "we are not going to play 'ring around the rosy' . . . we're not going to sit by and let this thing [the Farm Credit System] go,"

Senator Boren did not get a straight answer as to when the FCA chairman felt federal funds would be needed.

This was not to say there was a dearth of opinions regarding what ought be done with the Farm Credit System and when. Just about everyone connected with agriculture entered the fray. This, of course, meant another report from the GAO, the substance of which was presented at a hearing of Chairman Ed Jones' Agricultural Credit Subcommittee in early April 1987. At the hearings Comptroller General Charles Bowsher told the subcommittee that a bailout plan patterned after the Chrysler Corporation rescue would be the best short-term method to stabilize the Farm Credit System. Bowsher recommended a federal takeover with the setting up of a control board that would administer the infusion of federal funds or loan guarantees.

Among other proposals that appeared to be gaining momentum in early 1987 was the establishment of a secondary market for agriculture, one that would allow investors to purchase farm mortgages. There was so much interest, in fact, that the GAO was asked to make a study of it. GAO described a secondary market as one in which existing, rather than new, products are bought and sold—in this case, a market for the sale of mortgage loans. The sale of the individual loans or mortgage-backed securities returns funds to the loan originator, creating liquidity and allowing the originator to make additional loans or use the funds for other purposes. It was not a new idea, but would be patterned after the secondary market for housing.

The idea quickly picked up support, particularly among farm organizations. The National Grange, for example, felt that a secondary market would increase competition among investors, which would help reduce interest rates. Bob Frederick, veteran Grange legislative agent, noted in the March 27, 1987 issue of *Washington Update* that "a government guarantee of the mortgages would increase the investors' confidence and participation at little or no cost to the taxpayer. Traditional farm lenders would still make mortgages but would then resell loan packages to investors. Farmers are protected because investors only purchase the right to receive the mortgage principal and interest payments. They could not foreclose because all loan management rights would remain with the original lender who then collects a fee from the investor or retains part of the principal and interest."

The American Farm Bureau Federation was at least as enthusiastic, carrying a long, explanatory article in its March 9 issue of *Farm Bureau News,* complete with a flow chart explaining the process. The article noted that "The need for expanded sources of credit comes on the heels of widespread farm credit problems and financial difficulties among the traditional providers of credit. Events of the past four years underscore the inherent weakness of the present farm credit apparatus and show a critical need for a broader financial instrument for farm mortgage loans." AFBF president Dean Kleckner added that "A strong secondary market will blunt future lender problems by spreading the risk." Chief among proponents for an agricultural secondary market, of course, were commercial bankers through their representatives – the IBAA and the ABA. The ABA's Agriculture Committee made the market's establishment its top priority for 1987. The agricultural banking groups were urged by Congress and others to get together and form a task force and cooperate on the creation of a secondary market. This they did. The Farm Credit System was included in this effort and named President W. Malcolm Harding of the Central Bank for Cooperatives as its representative. Harding, a former FCA governor, was named to head the lender task force.

Although the Farm Credit System appeared to support the issue, certainly there have been grave reservations. With a secondary market, the System would be opening the door to let other lenders enter what had virtually been its sole province. At jeopardy in particular would be the Federal Land Banks. These long-term lenders held a 40 percent share of the farm real estate market, largely because commercial banks and insurance companies were not always interested in this lending area. A secondary market would enable these lenders to reenter the market at little risk. The market would also encourage others, like savings and loan associations and credit unions, to jump in. In any case, the land banks could depend on facing their greatest competition in history. This situation would not necessarily benefit all farmers because there was the danger that commercial banks and insurance companies might just scrape off the cream of the available loans, leaving the land banks to carry the rest.

However, the System felt it really did not have any choice if it wanted rescue legislation. To not participate would make it appear that it was opposed to competition. Whatever was to be done, the System needed to have a hand in it. It needed to participate if it were to attempt to minimize the negative effect a secondary market could have on its lending area. In any case, the situation was another reminder that the Farm Credit System had lost much of its clout in controlling the direction legislation might take. The System's reputation as a lender was greatly flawed. Perhaps it was becoming the lender of next-to-the-last-resort, just ahead of the FmHA. Yes, things were getting out of control.

But, despite its problems, the System was again able to pull itself together. Under heavy pressure from Congress and others to come up with its own proposals, Farm Credit presented them with a flourish on May 6, 1987, before Chairman Ed Jones' subcommittee. The presentation was made in what the FCC/A described as "an unprecedented demonstration of System unity." It was true that every district was represented by the thirteen directors of the Farm Credit Council, one from each district and the Central Bank for Cooperatives, and the managers of the thirty-seven Farm Credit Banks and the System's service entities.

However, based on past experiences, the question could legitimately be raised: Are the Farm Credit banks all in favor of the same thing? As evidence, a doubter could cite the "dog days" of 1971 when the System was attempting to gain its new charter act. All Farm Credit districts were represented then; unfortunately, two of them (the old Houston/Berkeley [now Texas/Sacramento] districts) were fighting against the legislation hammer and tong. There had been other instances later when a System leader might dutifully testify before a congressional committee in behalf of some proposed System legislation and, then, afterwards drop around to see his congressmen and tell them to disregard what he had said because his Farm Credit district was opposing at least certain portions of the legislation.

But the current situation seemed different. The System could no longer afford the luxury of dissent. Well, at least not as much dissent. After all, no one can be perfect, particularly when it comes to legislation.

In its financial recovery proposal the System asked for:

1. a $6 billion line of credit from the U.S. Treasury, to be handled by a seven-member Federal Farm Credit Assistance Board (not by the FCA chairman alone);

2. a seven-year period beginning with the date of enactment during which any borrower-held stock, participation certificates, or other allo-

cated equities in System institutions could be retired at not less than par value, thus assuring borrowers that their investment in their System institutions would be protected;

3. farmer-owners of the System to have "maximum flexibility" to determine the structure and the credit delivery systems of their institutions (a rather tentative attempt to address the merger issue);

4. the establishment of a Federal Farm Mortgage Corporation within the System, which would purchase, pool, and secure loans made or purchased by System institutions or other financial institutions (thereby establishing a secondary market for loans); and

5. Greater lender participation in the USDA Conservation Reserve Program (CRP), a program that pays participants to take erodible or marginal land out of production. To help convince Congress, the System produced and distributed a 25-page booklet, "Farm Credit System 1987–88 Business Plan."

After the unveiling of the financial recovery proposal, the Farm Credit legislative season began in earnest. A number of bills were dropped into the hopper. There was not much new about the legislative strategies, but there were some noticeable changes in the cast of characters. For one thing, the Beesley-Naylor conflict was removed from center stage. Announcing its neutrality, the FCA did not even testify in the early hearings in 1987. Naylor's curious rationale was that there were literally hundreds of variations in the proposed legislation and really "no right way" to do it. Naylor did, however, commend the committee for its "lengthy, very well thought out" hearings.

Beesley was not faring well, either. Although still the titular head of the System, Beesley seemed to have lost some of his drive. He seemed to have worn out his welcome with some congressional leaders, notably Chairman de la Garza. The two appeared seldom to be on the same wavelength. There was a feeling, too, that Beesley's grip on the System, never very firm, was beginning to slip a bit. Congressional leaders who appeared to sense this began asking others in Farm Credit for their views. One person legislative leaders relied on was Grant Lucas, chairman of the Farm Credit Council and veteran director in the Sacramento district. Lucas, a moderate not in the California Farm Credit tradition, brought considerable experience in Farm Bureau and cooperative activities to his position of leadership. Also, he had at his disposal the crack corps of Farm Credit district legislative agents who, along with the Farm

Credit Council staff, quietly and systematically pounded the congressional beat, visiting with key legislators, who were learning to rely on those agents for good information. Another System leader who played a more prominent role in the 1987 legislative effort, acting oftentimes as the System spokesman at congressional hearings, was Douglas D. Sims, president of the three St. Louis banks.

As one would suspect on the basis of their agricultural leadership roles, much more was heard from Chairman Leahy and Subcommittee Chairman Boren. The same was true for Sen. Rudy Boschwitz of Minnesota, ranking minority member of Senator Boren's subcommittee. The good news was that Boren and Boschwitz agreed on most farm issues;

FIG. 13.2. *Farm Credit officials testifying at House Agriculture Committee. The Farm Credit System used a team approach in pursuing passage of the Agricultural Credit Act of 1987. Grant Lucas (left) of California, chairman of the Farm Credit Council, and Douglas Sims (center), president of the Farm Credit Banks of St. Louis, were particularly effective. They are shown with Brent Beesley, CEO of the Farm Credit Corporation of America, testifying before the House Agriculture Subcommittee on Conservation, Credit and Rural Development in June 1987. Photo by William E. Carnahan.*

FIG. 13.3. *In 1987, the agriculture committees of Congress devoted months to an attempt to salvage the Farm Credit System. Among the principals in the House of Representatives were these members of the Subcommittee on Conservation, Credit, and Rural Development (left to right): Glenn English of Oklahoma, Berkley Bedell of Iowa, Kika de la Garza of Texas (who was chairman of the full committee), and Credit Subcommittee chairman Ed Jones of Tennessee. This subcommittee heard from more than one hundred witnesses, a fact confirmed by the weary faces of the subcommittee members above. Photo courtesy Rep. Ed Jones.*

the bad news was that one of the exceptions was on the issue of credit. However, they did manage to operate well enough to go along with fellow senators Lugar, Melcher, and Leahy on the Farm Credit legislation.

Another new, albeit negative, development was that presidential election politics were beginning to creep into the situation for the first time in four years. When Tip O'Neill was speaker of the House, he had essentially turned over all agricultural matters to his majority whip, former House Agriculture Committee chairman Thomas S. Foley of Washington. Not so when Rep. Jim Wright of Texas succeeded O'Neill. Speaker Wright could not refrain from doing things that were interpreted as indicating his preference for Rep. Richard A. Gephardt of

Missouri as the Democratic nominee for president. On the other hand, the onrushing presidential political campaign had a positive effect on Farm Credit legislation as well. All the presidential aspirants — Republican or Democratic — wanted to have the Farm Credit issue out of the way before hard-core campaigning began in earnest in 1988.

Perhaps the most refreshing new voice for Farm Credit legislation on the Senate side was that of Sen. Richard L. Lugar of Indiana, who became ranking minority member of the Agriculture Committee in 1987 and who chose to exert himself as an agricultural spokesman. Senator Lugar introduced a bill, which was mainly the product of a coalition made up of the AFBF, the National Cattlemen, the National Corn Growers, the National Cotton Growers, and the National Pork Producers. The proposal received a great deal of attention when first unveiled, although it was later obscured by other proposals.

Another farm organization coalition of note in 1987 was one made up of the National Farmers Union, the National Farmers Organization, the American Agricultural Movement, the League of Rural Voters, and the National Save the Family Farm Coalition. This combination developed a "working paper on agricultural credit" in which it insisted that "the Farm Credit System cannot be allowed to fail," and that "any legislation to restore the System should include protection of the borrowers." The paper urged mandatory restructuring of farm loans "when to do so would be less costly than foreclosure." Some of this coalition's proposals were adopted in modified form in the final bill, although not necessarily the provisions in which this coalition was most interested.

Thus, the 1987 credit debates featured a full-time return of the farm organizations to the credit arena. During the 1985 session they appeared to go their separate ways; in 1986 they played almost no role at all. The 1987 resurgence of interest was perhaps an attempt to avoid becoming irrelevant. A somewhat similar situation prevailed for the bankers, who did little about farm credit in 1985 and played no role in 1986 but were hot to trot in 1987, mainly because of the secondary market issue. That issue was, in fact, the commercial bankers' only interest in the legislation.

There was the usual name-calling and back-biting in the 1987 session, particularly as the congressional session wore on and time ran short. The most notable flap involved AFBF president Kleckner and Chairman Ed Jones. The July 6 issue of the *Farm Bureau News* carried an "Open Letter to Farm Bureau Members" signed by Kleckner and noted: "It appears that Congress is willing to let the Farm Credit System assistance issue go until the next crisis. Lawmakers must be convinced that action is needed now to avoid making hasty, poorly reasoned decisions when the next crisis develops."

Chairman Jones, who had just concluded fourteen days of hearings in which his subcommittee had heard from more than one hundred witnesses, took rather violent (for him) exception to the AFBF letter, firing back one of his own on the following Friday, July 10. Jones noted that attempts thus far had been to "shore up" the Farm Credit System without tapping the federal treasury, but that now it had become obvious that "multibillions of dollars" would be required over the next few years to prevent the System's collapse. After reminding Kleckner that "our focus on farm credit probably outweighs the amount of attention given to all other areas of interest combined," he closed his letter by slapping the AFBF president on the wrist: "I have come to expect sound judgment and cooperation from the Farm Bureau, not inflammatory rhetoric." Farm Credit, it should be noted, very wisely refrained from getting caught up in this fracas.

Despite all the stewing and fretting about the time constraints involved and the ebb and flow of day-to-day activity on legislation, the System was faring quite well as it moved toward the inevitable fall showdown. Things were fine until Congress was ready to adjourn for the annual Labor Day recess. Just before heading for his Texas home, Rep. Charles W. Stenholm, apparently piqued at the snail's pace in which System restructuring was taking place, began an aggressive effort to get results. He got House approval for a plan that would reduce the number of Federal Land Banks and Federal Intermediate Credit Banks from twenty four to six regional banks and combine the Central Bank for Cooperatives and twelve district BCs into one bank—all to be accomplished within one year.

A legislative move such as this is calculated to get attention, and it worked like a charm on the System. Doubtless it was the most dramatic point of the year. The System, which was scheduled to hold its annual National Conference of Farm Credit Directors in Sacramento in early September, decided to move the date up a week—to August 27–29. The rescheduling was intended as a show of interest in Rep. Stenholm's proposal. It was, however, a nightmare for the convention planners and for those attending the conference.

Despite the problems, Farm Credit directors unanimously agreed to go this far. Mergers of FLBs and FICBs are required in districts that receive federal financial assistance. Within six months similar merger initiatives would be placed before stockholders in all other districts. Within one year stockholders would vote whether to consolidate their FLBAs and PCAs in districts where the FLBAs and FICB had already merged. Within eighteen months stockholders would vote on proposals to consolidate the current twelve FC districts into no more than six districts. Stockholders in districts voting not to merge with another district would be ineligible for borrower stock guarantee; Bank for Cooperative stockholders in each district would vote on whether to be a part of a district, regional, or national BC or part of a merged FLB/FICB; and merger of unlike entities would be permitted, provided stockholders were fully informed and had the right to vote on such mergers.

The conference planners had made another adroit move—they invited Agriculture Committee chairman de la Garza to Sacramento to be their keynote speaker. According to the September 4 issue of *The Agricultural Credit Letter:* "He sounded a rousing call for the System to rally behind a realistic reorganization plan so as to win the support of Congress. 'Don't let your future be written in Washington,' he urged. 'Let's write it together.' He reiterated that his committee is concerned primarily with bettering the lot of farmers, not saving the FC System strictly as an establishment." The chairman's message was not entirely reassuring to his Farm Credit audience, but perhaps it was something the directors needed to hear.

The directors then headed home, probably with their fingers crossed, hoping that their actions would be enough to satisfy Rep. Stenholm. A comparison of the FC directors' proposal with Stenholm's guidelines indicated that Stenholm might not be satisfied. On the other hand, Stenholm's program was not entirely consistent. Although adamant on Farm Credit bank mergers, he would allow the local associations (the FLBAs and PCAs) to make their own merger decisions by stockholder vote.

One had to admire the Texas congressman for standing up to some of his fellow Texans. Certainly, you could not accuse Representative Stenholm of attempting to placate the Texas/Wichita district Farm Credit people, some of whom were still insisting that PCAs should never have been organized back in 1933 in the first place. A chief critic of the merger movement was Luman Holman, spokesman for the Texas FLBA stockholders and the interstate Grassroots organization, which claimed to champion System borrowers. This group charged that the mergers proposed by Representative Stenholm would destroy, rather than strengthen, local farmer control, and vowed to fight against the Stenholm merger formula. Grassroots was successful to the extent it was able to get Sen. David Prior of Arkansas to introduce a bill embodying its views in what came to be called "the Arkansas provisions."

According to Jim Webster, Farm Credit legislation moved "from crisis to crisis" through Congress in the fall of 1987. The System was not only fighting to survive, but to survive in a recognizable manner. There was need on one hand to gain government assistance, and quickly in some districts, lest the assets of the well banks become exhausted. Attaining such assistance, however, required satisfying the restructuring requirements of the Stenholm amendments, which could only come at a tremendous price to the System.

Another nagging issue was the development of a secondary market that would satisfy all elements, be helpful to farmers, and yet not destroy the Federal Land Banks in the process. The main proposal was to set up a secondary farm mortgage market backed by farm real estate loans and under the direction of a marketing corporation, to be called "Farmer Mac" (Federal Agricultural Mortgage Corporation). Farmer Mac was to be similar to those programs the government helped develop over the years for home mortgages, such as the Government National Mortgage Corporation (Ginnie Mae); the Federal National Mortgage Corporation (Fannie Mae); and the Federal Home Loan Mortgage Corporation (Freddie Mac).

Although Farmer Mac carried the enthusiastic support of commercial bankers and insurance groups along with some elements of the Farm Credit System, there was also some serious opposition, including some from the administration. Charles Sethness, Treasury's assistant secretary for domestic finance, expressed the Reagan administration's view. He strongly urged Congress not to adopt the proposal, arguing a secondary market would drain the Farm Credit System of its best performing loans and leave it with risky ones. "We don't need more credit [for farmers], as proponents of Farmer Mac argue," Sethness claimed. "We need [farm] income sufficient to make people more creditworthy."

As proof of the old axiom that politics makes strange bedfellows, among the other strong opponents to the secondary market was the Rural Caucus of Whitehall, Nebraska, a populist protest group of the first order. The Rural Caucus' opposition, however, was based on the fear that only the big farmers would benefit from the secondary market.

It was further pointed out that much of the difficulty facing Farm Credit was due to the fact that its bonds were locked in with the high interest rates of the 1970s and early 1980s. Carrying this burden meant that the Federal Land Banks would be hard put to compete with commercial banks and insurance companies that would be starting out fresh with the new secondary market. Fears over how a secondary market might affect the System almost scuttled the 1987 credit legislation, or at least delayed it until 1988. The issue almost caused a disruption in bipartisanship at a very crucial stage in the congressional negotiations. For example, Rep. Edward R. Madigan, a Republican from Illinois, the ranking minority member on the House Agricultural Credit Subcommittee, and an influential System spokesman, voted against H.R. 3030 (the House version of the 1987 act), in part because of his opposition to the secondary market.

To add to the difficulty there was the continuing turf struggle between the Agriculture and Banking committees (particularly in the House). In 1987 the Energy and Commerce Committee entered into the arena to get its piece of the action. The secondary market issue added fuel to the fire. The issue was compromised out when the Agriculture Committee agreed to Farmer Mac's being subjected to federal securities laws that included more specific standards for pooling farm loans. This meant also that Farmer Mac's securities would be registered under the Securities and Exchange Commission, something that Farm Credit securities heretofore did not have to do. This compromise is mentioned to illustrate the type of fast and furious action that is often necessary to move a legislative stalemate off dead center. Many feared that the compromise would include Farm Credit henceforth having to report to the banking committees of Congress. Amazingly, Farm Credit still presents its reports within the friendly confines of the agriculture committees.

Another example of this give-and-take was the manner in which problems on the budget were satisfied. The agriculture budget, which already faced a $1.2 billion cut in 1988, was a prime consideration. The administration did not want a Farm Credit bailout to offset these budget savings. These fears were satisfied by a plan advanced by Agriculture Committee Chairman de la Garza to have the first year of the System bailout be financed with a $2.5 billion appropriation that would be offset by the sale of assets from the FmHA loan portfolio. Again, this proposal was advanced at a time when it appeared that all was lost—at least for 1987—on the Farm Credit legislation.

One might assume that congressmen, like Christmas shoppers, would learn from the past and vow that they would avoid the mad dash at the close of the next session. These resolutions are seldom kept and such was the case for the Farm Credit legislation in the fall of 1987. The bill faced a December deadline problem that easily rivaled that of the passage of the Farm Credit legislation during the two previous years. Often delay is calculated; it can pave the way for greater compromise in the eleventh hour. This was true for the Agricultural Credit Act of 1987, which did not receive final approval until December 18 by the House and December 19 by the Senate.

Passage of the legislation was considered something of a miracle in view of the time allotted and the number of problems that had to be surmounted. Despite all the controversy, the House adroitly adopted its version of the Farm Credit Assistance Legislation (H.R. 3030) by a 365–49 vote on October 6, thereby putting the ball in the Senate's court. The Senate, however, was not able to get to the legislation until the first week of December.

It almost looked as though the legislation was jinxed. One of its prime movers, Sen. Richard Lugar, fell in a freak snowstorm that hit Washington, D.C., on Veteran's Day. Surgery was required to repair his broken jaw. He was able, however, to return to the Senate to assist Agriculture Committee Chairman Patrick Leahy in his efforts to ward off crippling amendments to the bill. The Senate voted 87 to 6 on December 4 to adopt its Farm Credit bill (S. 1665). As often happens in Congress, the lopsided vote was not necessarily indicative of the amount of opposition generated.

This action only got the legislation halfway home; there was the matter of compromising out differences in the joint conference of the two committees and getting the bill back to the respective Houses in time for floor action before the December 23 adjournment deadline. Considering the monumental issues involved, the odds were no better than fifty-fifty that the job could get done. As a matter of fact, in early December Senator Dole, a strong supporter of the bill, said the legislation did not have a chance. In fact it never would have happened had not House Speaker Wright and Senate Majority Leader Robert C. Byrd of West Virginia insisted that sufficient time be allotted for debate.

The stickiest issue for the Farm Credit System was the restructuring (reorganization) problem. Fortunately for the System, the Conference Committee did not go along with Representative Stenholm's hard deadline approach. This would have been devastating. Instead, the committee adopted the more permissive Senate version, one which more closely followed the plan advanced by Farm Credit directors at their conference in Sacramento. However, the House conferees did not make the restructuring open-ended. They set their own limitations.

Key structure provisions of the conference report mandated the merger of all Federal Intermediate Credit Banks and Federal Land Banks within six months after the signing of the act, which provided financial assistance to merged banks to prevent stock from being impaired as a result of the merger. The act also required the FLBA and PCA stockholders to vote on whether to merge their associations within six months of the merger of their FLB-FICB. Any merged association would have a PCA corporate structure and would maintain a discount relationship with its district bank.

The Banks for Cooperatives were not overlooked in the act. Their stockholders were required to vote within six months on merging into a consolidated bank for cooperatives. A two-tier vote was to be taken based on the number of cooperatives in the district as well as the total equity interest in the bank. As an added incentive, if eight or more BCs, including the Central Bank for Cooperatives, elected to merge, there would be no territorial limits on where the new national BC or the remaining district BCs may conduct business. If more than one, but fewer than eight district BCs elected to merge, a National Bank for Cooperatives would be formed, which could compete only within the territorial limits of the approving banks. The new National Bank for Cooperatives could maintain service centers in constituent districts and provide separate district BCs with the same services previously received from the Central Bank for Cooperatives.

System stockholders in each of the twelve Farm Credit districts were required to consider within eighteen months of the act's passage a plan for reorganizing the System into no fewer than six districts, and each district would be required to vote on its part of the plan. Interestingly, the act provided for a number of safeguards to assure local control to make the process as painless as possible and to help win over the recalcitrant, some of whom had even gone so far as to sue the System. Among these provisions to safeguard local control were those: (1) requiring a cooling-off period for all mergers, transfer of power and terminations and dissolutions; (2) allowing institutions to terminate Farm Credit System status when certain requirements were satisfied (i.e., when surplus in excess of 6 percent of assets is surrendered to the System); (3) requiring that district and association boards have at least one outside director; (4) permitting associations merged since the 1985 act and prior to enactment of 1987 legislation to petition to reorganize as separate associations; (5) prohibiting district banks from dismissing directors or managers of associations; and (6) prohibiting district banks from dismissing directors or managers of associations.

In looking at the fine print, Farm Credit System stockholders were free under the bill to vote down merger plans, but they faced a penalty for doing so. An effort was made to provide some freedom regarding territorial limitations. The proposal provided that for one year after enactment, an association whose services borders on another district was afforded the option to shift to another Farm Credit district if the association had more in common with the agriculture of that district. Rep. Glenn English, who sponsored this amendment, offered as an example an association in a limited cotton-growing area of his native Oklahoma might want to switch to the Texas Farm Credit District, which is more experienced in cotton production. Although such an amendment was not of earth-shaking importance, it did serve to indicate sensitivity and the desire of Congress to draft all-inclusive legislation, perhaps to avoid having to come back in 1988 for another Farm Credit bill.

The act also clarified the status of co-op borrower stock, making it clear that allocated equities of co-ops (patronage refunds to be paid later to borrowing co-ops), as well as stock and participation certificates, would be protected. It was determined that current stock would be protected for the "revolving cycle" of the loan (until the current loan was paid off), but on future loans stock would be at risk. However, the minimum legal stock requirement was lowered to $1,000, or 2 percent of the loan outstanding, whichever was less.

Traditionally, in a borrower-owned cooperative, ownership was expressed through the purchase of stock. The amount of stock required was between 5 and 10 percent of the value of the loan and was included as part of the loan. However, interest was paid on the full amount borrowed. This requirement irritated some borrowers, but it was not a serious problem until the question of risk was at issue. In the congressional discussions, System borrowers were characterized as being like stockholders in a corporation in the sense that both own equity shares in the cooperation. When a corporation fails, the shareholders receive only what is left after the creditors are satisfied. However, a case was made in behalf of System borrowers that they did not purchase the stock voluntarily; thus they were not investors who had chosen to bear the risk of ownership. Also, realistically, Congress recognized that loss of equity would lead to further borrower flight from the System, making the System's prospects even more bleak.

Of course all the restructuring in the world would not be sufficient without immediate government assistance—a "bailout." An equal amount of finesse was required by the Conference Committee in developing a package agreeable to all parties involved. What evolved was a plan to set up a Farm Credit System Financial Assistance Corporation (replacing the Farm Credit System Capital Corporation), which would administer aid to faltering Farm Credit System institutions. For this purpose, the corporation would be permitted to raise funds up to $4 billion through the issuing of special purpose, fifteen-year uncollateralized and guaranteed bonds. Under the plan, the government would pay all the interest on the bonds for the first five years and one-half of the interest for the second five-year period. Meanwhile, the System pays one-half of the interest for the second five years and all of the interest during the remaining five years in the fifteen-year period.

However, availability of government assistance did not have to await the establishment of the new bond program. Provisions were made for the board of the assistance corporation to dip into the $260 million revolving fund still held by the FCA, which had accumulated as the System paid off the original seed capital provided by the government. Early action on this provision was perhaps triggered by alarms from the System—notably from the Jackson, Mississippi, and Spokane, Washington, Farm Credit districts—that the time for government capital was at hand.

To meet any immediate need for assistance, a three-member assistance board was set up, consisting of the secretary of agriculture, the secretary of the treasury, and a designated third member appointed by the president (a farmer with financial affairs credentials). Two of the three board members (a majority) were already on the job and could act immediately because their appointments would not require Senate confirmation. The assistance board's existence was scheduled to be terminated on January 31, 1992. Eventually, the Financial Assistance Corporation would have the same board as the Farm Credit Funding Corporation, which markets Farm Credit securities. Although prohibited from managing assets of the Farm Credit System, the assistance board was granted far-reaching powers over those institutions receiving federal assistance, an indication of the erosion of farmer control of the System. This includes the authority to approve a receiving institution's business, operating, and investment plans and policies.

Also, during the interim between passage of the act and its implementation, the Farm Credit Administration was to play a key role in determining what action was needed to deal with an immediate threat of failure of a Farm Credit bank. The FCA was allowed not only to determine whether financial help was needed, but whether a bank should be merged, or liquidated. Pending availability of funds from the assistance bonds program, the FCA was authorized to use monies from its $260 million revolving fund to provide the government assistance. The FCA's future role was less clear, an indication that the Treasury would continue to be a force in Farm Credit.

As for System loss-sharing, all assessments of the old Capital Corporation were to be returned to the contributing bank, as well as all voluntary loss-sharing accruals since the third quarter of 1986. Simultaneously, there was to be the creation of an accounts payable from the new assistance board to institutions that would have benefitted from the third quarter loss-sharing. A one-time assessment on surplus (i.e., unallocated retained earnings) was imposed on the Farm Credit banks. This was limited to that amount in excess of 5 percent of assets (in the case of the banks) and in excess of 13 percent for the Farm Credit associations. Whether the stronger banks and associations could be persuaded to continue with loss-sharing will go a long way in determining if the System would be able to survive. First it must dig itself out from under a stack of lawsuits and resolve internal conflicts.

Congress also took precautions for the future. The act authorized the creation of an insurance reserve fund to be operated by the FCA. This fund (which was to become available in 1990) was intended to assist Farm Credit institutions and protect investors. Starting in 1989, System institutions were to be required to pay an amount equal to fifteen basis points of their accruing loan volume and twenty-five basis points of their nonaccruing loan volume into the fund. This action also indicated that the System would no longer be permitted to make such judgments on its own.

The 1987 act also contains a Senate provision that any institution has the right to withdraw from the Farm Credit System with stockholder and FCA approval. In so doing, however, the departing institution would have to forfeit all of its capital exceeding 6 percent of its assets to the System's reserves. This was another example of the flexibility written into the legislation. Elements of the System were permitted to secede, but do so at a price.

Although in 1987 the Farm Credit System was successful in its efforts to gain government assistance, there were strings attached. Perhaps the most formidable obstacle was restructuring—not only restructuring of the Farm Credit System itself, but the mandatory restructuring of loans. The loan restructuring provision was included to make sure each farmer's loan was given due consideration before foreclosure action could be taken. Generally, restructuring of loans was called for if such action would be less costly to the System than foreclosure. Repayment capacity of the borrower would be a key factor in making such determinations, too, perhaps a reminder to the System that if this factor had been given more weight over the years, much difficulty could have been avoided.

The loan restructuring program would not come without additional bureaucracy, however. To monitor this activity a Special Assets Council was established in each district, with even more extensive policing to be applied to districts receiving financial assistance. In addition the FmHA was directed to be more liberal in writing down principal and interest in order to avoid putting a borrower off the farm. The thrust of the program was admirable—to make every effort to keep the farmer on the farm.

Another part of the act that had a far-reaching impact on the System was the establishment of a secondary market. The Federal Agricultural Mortgage Corporation—Farmer Mac—was established as a government-sponsored enterprise. It serves as a secondary market and has the power and resources to guarantee its securities. Although chartered as a unit of the Farm Credit System, Farmer Mac has a neutral directorship. It began with a nine-member board appointed by the president, but ultimately Farmer Mac was to be governed by a fifteen-member board—five members elected by the System, five by commercial lenders, and five appointed by the president and confirmed by the Senate. At least two of the five appointed by the president were to have farm connections and no financial connections.

Farmer Mac was limited to real estate mortgages only, including farm and rural housing mortgages. A move to include a separate market for System production and intermediate-term loans was dropped. The act granted clear authority for the System to form one or more pool entities and grants System borrowers a choice between taking a loan with the regular borrower rights protection or one sold in the secondary market. The act did place some limitations on the use of Farmer Mac by commercial banks and insurance companies. The total annual volume cap on loans permitted was $1.6 billion, $3.2 billion, and $6.4 billion for each of the first three years, respectively. Those caps did not apply to loans originated by System institutions.

By the time the Agricultural Credit Act of 1987 was sent to the White House on December 19, 1987, much of the anxiety as to whether President Reagan would sign had been removed. The administration did feel that the terms for Farm Credit System assistance were too easy — that the System should get nothing "interest free." Also, the administration opposed the secondary market, in part because of its possible adverse effect on the System but also because it was strongly opposed to "government-sponsored enterprise" of any kind. In addition, the administration objected to the higher cost assistance programs heaped on FmHA.

Apparently, enough people had conceded on enough points that the administration was persuaded to go along. In any case, President Ronald Reagan, with mixed feelings, signed the measure (Public Law 100-233) on January 6, 1988, with the usual media attention. There were nearly fifty people on hand to witness the signing — mostly members of Congress, but some representing the farm community, including five from the Farm Credit System. Only members of Congress, however, appeared with President Reagan in official photos of the signing.

Celebration was as much for the fact that the legislation was passed as for what it contained. President Reagan's comments were guarded at the signing ceremony. On one hand, the president said that the act "ensures that the Farm Credit System will continue as a principal source of private credit to America's farmers, while at the same time [the law] implements many needed reforms to the System to ensure its long-term viability." On the other hand, he voiced objections to secondary market provisions as being "potentially expensive," urging Congress to remove the new secondary market "as soon as possible," as well as easing the cost burden of the government refinancing program placed upon

FmHA. "It makes little sense to add on new and unnecessary spending in this time of deficits," President Reagan said, urging Congress "to work with us to amend or remove these provisions as soon as possible."

The battle-weary chairman of the Senate Agriculture Committee— Patrick Leahy—indicated to reporters at the signing that he did not think the Senate would respond to the president's request. "We have the Farm Credit bill that's there," Senator Leahy said. "I cannot believe that we're going back to have another Farm Credit bill next year, that it would even be possible."

The Farm Credit System had to be greatly relieved, if not jubilant

FIG. 13.4. *Following ten months of effort and debate, President Ronald Reagan on January 6, 1988, signed the Agricultural Credit Act of 1987 as key congressmen look on. From left to right: Sen. David Karnes of Nebraska; Sen. Richard Lugar of Indiana, ranking Republican on the Senate Agriculture Committee; Sen. Patrick Leahy of Vermont, chairman, Senate Agriculture Committee; Rep. John Dingell of Michigan, chairman of the House Energy and Conservation Committee; Rep. James Jeffords of Vermont; Rep. Bill Schuette of Michigan; Rep. Larry Combest of Texas; and Rep. Edward Markey of Massachusetts. White House photo.*

over the signing. Speaking for the System at the signing, Hugh F. Dailey, long-time director of the Baltimore District and vice-chairman of the Farm Credit Council board, noted that the legislation "reaffirms the importance of the Farm Credit System as a good, solid source of credit for the nation's farmers, ranchers and their cooperatives." Dailey commended Congress for keeping "the needs of System's farmer-borrowers in sharp focus throughout the legislation . . . (and recognizing) the unique nature of the Farm Credit System."

It seemed to this writer that Congress showed great patience with and understanding of the System, particularly as regards reorganization. There was a lot Congress did not know about the complicated Farm Credit System but seemed to take the trouble to learn during enactment of legislation in 1985, 1986 and 1987. On the other hand, Congress has made it plain that there are limits to its patience. As the System was admonished by Senate Agriculture Committee Chairman Leahy at the signing of the 1987 act: "The Farm Credit System exists only to serve farmers . . . and we [the Congress] will not tolerate disregard of this." In drafting the legislation, Congress made a concerted effort to treat all parties fairly. It was obvious, too, that Congress intends to maintain the Farm Credit System.

However, it was also clear that Congress no longer had confidence that the System could put its house in order on its own. There will be continual and everlasting oversight. True, the Agricultural Credit Act of 1987 makes provisions for government money to be paid back when and if the System fully recovers, much in the manner as it was able to repay the original seed capital. However, the System will never be able to regain the independence and status it once held. When the first of the government capital began to flow back into the Farm Credit System, it signified the fall of an empire, but, hopefully, the rebuilding of a new. Whatever happens, it was clear that the cooperative Farm Credit System would never be the same again.

Epilogue

 Wherever and whenever the "fall of the Farm Credit empire" is discussed, the first question asked is: "What went wrong?" Or perhaps more appropriate to matters governmental: "Who is to blame?" Obviously, as these pages have indicated, a lot of things went wrong and a number of people were at fault.

It has been my contention throughout that the number one culprit was the prolonged agricultural depression of the 1980s. Although people become weary (and wary) of statistics—and I have purposely used them sparingly here—there are some that cannot be ignored. For example, agricultural asset values and commodity prices declined drastically during the period. Farmland values across the United States declined some 35 percent between 1981 and 1987. In some parts of the Midwest it was much worse. According to the United States Department of Agriculture, asset values in the Corn Belt fell an average of 50 percent and as much as 66 percent in some states during that period.

While asset values plummeted in the early 1980s, real interest rates moved upward. Federal Reserve Board Chairman Paul A. Volcker was bent on curbing inflation through higher interest rates. Although Volcker achieved a high degree of success, it was partly at the expense of highly leveraged farmers and others who were relying heavily on debt capital. Farmers who succeeded at a time when real interest rates charged by the Federal Land Banks were negative, now were confronted with interest rate payments beyond their capability to service. Higher interest rates were proving to be too heavy a burden for many farmers.

Falling farm prices were also at the heart of the System's problems. Farmers stood by almost helplessly as their markets dwindled, particularly overseas. Historically, moving food and fiber overseas served as something of a safety valve in surplus situations. Generally, too, there had been the option of switching to other crops. In the 1980s none of these options appeared available to farmers. Each problem seemed to compound itself, impacting severely on the farmer and, therefore, on the lender as well.

By early 1987 the System had sustained nearly $5 billion in losses during the two preceding years and was carrying $6.8 billion in what were tagged nonaccrual loans; $5.8 billion in other high-risk loans; and over $1 billion in acquired properties. Farm Credit System loan volume—in the $80 billion range in the early 1980s—dropped to below $56 billion by 1987.

Digging out was proving to be a slow, arduous task. By the end of 1988 nonaccrual loans had decreased to $3.3 billion. High-risk loans, excluding nonaccruals, decreased to nearly $4.6 billion in the same period. The System's nonearning assets, which consist of nonaccrual loans and other property owned, declined by $2.1 billion to $4 billion during 1988, a reduction of 34.7 percent in a year's time. Nevertheless, the level of nonearning assets remained high at the end of 1988, constituting 7.7 percent of the System's loans.

There are those who blame the ever overoptimistic farmers for the inflationary pickle they had gotten themselves into. Certainly farmers were influenced by accounts of worldwide demands for food and fiber. Agricultural journalists, including yours truly, were among those contributing to this undue optimism, visualizing unlimited opportunities in agriculture. In the late 1970s and early 1980s agricultural trade was skyrocketing, and it appeared there would be no end to foreign demand for United States farm products.

Lauren Soth of the *Des Moines Register,* an elder statesman of agricultural journalism, explained the situation this way: "The farm people who are hurting now made what turned out to be unwise investments and incurred large debts in the 1970s, or speculated in land up until 1982."

One could not blame the farmers entirely for some of the decisions they made. For example, the February 20, 1980, issue of the *Kiplinger Agricultural Letter* told its readers that land prices would continue to rise: "a tripling by 1990 is a fair expectation, average for the U.S. Farmland costing $1,000 an acre now will sell for about $3,000 in nine years." *Kiplinger* indicated that there was little chance of bringing inflation

FIG. E.1. *According to Lauren Soth of the* Des Moines Register, *dean of American agricultural journalists, many nonfarming agricultural specialists contributed to the boom psychology that permeated agriculture from the 1970s up to 1984. Photo courtesy Lauren Soth.*

down, and "the necessary ingredients for continued expansion of farm exports seem to be pretty well in place."

There are many other examples. During this period Merril J. Oster, president of the Professional Farmers of America, predicted that "The exciting decade of the 1980s will create new wealth for the alert, well-informed farmer . . . before 1990 you'd sell $5 bushel corn, $15 soybeans, $8 bushel wheat . . . ."

Most so-called experts were painting the same rosy picture at the turn of the 1980s. As Soth pointed out, "Bankers, including Farm Credit System bankers, agricultural colleges, agribusiness companies, and others were saying the same thing. The press shares responsibility for the boom psychology, but journalists can cite renowned economists who predicted that inflation would continue and that world population would outstrip farm production."

Ed Curran, veteran agricultural observer, was less kind in his analysis:

In our way of thinking, too many in agriculture began carrying the "genius" label because they [farmers] made it big during a time it was all but impossible to fail. The ag economists were there to predict better things (which turned out to be better); the bankers were there to provide loans when needed (after all, farm land values were rising). And, didn't those ag economists say farmers didn't owe enough money? That they had to expand—and go out and borrow more to do so—to get ahead? Finally, there was good old Uncle Sam (in the form of government payments from USDA) to fall back on if things didn't work out.

Inevitably, there were charges of poor management on the part of many in the Farm Credit System and there was a general claim of laxity against the regulatory agency—the Farm Credit Administration—for not recognizing the problem earlier and doing something about it. For the most part, these charges centered around two main areas, both of which could have been avoided by twenty-twenty hindsight. The first misfortune was the timing of bond sales that left the System stuck with high-cost funds. The other was the rapid expansion of loans, caused by more liberal lending practices brought on by the Farm Credit Act of 1971. Land values were elevated well beyond what the land could produce to pay off the loans. Most observers feel Farm Credit System management must bear some responsibility in both instances.

There has been a tendency to equate the Farm Credit System dilemma to that in the savings and loan (S & L) industry, an exercise that tends to put the System in a better light. For one thing, by early 1989, the extent of the government bailout of the System was estimated at around $1 billion. The projected cost of rescuing the S & Ls was set at upwards of $200 billion. Also, although many charged that some actions (or inactions) of Farm Credit management were irresponsible, only in a few instances was it contended that any laws were broken. On the other hand, there will probably be many court actions before the S & L crisis is sorted out.

Actually, by late 1988, the System was being complimented for its recovery efforts. Perhaps the greatest praise at the time was the suggestion—first made by Weldon V. Barton, agricultural representative for the Independent Bankers Association of America—that the "Farm Credit bailout sets a pattern for a FSLIC (Federal Savings and Loan Insurance Corporation) solution." Barton noted that:

> The Farm Credit System and the S & L industry—and their problems—are remarkably similar. Each is a loose conglomeration of hundreds of local lending institutions serving more or less a special class of borrowers: farmers and home buyers. . . . Legislation passed in 1985 and 1987 put real muscle into government regulation of the Farm Credit banks, and is restoring the $50-billion financially troubled to viability.

In any case, a blanket indictment of Farm Credit System management seemed grossly unfair. After all, there were six Farm Credit districts—Springfield, Baltimore, Columbia, St. Louis, Texas, and Sacramento—that managed to remain solvent throughout, without any assistance from their sister banks. In fact, the Farm Credit banks of Springfield, Baltimore, and Texas did rather well, thank you.

Except for adequate management, how does one explain survival of the Farm Credit banks of Texas? Government subsidies of nearly $2 billion had to be pumped into failing Texas savings and loan associations in 1987 alone, and at least one hundred failed Texas S & Ls were consolidated into bigger, healthier units? Also, the comptroller of the currency at that time (1987) reported that Texas had a large number of failed commercial banks that served agriculture.

The Federal Deposit Insurance Corporation (FDIC) reported 184 bank failures in 1987, including 54 agricultural banks (those with 25 percent or more of their lending in agriculture). This figure did not include an additional 21 banks that were bailed out by infusions of capital from FDIC. Indeed, there were more bank failures in 1987 than there have been in any one year since the Great Depression of the 1930s. The record was broken again in 1988, when FDIC reported 200 failed banks in the nation, over half of which (113) were in Texas.

The Texas situation leaves one wondering whether the Farm Credit System's problems were due to environment or to bad management. Or both. Certainly, bad Farm Credit management was a factor. The last FCA governor, Donald E. Wilkinson, has come in for considerable criticism. For some time following his departure from the FCA on March 3, 1986, Governor Wilkinson observed a strict silence, but he did grant an interview soon after his departure to Alan Guebert, of *Top Producer* magazine. He described the FCA's regulatory stance over the years as "free and easy."

Governor Wilkinson admitted that "errors were made," describing the FCA's regulator-to-the-regulated relationship with the System as "incestuous, fatally flawed." Wilkinson said that he "wasn't cold-blooded enough" for the job at times and that he "waited too long to crack the whip on the System."

Perhaps even more significant, Wilkinson did not appear optimistic about the System's future, barring drastic changes. "I do not yet see this private structure [the independent but federated cooperatives of the FCS] making the changes it needs in order to survive. The current structure will surely be its downfall if it doesn't act quickly. It needs to modernize." It is significant to note that Wilkinson's observations were made prior to the passage of the 1987 credit act; otherwise, his outlook for the System might have been more optimistic.

There are just as many in Farm Credit who will argue that the System was doomed to failure in the 1980s because of its roots. Many maintain that the chief problem was that Farm Credit had too many philosophical hangups. It was born in the depression of the 1930s to help farmers. Through the years the Farm Credit System generally had set the ground rules by which production and farm real estate lending was to be conducted. Farm Credit was emotionally, philosophically, and financially tied to agriculture; it had all it eggs in one basket. When agriculture began to deteriorate, many commercial banks and insurance companies were able to pull out. The Farm Credit System was not.

Some of these same people claim that the System was always consumed by a "cockeyed optimism," that rendered it incapable of recognizing its own desperate situation. Additionally, there was a widespread feeling that the cooperative Farm Credit System could never break faith with its own constituents who, after all, had always been assured they were the owners. Nor would Congress let the System off the hook. There always was pressure from members of Congress not to foreclose—not to put the brakes on the already shaky marginal loans, at least not on the loans of their constituents.

Apparently, when push came to shove, Farm Credit could not bring itself to tighten up immediately on its borrowers, who were considered friends and neighbors. The System tried mightily to avoid confrontation with its borrowers. Later, the System realized it had no choice but to jump in and try to cut its losses, lest there be no System available to anyone.

Another school of thought in 1987 was that the System had gotten

FIG. E.2. *The Farm Credit Administration "waited too long to crack the whip on the System," claims Donald E. Wilkinson, the last of the Farm Credit Administration governors. FCA photo.*

too big for its breeches — that it was never the intention of the System's founders for the System to become such a colossus. The most effective spokesman for this view was John Kenneth Galbraith, who, as a young Harvard professor in 1933, developed a paper for the Brookings Institution on the role of Farm Credit in President Franklin D. Roosevelt's New Deal. Galbraith, back at Harvard following a distinguished public service career, claims that "it [Farm Credit] was never intended to be so bank-like as it is today. That's why it is experiencing so many financial problems."

"During the Depression," Galbraith said in 1986, "Farm Credit was a lender to farmers who could not get credit elsewhere. It never tried to compete with the banks, and thus stayed clear of the profit motivation. With the support of Congress, it should once again be redirected to refinance farmers."

Certainly, the remaking of a Farm Credit System as a combination

FIG. E.3. *Dr. John Kenneth Galbraith, Harvard University, claims that farm credit was intended as a lender to farmers who could not get credit elsewhere and that in abandoning its original mission farm credit has invited its own failure. Jane Reed photo, Harvard University.*

cooperative/government lender has been considered. Almost every administration—Republican and Democrat—has approached either the governor of the FCA or the Federal Farm Credit Board with this very proposition. Why not have the System, with all its credit know-how, do both—its own cooperative lending, but also the government-subsidized credit (now handled by the Farmers Home Administration, an agency in USDA)? Just operate out of two "windows," was the proposal—one for "soft" credit, one for "sound" credit. The System declined repeatedly and not always diplomatically. The System simply was too proud of its independent, nonsubsidized status and could not visualize itself handling soft credit. As a result of the troubles of the 1980s, the proposition surfaced again and could not be dismissed out of hand because of the System's weakened condition. Even so, the System has never really changed its position and appears to have dodged the bullet another time.

The System has a useful vehicle for recovery in the Agricultural Credit Act of 1987, but government assistance alone has seldom proved to be a panacea. While the 1987 act was being put together, there were those who joked that the legislation should more properly be called the Agricultural Adjustment Act of 1987, because it is the Accountants, the Attorneys, and the Appraisers who stand to gain the most from its passage.

Given that the rebirth and revitalization of an institution like the Farm Credit System will not be accomplished by laws alone, will the people involved respond sufficiently? Will the System be able to stem the tide of borrower flight and alienation and to convince farmers to return to the fold? Do farmers still have the determination, the desire, and the time for rebuilding their own credit resource? The answers to these questions, not the 1987 act alone, will determine the outcome in the years ahead.

Another "people" question: Does the Farm Credit System have the necessary professional know-how to make a comeback? Many old-timers do not think so. One System veteran decided to take early retirement in the spring of 1988 because "life is too short to stick around for what may come to the Farm Credit System. . . . The System has changed, is changing, and I'm not sure to what good. It's another ballgame altogether, with more and more bankers on boards to run the show."

The old-timer felt that Farm Credit "has lost touch with what really goes on down on the farm. The business is no longer a one-on-one proposition. A lot of our new employees are not farm backgrounded, and aren't all that interested in how things turn out on today's farms. They do not link their own job to it." But, then, as if recalling the nightmare of his past few years on the job, the old-timer sighed and shrugged, "Perhaps that's progress."

There are many who would agree that some change in attitude constitutes progress. Younger System employees sometimes explain it this way: "Agriculture is changing and financial services must change along with it. We're in a larger, much more sophisticated and competitive market. We can no longer survive as a 'mom-and-pop' operation. We must show more vision and avoid some of the pitfalls of the past."

This viewpoint also argues for the Farm Credit System becoming more like regular commercial banks — that is, becoming full-service institutions. By so doing, the System would be in a better position to compete. The System must do this, some argue, if it is to continue as a reliable source of credit and continue to set the standards for agricultural lending. However, this expanded service would require authority from Congress, a move that would doubtless be opposed by commercial bankers.

Some critics point to the System's long-held practice of using average cost pricing, rather than marginal pricing, in its loan rates as an example of past pitfalls. The System got in trouble, they claim, because for a period of time the System was underselling the competition on loans. What it should have been doing was to be charging the going rate and building up reserves. This is easy to say in retrospect, but one cannot fault the System for continuing a policy that had worked so well for so many years. The System's "liberal" lending policies (encouraged by the Farm Credit Act of 1971) are faulted for escalating the price of land, encouraging new farmers to come into farming, and encouraging current farmers to expand. The PCAs are equally blamed for "loaning on just about everything imaginable."

The commercial banks had developed a competitive edge and were in a position to attract some of the borrowers who had fled the System. Although the return to profitability by agricultural banks was slow in 1987, they had progressed to the point of being the largest source of agricultural production lending at year's end, holding nearly 44% of loans outstanding. Production credit associations, on the other hand, held only 15.3 percent. FmHA held 22.8 percent of such debt.

Changing patterns in long-term farm lending, an area in which the Federal Land Banks traditionally had been the dominant lender, were even more striking. The proportion of the long-term loan market held by commercial banks figured to increase substantially with the creation of Farmer Mac (Federal Agricultural Mortgage Corporation), which gives commercial bankers access to a secondary market. By early 1989 over 1600 commercial bankers had become members of Farmer Mac by purchasing stock and becoming part owners. Farmer Mac's initial capital offering was oversubscribed. On the basis of the interest evidenced by the commercial banks and other indicators, Farmer Mac officials were predicting it would account for about $5 billion a year in real estate loans. Even though the System faced tougher competition with the availability of Farmer Mac, the fact that the commercial banks were showing profitability in farm lending had a positive impact on Farm Credit. It was an indication that agriculture must be headed out of the doldrums.

There were other indications of a rising confidence in agriculture. The *Report of the National Commission on Agricultural Finance* was released in February 1989. The thirteen-member commission authorized by the Farm Credit Act of 1985 got off to a slow start because of funding problems but was in action in time to proclaim that the "the agricultural sector has adequate total credit available. Intermediation mechanisms are generally working. A healthy degree of competition exists."

The commission claimed that "the marketplace should allocate credit flows, and restrictions, where they exist, should be removed." It was time for the federal government to back off, the commission declared, voicing its concerns "that national policies which use subsidized credit programs to address farm income problems misdirect resources and create inefficiencies." In other words, business as usual.

Outwardly, the course of the Farm Credit System since the passage of the 1987 act appeared to give credence to its claim of recovery. True, the Federal Land Bank of Jackson had failed, the first time in Farm Credit System history that a bank had been placed in liquidation. This served as a constant reminder of the System's "fall," but this black mark was also being erased. The Farm Credit Banks of Texas purchased the loans of the Jackson Land Bank and had its charter changed so it could serve the three states of the Jackson District — Alabama, Mississippi, and Louisiana.

The fate of the FICB of Jackson and the two PCAs serving the district had not been determined at the turn of 1989, but it was presumed that it would be taken over by neighboring Farm Credit districts. The Jackson Bank for Cooperatives presented no problem; it had been merged into the new National Bank for Cooperatives.

There was fairly good news, too, from the Farm Credit Banks Funding Corporation in New York City. On March 1, 1989, a 1988 net income for the System of $704 million was reported, compared to a net loss of $17 million in 1987. The figures included increases over the previous year of $278 million in net interest income and of $81 million in gain on the sales of other properties owned, which contributed to the improvement. The second quarter 1989 figures looked even better.

Detracting from the year's performance by the System was the fact that the well banks still faced some set asides for losses, including $140 million additional for the Jackson Land Bank liquidation. In addition, there were other financially strapped units within the System that needed help. There was, for example, an $81 million "extraordinary" charge relating to the Farm Credit Bank of Omaha's restructuring of liabilities, and $93 million more was required by two other banks, for a total of

$174 million in debts. This provided a severe drag on the System's overall performance for the year.

As FCA Board acting chairman Marvin R. Duncan observed early in 1989, "Although progress has been made, the System still had $9.5 billion in adversely classified loans and more than $700 million in acquired properties at the end of the third quarter of 1988." Despite the degree of difficulty, Duncan said that in the Agricultural Act of 1987, "the (System) banks and associations not only have the tools to restructure themselves, but the tools with which to return to financial stability."

In part, Duncan was referring to that portion of the 1987 act that had established a Farm Credit Assistance Corporation and a board to manage the issuance of up to $4 billion in government-guaranteed bonds. Of that amount, nearly $3 billion in bonds were authorized for 1988 and 1989. However, because of improvements in the farm sector and the success of some of the System's reorganization actions, it began to look as though less financial assistance would be needed than anticipated—perhaps only $1 billion of the $4 billion authorized. In fact, Eric Thor, CEO of the FC System Assistance Board, indicated in mid-February 1989 that "most of the financial institutions in the Farm Credit System do not need any more [help]."

In 1989 the System's report card showed improving grades. The news was good, prompting some in the press, including the American Farm Bureau Federation to proclaim, "Farm Credit System Recovering After 1987 Assistance Act." This improvement was confirmed in an updated *Issue Brief of the Congressional Research Service of the Library of Congress*. Compiler Ralph Chite, former economist with the Farm Credit Administration, provided a positive analysis of the implementation of the Agricultural Act of 1987.

Although guardedly optimistic, the perception was that the agricultural economy was getting better, despite some lingering concern in many areas over the drought. Editors of *Agricultural Outlook* magazine observed in early 1989 that "The farm finance outlook is favorable, in large part because of the continued strength of crop and livestock sales. Slightly higher commodity sales totaling $148–$152 billion, are forecast."

Part of this optimism stemmed from rosier reports on world trade. Export tonnage for fiscal 1988 was pegged at nearly 148 metric tons, up about 15 percent from 1987. According to a USDA forecast, export volume was expected to drop about 8 percent in 1989, but the value of these exports was expected to continue upward—to about $36.5 billion.

As Peter J. Heffernan, economist for the Federal Reserve Bank of Chicago, commented: "With U.S. agricultural exports expected to rise again this year, the U.S. agricultural surplus will likely register a third consecutive annual increase. At 15.5 billion, the agricultural trade surplus is expected to be up almost 7 percent from last year and almost triple the low recorded in fiscal 1986." This is still well below the record excess of exports over imports set in fiscal 1981 ($26.6 billion), but it is encouraging.

Another positive factor in the trade equation was President George Bush's appointment of former U.S. special trade representative Clayton K. Yeutter as Secretary of Agriculture. Yeutter is a former president of the Chicago Mercantile Exchange and a former assistant secretary of agriculture. An agriculturally oriented Nebraskan, Yeutter was once considered as a possibility for governor of the Farm Credit Administration. Even so, Yeutter has never been considered particularly favorably dis-

FIG. E.4. *When the district Federal Land Banks merged with the Federal Intermediate Credit Banks in 1988, the "s" was dropped from the office signs throughout the country, shown above symbolically by Gene L. Swackhamer, president in the Baltimore district. Swackhamer was one of the few top Farm Credit executives able to survive the System trauma of the 1980s. Photo courtesy Farm Credit Banks of Baltimore.*

posed toward farmer cooperatives—and that includes the cooperative Farm Credit System.

The Agricultural Credit Act of 1987 also mandated much restructuring within the System. Has the System carried out these dictates? What kind of report card does the System rate here? Perhaps, a C-minus. The Farm Credit System did what it was forced to do and little more. By July 6, 1988, the Federal Land Bank and the Federal Intermediate Credit Bank in eleven of the twelve districts (the Jackson district no longer a factor) merged to form a single Farm Credit bank in each district, for example, the Farm Credit Bank of Baltimore.

There is a feature in the 1987 act that would permit PCAs to merge with their FLBA counterparts. Some of this action was going forward but with considerable difficulty. Local PCAs and FLBAs most often do not serve the same territories, and their federal income tax status is different (FLBAs are not subject to tax; PCAs are). PCAs are also direct lenders while FLBAs are essentially agents of the FLBs. The tax issue is perhaps the most significant roadblock. Instinct tells the System that when a taxed organization is merged with one that is tax exempt the entity that emerges shall be taxed. With all the other problems standing in the way of the System's remaining competitive, an additional tax burden was unwelcomed. Interestingly, the long-standing animosity between FLBAs and PCAs appeared to be less of a deterrent to merger. Survival had become the overwhelming issue.

Another controversial provision in the 1987 act would permit an association whose chartered territory adjoins another Farm Credit district to petition to become affiliated with that district. It is possible, too, for a Farm Credit institution to terminate its federal charter (to leave the System) and obtain another type of charter. One can easily recognize that although the 1987 act offers much to the System in the way of healing powers, it also contains a great potential for added chaos.

Another provision of the act would allow the merger of entire Farm Credit districts. During the legislative process on the act, Rep. Charles W. Stenholm of Texas, among others, sought to make such mergers mandatory, aiming to reduce the twelve districts down to at least six. Based on his past experience with the Farm Credit System on such matters, Stenholm even proposed a deadline for completion. Neither the mandatory nor deadline provisions survived in the final version of the bill, perhaps a great mistake. At this writing no mergers of Farm Credit districts had taken place and none were contemplated.

The Banks for Cooperatives, on the other hand, fulfilled their obligations to the 1987 act. The BCs accomplished a merger, but not without considerable difficulty. At least, eleven of the thirteen banks did. On January 1, 1989, these eleven banks, including the Central Bank for Cooperatives, started operations in Denver as the National Bank for Cooperatives (CoBank). This bank is not to be confused with (but doubtless will be) the National Cooperative Bank (initially the National Consumer Cooperative Bank) of Washington, D.C. The fact that two of the district Banks for Cooperatives — Springfield, Massachusetts, (which serves New England, New York, and New Jersey), and St. Paul (serving Michigan, Minnesota, North Dakota, and Wyoming) — did not join in the new CoBank presents a curious situation. Under the law, these two banks and the bank created by the merger are both permitted to serve all fifty states and Puerto Rico.

The System must concede that no great strides have been made by way of simplification of the System, not even in terms of its bulky nomenclature. For every organization that has been abolished or merged, others were added, the Farm Credit Corporation of America and the Farm Credit Financial Assistance Corporation, for example. True, the Assistance Corporation is scheduled to be phased out when the System is able to pay off its obligations to the government. Farmer Mac — although definitely not exclusively a vehicle of the System — also contributes to the complexity of agricultural finance.

At one point in the restructuring, it was taken for granted by many that the FCC/A, the FC Council and System's fiscal agency. (Farm Credit Banks Funding Corporation) would be merged. In 1989 there has been less talk of this because the System was not prepared to permit any one entity so much power. An ad hoc board/management workgroup on System services came up with a recommendation to divide the responsibilities. The Farm Credit Council and the Farm Credit Corporation of America would be consolidated into a trade association under the plan, focusing only on two main areas — providing various services to the banks and the leadership for the political action.

According to the workgroup's recommendation, the Funding Corporation would not merge but rather would take on a wide range of other responsibilities. In addition to handling the sale of securities for the System, the FCBFC would take over the audit committee and the handling of the Systemwide audit. In addition, it would set accounting and financial guidelines and standards; credit guidelines, standards, and monitoring; and would handle financial reporting and forecasts, financial planning, and business planning. Many of these responsibilities were originally handled by the Farm Credit Administration and were transferred to the FCC/A when the FCA decided to put itself at "arm's length" from the System.

There were those who had hoped for the emergence of a strong, single-voiced central entity to guide and lead the System and maintain proper discipline over it. It was not to be. The System will apparently continue to speak in many tongues. Since the signing of the 1987 act, much has been accomplished by the System, but much was left undone.

If anything, the Farm Credit System will probably act less like a nationwide system. As pointed out by economist David Freshwater: "The FCS (Farm Credit System) is still a federated cooperative where loyalties are primarily to the local organization, not the FCS as a whole. By strengthening the associations at the expense of the banks the Act may have weakened the FCS in the long run. Without the banks to act as a centralizing or unifying force, the associations may move toward even more autonomous behavior."

In the area of minimizing politicization, the Farm Credit System flunked out. A higher degree of federal control accompanied federal assistance and has been partly manifested through political appointments at the top levels, notably in the Farm Credit Administration and the Assistance Corporation. This is a condition that will likely prevail long after the System repays the government bailout.

It became obvious as the System moved into 1989 that any further actions would be handled by a new staff. The flight of farmers and employees had been widespread. In 1989 there was no indication that a new "phantom group" would emerge. Most of the old members were gone. Many other potential leaders slid into early retirement, some were forced out by mergers and other career-threatening circumstances. The principals in the battle over the Farm Credit Act Amendments of 1986—H. Brent Beesley, CEO of FCC/A, and Frank W. Naylor, Jr., chair of the FCA Board—had departed. Gone also from the FCA Board was Naylor's chief adversary—Jim Billington, the Democratic representative. Although congressional changes were minimal, the System had lost one of its greatest friends—Chair Ed Jones of the House Agricultural Credit Subcommittee, who retired.

Because of the newly acquired partisan political orientation at the top and other frailties, doubts remained as to Farm Credit Administration's competence as a professional organization capable of regulating the cooperative Farm Credit System. The jury is still out at this writing, but the consensus seems to be that things will be "ok," thanks to the number of professionals the FCA had inherited and retained and to a few prudent selections made since 1985. Also, some are comforted by the fact that the FCA will remain under the watchful eye of Congress and the public and will receive greater scrutiny from the United States Treasury.

The FCA also obtained another safeguard, a full-time inspector general, an appointment necessitated by the Inspector General Act Amendments of 1988. Interestingly, the FCA selected Eldon W. Stoehr (a long-time FCA employee, not a political partisan) for the post.

All in all, at the turn of 1989, one would have to concede that a spirit of optimism prevailed over Farm Credit. Confidence was returning. One observer who attended the annual meeting of the Farm Credit Council in Hawaii in January 1989 observed, "The atmosphere was as though nothing bad had ever happened. It was like business as usual."

Once again, favorable press for the Farm Credit System began to reappear in 1989. For example, the June 18 *Washington Post* ran a lengthy article headlined "Farm Credit System: Back from the Brink. Rescue of Banks Abounds with Lessons on Bailouts." The May 14 *Denver Post* headlined its piece "Farm Credit Sees Black Ink. Bailout Critics Change Tune as Lenders' Losses Disappear." The Farm Credit Corporation (FCC/A) thought enough of both articles to reprint and distribute them far and wide.

However, in early 1989 the best advice for the Farm Credit System was not to become overconfident. According to Eric Thor, the CEO of the Farm Credit Assistance Board, "We will not know whether this thing [the bailout] is as highly successful as some people are touting for two to three years."

Is confidence in the cooperative Farm Credit System justified? Or is it just more of the same "cockeyed optimism" that permeates agriculture with the advent of another spring? One cannot be sure. Many issues still have to be worked out before a determination can be made. There remains, for example, the question of whether the elements of the System will be able to cooperate and operate as a System. But in view of its past — and in spite of all that happened in the 1980s — one has to like the System's chances. Certainly, I would never bet against the cooperative Farm Credit System!

References

BOOKS

Hoag, W. Gifford. *The Farm Credit System . . . History of Financial Self-Help.* Danville, Ill.: Interstate Printers and Publishers, 1987.
Knutsen, Fred A. *Origins of the Federal Farm Credit Board.* Washington, D.C.: Farm Credit Administration. 1978.

ARTICLES

Berry, John M. "Farm Credit System: Back From the Brink." *Washington Post* 18 June 1989.
"Business Failure Record." *Dun & Bradstreet.* 1987.
Barton, Weldon V. "Commentary: FC Bailout Sets Pattern for FSLIC Solution." *American Banker.* 7 Dec. 1988.
Cameron, Zita. "American Expert Doesn't Understand." *Atlantic Cooperator.* Sept. 1986.
"Capitol People." *American Banker.* 6 Oct. 1986.
"The Debt Is as High as an Elephant's Eye." *The Economist* [London]. 20 Sept. 1985.
Dietrich, Barbara. "Suing the PCA." *Farm Futures.* Mar. 1986, 10–11.
Freshwater, David. "The Political Economy of Farm Credit Reform: The Agricultural Act of 1987." 5 May 1989.
Galbraith, John Kenneth. "The Reagan Syndrome." *Top Producer.* Sept. 1986.
"The Golden Years Are Gone for Co-ops." *Business Week.* 23 July 1984, 156–59.
"Government Fat Cats Harvest Big $$$." *National Enquirer.* 7 Jan. 1986.
Guebert, Alan. "Errors Were Made." *Top Producer.* June/July 1987.
Harl, Neil E. "A Proposal for Interim Land Ownership and Financing through an Agricultural Financing Corporation." *Journal of Agricultural Taxation and Law.* Spring 1986, 19–33.

_____. "Harl on Ag Law." *Agri Finance*. Apr. 1986, 12–13.

Harsh, Jonathan. "Easy Money Is No Favor." *Farm Futures*. May 1984, 20–27.

"Heartland Rebellion." *Village Voice*. 5 March, 1985.

Hoag, W. Gifford. "Joint Ventures Result in Savings." *NCBA Cooperative Business Journal*. Nov. 1987.

"How the Farm Credit Crisis Is Crushing America's Breadbasket." *Business Week*. 18 Feb. 1985, 124–26.

Kaplan, Kim. "Farm Lending's Chairman Eyes Credit Crisis." *American Banker*. 12 Aug. 1985.

Nyberg, Bartell. "Farm Credit Sees Black Ink." *The Denver Post*. 14 May 1989.

Palmer, Lane. "Why Mergers Are Necessary." *Farm Journal*. Aug. 1985, 40.

Richter, Jay. "Farm Credit System Still on Sick List, but 'Demise Greatly Exaggerated.' " *Farmland News*. Mar. 1987.

_____. "Political Meddling over Farm Credit Helm." *Farmland News*. 30 May 1973.

Soth, Lauren. "Commentary." *Choices*. 1st Quarter 1987, 18.

Swank, C. William. "Up with Agriculture." *Buckeye Farm News*. Dec. 1986.

Taylor, Marcia Zarley. "Why You Pay Millions in Bad Farm Loans." *Farm Journal*. Aug. 1983, 17–19.

_____. "It May Take the Entire Farm Credit System to Keep the Lights on in Louisville." *Farm Journal*. Aug. 1985.

"Tough Talk from Farm Credit Regulator." *Banking Journal*. Nov. 1986.

TRADE PUBLICATIONS

ABA Bankers Weekly
"RAP Replaces GAAP." 14 Oct. 1986.

ABA Banking Journal
"Profitability Returns to Ag Banks." Jan. 1989.

Agricultural Credit Letter
"Billington Clashes with FCA Board Majority." 5 June 1987.
"Congress Puts Watch on Farm Credit Losses." 19 Sept. 1986.
"Grassroots Opposition to Mergers." 18 Oct. 1985.
Webster, Jim. "Board Decides against Firing Governor, but He's Not out of the Woods." 4 Oct. 1985.
_____. "FCS Works Up Alternative to House Bill's 'Stenholm' Reorganization Plan." 4 Sept. 1987.
_____. "Iowa Governor Invokes Emergency Law, Sets Partial Farm Foreclosure Moratorium." 4 Oct. 1985.

Banking Report [Bureau of National Affairs, Washington, D.C.]
"GAO Proposes Federal Takeover of Farm Credit System." 13 Apr. 1987.
"Secondary Market Provisions." 21 Sept. 1987.

Cooperative Business Journal

"Regional Co-ops and Consolidation Talks." Jan.–Feb. 1989.

Drover's Journal
12 Nov. 1986.

FCA Money and Marketing Report
"System Farm Lending Continued Steep Decline in First Quarter." 31 July 1986.

Farm Bureau News
Baier, Dana. "System Recovery after 1987 Assistance Act." 21 Nov. 1988.
King, Jack. "By Spreading Risk, Secondary Market Could Help Borrowers." 9 Mar. 1987.
Kleckner, Dean. "Open Letter to Farm Bureau Members." 6 July 1987.
Lipton, Don. "FB Calls for Prompt Federal Aid for Farm Credit System." 30 Mar. 1987.

Farm Credit Letter [Farm Credit Corporation of America]
"Farm Credit System's Recovery Proposal for $6 Billion in Federal Assistance." May 1987.
"Farm Credit System Sets Strategic Objectives." Mar.–Apr. 1986.
"High Interest Rates Hurt Farmers and Lenders." Sept.–Oct. 1986.
"New Legislation Would Change FCA's Approval Authorities." Sept.–Oct. 1986.
"Offering Competitive Interest Rates." Mar.–Apr. 1986.
"Ten Principles." Oct. 1985.

Farm Credit Update, Farm Credit Administration, Apr. 1984.

Farm Paper Letter
Curran, Ed. "Critics Say USDA's Information Became Politicized." 19 Feb. 1988.
_____. "Most People Who Survived." 8 Jan. 1988.

Food and Fiber Letter
Webster, Jim. "Grapevine: Shakeup at FCA Continues." 2 June 1986.

Inside FCA
"ACC Concept Launched." 2 May 1985.
"Are You Safe?" 9 Jan. 1986.
"Bankruptcy Options." 13 June 1985.
"Ed's Answers." [Report on Ed Harshbarger's appearance at 1986 Denver Farm Forum.] 20 Mar. 1986.
"Family Farm Bailout?" 16 Aug. 1988.
"Farm Relief Bill." 27 Feb. 1986.
"Hardest Decision." 7 Nov. 1985.
"Help or Harm?" 2 Aug. 1984.
"Local Control—The Central Issue." 15 Aug. 1985.
"More Reactions." 19 Sept. 1985.
"NFU Convention." 7 Mar. 1985.
"Rejoins Family." 29 May 1986.
"Violence: Growing Rural Concern." 27 Feb. 1986.
"What Would You Do?" 20 Feb. 1986.

The Insider [Farm Credit Council]
  "Gratitude Expressed for Vote by Congress." 19 Dec. 1987.
  "Sen. Lugar Introduces Farm Credit Bill Today." 10 July 1987.
  "System Structure Proposal Calls for Orderly Down Sizing." 4 Aug. 1987.
Legislative Report [St. Louis Farm Credit Council]
  O'Day, John J. "Farm Credit Act Amendments of 1986."
Northwestern Banker Newsletter
  "Mixed Reaction to Iowa Moratorium." 7 Oct. 1985.
Washington Update
  Frederick, Bob. "Secondary Farm Mortgage Market Worth $27 Billion to U.S. Farmers." 27 Mar. 1987.
Washington Weekly Report [Independent Bankers Association of America]
  "Agricultural Supplement, Debt Restructuring Proposals." 12 Oct. 1984.

NEWSPAPERS

Columbus [OH] Dispatch
  "Four Countrymark Leaders to Leave." 16 Aug. 1986.
Des Moines Sunday Register
  Perkins, Jerry. "Omaha Banks in Dire Peril." 19 Oct. 1986.
Des Moines Register
  Marbry, Drake. "Farmer Madness."
Fargo Forum
  "Land Bank Officials Discuss Dismissals." 10 Feb. 1985.
Hagerstown [MD] Herald-Mail
  "Brains? Who needs brains . . . ?" (cartoon), 21 Sept. 1985.
Lincoln [NE] Star
  Donaldson, Curt. "Farmers Anonymous."
Omaha World Herald
  "To Stabilize Land Market Ag. Authority Would Buy Farm Land to Resell." 9 Jan. 1986.
Saint Louis Post Dispatch
  "Muzzled (Washington Notebook)." 19 Aug. 1985.
Savannah Morning News
  Anderson, Jack. "Boondoggle." 4 Oct. 1985.
USA Today
  "The Third Time's a Charm for Farm Aid." 21 Sept. 1987.
  "Way to Held Farmers Is to Cut All Aid." 16 Aug. 1985.
Wall Street Journal
  "Blighted Ledgers." 7 Oct. 1985.
  McCoy, Charles F. "Out of Options, Farm Credit System Buried in Bad Loans." 4 Sept. 1985.
  _____. "Many Farmers May Face Loan Cutoffs." 24 Feb. 1986.

"Plan Speeding through Congress to Let Farm Credit System Mask Huge Losses." 3 Oct. 1986.

Washington Post

"Bank Board to Bail Out Insolvent Texas S&Ls." 4 Feb. 1988.

Berry, John M. "Farm Credit Ready to Paper over Its Red Ink." 12 Oct. 1986.

"Farm Aid III Draws 68,000." 21 Sept. 1987.

McAllister, Bill. "Reagan Signs Farm Credit Bill." 7 Jan. 1988.

Sinclair, Ward. "Aiding Farm Credit Agency Has Funds for Board Members to Travel Abroad." 24 Nov. 1987.

_____. "Sandpapery 'President's Man.' " 8 Dec. 1986.

Marjorie Williams. "Lean and Hungry." 5 Aug. 1986.

Wichita Eagle-Beacon

"Farm Credit Bailout Exec. Sees Hope for the System." 20 Feb. 1989.

WIRE SERVICES AND PRESS RELEASES

"Branstad Urges Reagan to Endorse System Bailout." Associated Press wire story, 17 Oct. 1985.

Cenex Corporate Communications Department, "Young Farmers See Farming as a Way of Life." Press release, St. Paul, Minn. 28 Jan. 1986.

Currier, Chet. "Tough Times for the Farm Credit System." Associate Press Business Wire, 18 Oct. 1985.

"Farm Credit to Need Bailout?" Associated Press (wire story), 24 Feb. 1987.

Federal Farm Credit Banks Funding Corporation. "Farm Credit System Reports Net Income of $704 Million for 1988." News release, 1 Mar. 1989.

Hillgren, Sonja. "Creative Accounting May Help Farm Credit System." United Press International (wire story), 10 Oct. 1986.

ADDRESSES

Block, John R. Address to the National Corn Growers Association, Cedar Rapids, Iowa, 29 July 1985.

Duncan, Marvin R. "The Restructuring of the Farm Credit System." Address to the Western Regional Coordinating Committee of the FCA Board, Phoenix, Ariz., 12 Jan. 1989.

Fredrickson, C. T. "The Future of Cooperatives." Address to the 1986 annual meeting of the National Council of Farmer Cooperatives.

Galbraith, John Kenneth. "Agricultural Policy: Ideology, Theology, and Reality Over the Years." Address to the National Governor's Conference, Traverse City, Mich., 27 July 1987.

Jones, Ed. Address to National Conference of Farm Credit Directors, Jackson Hole, Wyo., 17 Sept. 1985.

Wilkinson, Donald E. Address to the American Institute of Cooperation, University of Kansas, Manhattan, Kans., 1 Aug. 1985.

———. Address to the National Conference of Farm Credit Directors, St. Louis, Mo., Sept. 1985.

UNPUBLISHED MATERIAL

American Bankers Association. "Transition in Agriculture: A Strategic Assessment of Agricultural Banking, 1986." Research study.

Cooperative League of the USA. Policy resolutions, 1984.

Farm Credit Board of Spokane. "Restoring Financial Viability." Proposal to the Federal Farm Credit Board, Nov. 1984.

Farm Credit Corporation of America. *Project 1995 — A Look to the Future.* Report, 1986.

Farm Credit Corporation of America. "A Proposal to Consolidate the Banks for Cooperatives." Report, July 1987.

Federal Farm Credit Board. "Dealing with Stress in Agriculture." Resolution adopted by the Federal Farm Credit Board, Feb. 1985.

———. Minutes of meeting, Oct. 1985.

———. Resolution adopted for approval of Farm Credit District Boards, Mar. 1985.

Fredrickson, C. Terry, and Ben Sunbury. "Failure: The Farm Credit System . . . A Funny Thing Happened on the Way to Dominance." Program presented at the Annual Planning Conference of the Federal Farm Credit Board, Point Clear, Ala., Feb. 11–14, 1982.

———. "Success: The Farm Credit System . . . Where the Best Provide Themselves with the Best." Program presented at the Annual Planning Conference of the Federal Farm Credit Board, Asheville, N. C., April 26–28, 1983.

Irwin, George. "Agency Status." Policy paper, 1983.

Louisville Farm Credit District Presidents' Committee. "August *Farm Journal* Article." Memo to all Farm Credit Bank Presidents and to the FLBAs, PCAs, and cooperative borrowers with the Louisville Farm Credit District and to all employees of the Louisville Farm Credit Banks, 28 July 1983.

National Farmers Union. "Working Paper on Agricultural Credit," 1987.

National Rural Electric Cooperative Associations. Policy resolutions, 1984.

Powers, Michael J. "Interest Rate Reductions." FCA memo to CEOs of each Farm Credit System institution, 28 Oct. 1986.

CORRESPONDENCE AND INTERVIEWS

Farm Credit Administration staff members. Interviews granted at a public hearing in Ames, Iowa, Aug. 1985.

Farm woman. Letter to director, Federal Farm Credit Board, Aug. 1985.

Hendrix, Bill. Letter to White House, 25 Aug. 1986.

Hovendick, Donald L. Personal letter to author, 29 Aug. 1985.

Irwin, George D. Interviews with author.

Jones, Ed. Letter of response to the Farm Bureau, 10 July 1987.

Smith, Virginia, Rep. "Dear Colleague Letter," July 1985.

Terrell, Joseph. Farm Credit Council. Interview with author, 18 Oct. 1985.

GOVERNMENT PUBLICATIONS

Department of Agriculture. Agricultural Cooperative Service. "Cooperative Principles and Practices." *Farmer Cooperatives.* Washington, D.C.: GPO, July 1984.

_____. "Hofstad Urges Co-ops to Gather under Umbrella of Cooperation." *Farmer Cooperatives.* Washington, D.C.: GPO, Oct. 1986.

Department of Agriculture. Economic Research Service. *Year-End Update of U.S. Agriculture, 1987.* Washington, D.C.: GPO,

Farm Credit Administration. *Banks for Cooperatives . . . A Quarter Century of Progress.* Circular E-47.Washington,D.C.:GPO,

_____. *The Farm Credit System in the 70's and Appendix.* Report of the Commission on Agricultural Credit, Mar. 1970.

_____. [Arnold, C. R. (Cap).] *Farmers Build Their Own Production Credit System.* Circular E-45.

_____. "FCA Board Approves Regulations Implementing Regulatory Accounting." *FCA Bulletin.* Dec. 1986.

_____. *1988 Farm Financial Outlook-Cautious Optimism.* Agricultural Situation Report. USDA. 18 Dec. 1987.

_____. *Salaries of CEOs of Farm Credit Banks.* Farm Credit Administration, 1985.

Federal Deposit Insurance Corporation. *1988 Bank Closings and Assistance Transactions by States, as of 31 Dec. 1988.*

_____. "U.S. Bank Failures and Assistance Actions, 1987."

Federal Reserve Bank of Chicago. "Agricultural Exports." *FRD of Chicago Agricultural Letter,* 31 Dec. 1988.

General Accounting Office. "Farm Credit—Action Needed on Major Management Issues." Report to the Chairman, Subcommittee on Conservation, Credit, and Rural Development, Committee on Agriculture, House of Representatives. Washington, D.C.: GPO, 1986.

_____. "Farm Finance—Secondary Markets for Agricultural Real Estate Loans." July 1987.

———. General Government Division. *Farm Credit Administration's Liquidation of Production Credit Associations.* Report to Congress. Washington, D.C.: GPO, 1985.

———. *Preliminary Analysis of the Financial Condition of the Farm Credit System.* Report to Congress. Washington, D.C.: GPO, 1985.

Library of Congress. Congressional Research Service. *Implementation of the Agricultural Credit Act of 1987.* Washington, D.C.: GPO, 1989.

U.S. Congress. House. Committee on Government Operations. *FCA's Role in the System's Crisis: 29th Report by the Committee on Government Operations.* 99th Congress, 2nd Session, 1986.

U.S. Congress. Senate. *Beesley, H. Brent. Statement to the Committee on Agriculture, Nutrition, and Forestry.* 99th Congress, 2nd Session, 1986.

LEGISLATION

Agricultural Credit Act of 1987.

Cooperative Marketing Associations Act [Capper-Volstead Act]. U.S. Code. Vol. 42, stat 388 (1922).

Family Farmer Bankruptcy Act of 1986, PL 99-554 [H.R. 5316], Oct. 27, 1986.

Farm Credit Act Amendments of 1980. U.S. Code. Vol. 94, stat 3437 (1980).

Farm Credit Act of 1933. U.S. Code. Vol. 48, stat 257 (1933).

Farm Credit Act of 1971. U.S. Code. Vol. 85, stat 583 (1971).

Farm Credit Amendments Act of 1985. U.S. Code. Vol. 98, stat 1678 (1985).

Farm Credit System Borrower Interest Rate Relief Act of 1986, in OMNIBUS Budget Reconciliation Act of 1986, PL 99-509 (Subtitle D—Farm Credit Institutions), Sec. 1031-37 (1986).

Federal Farm Loan Act. U.S. Code. Vol. 39, stat 360 (1916).

COURT CASES

Federal Land Bank of Springfield, Federal Intermediate Bank of Springfield, Springfield Bank for Cooperatives, Federal Land Bank of Texas, Federal Intermediate Bank of Texas and the Texas Bank for Cooperatives v. Farm Credit Administration and Farm Credit System Capital Corporation. United States District Court, District of Massachusetts, 19 Feb. 1987.

Holdman et al. v. FCA. Aug. 1984.

Index

Advertising Council of Cooperatives, International, 149
Agency for International Development, xii, 24
"Agency Status," 17–18
"Aggie bonds," 104
Agricultural Conservation Corporation, 106
Agricultural Credit Act of 1987, 8, 10, 14, 165, 224, 230, 232, 244, 246
Agricultural Credit Letter, 59, 221
Agricultural Extension Service, 25
Agricultural Outlook, 244
Agway, Inc., 161
Aiken, George D., 134, 140
Allbee, Roger, 130, 207
Amdahl, Burgee, 88, 118
American Agriculture Movement, 110, 126, 219
American Bankers Association, xiv, 17, 182, 197, 203, 214
American Institute of Cooperation, 42
Anderson, George (Bus), 174
Anderson, Jack, 63
Andrews, Mark, 25, 210
Andrus, Dwayne, 160
Archer Daniels Midland, 160
Atlantic Cooperator, 159
Auberger, Kenneth J., 177
Auer, Ken, 129

Bacon, Larry H., 177–78
Baer, Kenneth, 164
Bandow, Doug, 54

Banking Journal, 182, 200
Banks for Cooperatives, 7, 69, 145, 153, 220, 225
Banner, Delmar K., 93, 118, 129
Barratt, William F., 33
Barton, Weldon V., 236
Bedell, Berkley, 218
Beesley, H. Brent, 92, 124, 175, 189, 190, 195, 211, 248
Bellmon, Henry, 111
Bennett-White, Reider J., 130
Benson, Ezra Taft, 137
Bergland, Bob, 137, 151
Billington, James R., 186, 207, 209, 248
"Black Wednesday," xiii, xiv, 29
Block, John R., 42, 62, 137, 174
Boren, David L., 70, 186, 208, 212, 217
Borrower flight, 31
Boschwitz, Rudy, 89, 217
Bowersox, Kim C., 178
Bowsher, Charles, 213
Boyd, Francis J., 178
Branstad, Terry, 53, 61–62
Bronson, Michael A., 177
Brooks, D. W., 156
Buffington, Arthur C., 36–37, 88
Bush, George, 62, 163
Business Week, 40, 154
Byrd, Robert C., 225

Cameron, Zita, 159
Capper-Volstead Act of 1922, 147–48, 151
Carpenter, Cy, 105

Carter, James E., 135, 140, 151
Catholic Rural Life Conference, 33
Cato Institute, 54
Cenex, 155, 160, 165
Central Bank for Cooperatives, 7, 17,
    162, 164, 220, 225
Chite, Ralph, 244
Clark, Vance, 113
Clayton Act, 147
CoBank, 165
Cochran, Thad, 193, 200
Coleman, Tom, 125, 199
Columbus Dispatch, 161
Commission on Agricultural Credit, 143
Competitive Banking Act of 1987, 198
Congressional Research Service, 244
Conrad, Kent, 210
Consolidated Family Farms, 105
Cook, Alton B., 32, 92, 118
Cooley, Harold D., 134–35
Cooperative Communicators
    Association, 149
Cooperative Editorial Association, 149
Cooperative League of the USA, 100,
    102, 149
Countrymark, Inc., 155, 161
Cowden, Howard A., 156
Curran, Ed, 39, 181
Currier, Chet, 50

Dailey, Hugh F., 232
Daniels, Gloria Conant, 141
DeBaghi, Bill, 129
Debt Adjustment Program, 109, 114
de la Garza, E. (Kika), 123, 199, 210,
    221, 224
Denver Farm Forum, 78
Denver Post, 249
Des Moines Register, 39, 52
DeVuyst, Larry, 139
Dole, Robert, 125, 151, 212, 224
Donaldson, Curt, 51
Drovers Journal, 193
Duel directorship, 74
Duncan, Marvin, 173, 208–9, 244

Eberly, Sam, 71
Economist, 46
Edwards, Larry W., 58

Eidam, John E., 156
Eisenhower, Dwight D., 134–35, 138
Ellender, Allen J., 134
English, Glenn, 58, 226
Erickson, Ronald H., 41, 57
Evans, Cooper, xi, 41, 60
Exon, James J., 128

Family Farm Bankruptcy Act of 1986,
    108
Family Farm Movement, 33
"Farm Aid," 109–10
Farm Bloc, 55
Farm Bureau Federation, American, 73,
    100, 102, 110, 126, 213, 219, 244
Farm Bureau Federation, Kentucky, 104
Farm Bureau Federation, Ohio, vii, 102,
    155
Farm Bureau News, 214, 219
Farm Credit Act Amendments of 1980,
    20, 123, 169
Farm Credit Act Amendments of 1986,
    197–98, 203, 248
Farm Credit Act of 1933, 6–7, 147
Farm Credit Act of 1953, 9, 12, 133,
    135, 138
Farm Credit Act of 1955, 70
Farm Credit Act of 1971, xiv, xv, 65,
    70, 129, 142, 168, 236, 242
Farm Credit Administration, 12, 64, 89,
    135, 167, 187
Farm Credit Amendments Act of 1985,
    xiv, 9, 13, 90, 126, 129, 133, 141, 144
Farm Credit Assistance Corporation, 14,
    244, 247
Farm Credit Assistance Legislation, 224
Farm Credit Banks: of Baltimore, 237,
    247; of Columbia, 237; of Jackson,
    243; of Louisville, 32, 83; of Omaha,
    35–36, 57, 243; of Sacramento, 157,
    173, 237; of St. Louis, 237; of
    Spokane, 33; of Springfield, 96, 202,
    237; of Texas, 77, 96, 202, 226, 237,
    243; of Wichita, 38
Farm Credit Corporation of America,
    13–14, 88, 91–92, 205, 247
Farm Credit Council, 13, 19, 67, 93,
    100, 216, 247
Farm Credit Leasing Corporation, 14
Farm Credit Letter, 198

Farm Credit System Capital Corporation, 14, 36, 95, 127, 174, 196, 203, 227
Farm Credit System Financial Assistance Corporation, 111, 121, 227
Farm Credit System member stock, 198
Farm Futures, 81
Farm Journal, 32, 73, 83
Farm Loan Act of 1916, 4, 133
Farmer Cooperatives, 146, 163
Farmer Mac, 222, 230, 242, 247
Farmers Home Administration, 26–27, 109, 112
Farr, Thomas N., 32, 88
FCA Board, 90, 127, 180, 208–9
Federal Deposit Insurance Corporation, 237
Federal Farm Credit Assistance Board, 215, 249
Federal Farm Credit Banks Funding Corporation, 10, 14, 243
Federal Farm Credit Board, xi, xv, 9, 56, 127, 133–44
Federal Farm Loan Act, 4–5
Federal Farm Mortgage Corporation, 111, 216
Federal Intermediate Credit Banks, 6–7, 220
Federal Land Bank of St. Paul, 137
Federal Land Banks, 4, 6, 10–11, 68–69, 203, 220
Federal Reserve Board, 90
Federation of Southern Cooperatives, 111
Feland, Armstead M. III, 86, 118
FELCO, 164
Ferguson, Francis E., 95
Financial Assistance Corporation, 14
Foley, Thomas S., 151, 218
Fortune Magazine, 153
Franklin, Ben, 150
Frederick, Bob, 213
Fredrickson, C.T. (Terry), 29–30, 87, 88, 158
Freeman, Orville, 169
Freshwater, David, 200, 247

Galbraith, John Kenneth, 239–40
Gaston, William, 164

General Accounting Office, 60, 195, 198, 213
Gephardt, Richard A., 218
Gold Kist, 156
Graham, Donald E., 153
Grassley, Charles, 57, 125
Great Depression, 6, 21, 68
Greeneisen, Jon F., 130
GROWMARK, Inc., 160
Guebert, Alan, 237

Hagerstown Herald Mail, 54
Hale, Evan, 130
Hammil, David, 137
Hanes, Donald K., 151
Hanlin, Russell, 164
Harding, W. Malcom, 164, 214
Harding, Warren G., 77
Hardy, David M., 156
Harl, Neil, 55, 107–8
Harling, John, 38, 164
Harshbarger, Ed, 78
Harvest States, 155
Harvey, Crete B., 141
Hauenstein, Ben, 95
Heffernan, Peter J., 245
Heitz, Glenn E., 86, 153
Helms, Jesse, 125, 141, 207
Hendrix, Bill, 187
Heritage Foundation, 19
Hiller, Bill, 164
Hillgren, Sonja, 39, 197
Hoag, W. Gifford, viii, 16, 146
Hofstad, Ralph, 160, 163
Holman, Luman, 222
Hope, Clifford R., 134
Hovendick, Donald L., 36–37

Illinois Farm Development Authority, 104
Independent Bankers Association of America, 20, 113, 214, 236
Ingalsbe, Gene, 146
Ingraham, Charles, 162
Inspector General Act Amendments of 1988, 122
Institute for Agriculture and Trade Policy, 111

Iowa Bankers Association, 61
Irwin, George, 17, 144

Jaenke, E. A. (Ed), 74–75, 129, 136,
    142, 170
James, Gene, 164
Johnson, Lyndon B., 135
Jones, Ed, 114, 121–23, 194, 199, 210,
    213, 219, 248

Katz, Jeff, 57
Kendall, Don, 39
Kennedy, John F., 135
Kleckner, Dean, 56, 102, 214, 219
Krueger, Kenneth P., 34
Krumme, Richard, 109

Lake, James, 129
"LaMoure Incident," 84
Land O'Lakes, 160, 163
LaVerghetta, Michael J., 49
Lawrence, J. D., 156
Lawsuits, 77, 80, 202
Leach, Jim, 58
League of Rural Voters, 219
Leahy, Patrick J., 207, 217, 224, 232
Loan moratoria, 103
Lincoln, Murray D., 155
Lincoln Star, 33
Loans to fishermen, 33
Long, Russell, 151
Louisville Courier Journal, 39, 84
Lucas, Grant, 118, 216, 217
Lugar, Richard L., 219, 224
Lyng, Richard, 129

Mabry, Drake, 52
McCarty, Rick, 130
McCoy, Charles F., xii, 112
McDougal, Robert, 86–87
Macklin, Hugh, 54
Madigan, Ed, 125, 199, 223
Martin, Marsha, 130
Mason, Harold T. (Bill), 168
Maziruddin, Junab Kazi, 24
Medero, Fred, 58

Melcher, John, 40
Meriwether, J. Bruce, 61
Mid-America Dairymen, Inc., 160
Minneapolis Star and Tribune, 39
Morgenthau, Henry, Jr., 68
Mowery, Phyllis, 177
Muleta, Joseph, 68
Myers, Bob, 140
Myers, William, 156

National Association of Wheat Growers,
    100
National Bank for Cooperatives, 225,
    247
National Cattlemen's Association, 100,
    219
National Commission on Agricultural
    Finance, 242
National Consumer Cooperative Bank,
    247
National Cooperative Business
    Association, 100
National Conference of Farm Credit
    Directors, 87, 90, 117, 171, 220
National Corn Growers Association, 219
National Cotton Growers Association,
    219
National Council of Churches, 111
National Council of Farmer
    Cooperatives, 100, 137, 149
National Enquirer, 46
National Farmers Organization, 100,
    105, 110, 219
National Farmers Union, 100, 105, 110,
    219
National Federation of FLBAs, 69
National Grange, 100, 213
National Milk Producers Association,
    100
National Pork Producers Association,
    219
National Rural Electric Cooperative
    Association, 100, 101, 137
National Tax Equality Association, 148
National Save the Family Farm
    Coalition, 219
Nationwide Insurance Companies, 155
Naylor, Frank W., Jr., 49, 114, 173, 176,
    181, 184, 190, 200–201, 209, 248

Nelson, Willie, 109–10
Nixon, Richard M., 135, 176

O'Day, John J., 130
Olson, Snell, 157
Omaha World Herald, 39, 104
O'Neill, Tip, 218
Oster, Merril J., 235
Other financial institutions, 7

Palmer, Lane, 73
Pearson, Drew, 64
Peck, Francis W., 156
Pepper, Jerry, 51
Perkins, Jerry, 39
Phantom group, 85
Policy Coordinating Committee, 87
Powers, Michael J., 200
Pranger, Sylvester B., 177
Prior, David, 222
Privatization, 19
Production Credit Associations, 6–7, 10, 68, 203
Professional Farmers of America, 235
Project 1995, 88, 91, 115
Protest groups, 33
Public relations and advertising, 82

Rather, Dan, 40
Reagan Administration, 171–72, 181, 223
Reagan, Ronald, 19, 62, 135, 139, 141, 230
Reclamation Act of 1902, 140
Redmer, Paul C., 185
Reese, Monte, 130
Regulatory Accounting Procedures, 197, 201
Remsberg, J. Homer, 136
Richter, Jay, 39, 136
"Robin Hood principle," 96
Roosevelt, Franklin D., 10, 68, 117
Row, Charles R., 176
Rural Caucus, 223
Rutherford, Edgar C., 140

St. John, John, 93, 156

St. Louis Post Dispatch, 181
Savings and loan association crisis, 236
Scarboro, W. Proctor, 141
Schlader, Raymond L., 32
Schwendiman, Gary, 158
Securities and Exchange Commission, 223
Sethness, Charles O., 200, 223
Shuman, Charles B., 73
Sims, Douglas D., 118, 217
Sinclair, Ward, 39, 185
Smith, Virginia, 60
Soth, Lauren, 234
Special Assets Council, 229
Stark, Pete, 46
Steele, George, 137
Stenholm, Charles W., 220–21, 225, 246
Stockdyk, Ellis A., 156
Stromberg, Roger, viii, 179, 182
Successful Farming, 109
Swackhamer, Gene, 117, 245
Swank, C. William, 102

Taft, Robert A., 150
Talmadge, Herman, 121–22
Taylor, Marcia Zarley, 39
Terrell, Joe, 63, 129
Thatcher, W. M. (Bill), 155
Thayer, Julian B., 142
Thor, Eric, 249
Todd, Melvin J., 106
Tootell, Robert B., 68, 147
Top Producer, 237
Tripp, Dwight, 26
Tucker, Ray Moss, 32, 62, 97, 118

User fee, 20, 174
USA Today, 54, 55

Village Voice, 46
Volcker, Paul A., 233

Waits, John, 93, 129
Wall Street Journal, xii, 47–48, 49, 112, 197
Washington Post, 39, 151, 185, 197, 249

Wasserman, Craig, 208
Weaver, James, 33
Webster, James C., 39, 59, 130, 171,
  176, 222
Whitten, Jamie L., 168
Wichita Bank for Cooperatives, 24
Wilkinson, Donald E., xii, 42, 43, 50,
  58, 90, 114, 170, 175, 237, 239
Williams, E. Morgan, 102

Wilson, Ron, 130
Wilson, Woodrow, 5
Women in Farm Credit, 141
Wright, Jim, 218, 224

Yeutter, Clayton K., 245

Zorinsky, Ed, 121–23